D0999486

WOMEN'S STUDIES QUARTERLY

VOLUME 48   NUMBERS 1 & 2   SPRING/SUMMER 2020

An educational project of the Feminist Press at the City University of New York, the College of Staten Island, City University of New York, Hunter College, City University of New York, and LaGuardia Community College, City University of New York, with support from the Center for the Study of Women and Society at the Graduate Center, City University of New York

WSQ: Women's Studies Quarterly, a peer-reviewed, theme-based journal, is published by the Feminist Press at the City University of New York.

COVER ART
strange fruit 16 by Debra Priestly

WEBSITE
feministpress.org/wsq

EDITORIAL CORRESPONDENCE
WSQ: Women's Studies Quarterly, The Feminist Press at the City University of New York, The Graduate Center, 365 Fifth Avenue, Suite 5406, New York, NY 10016; wsqeditorial@gmail.com.

PRINT SUBSCRIPTIONS
Subscribers in the United States: Individuals—$60 for 1 year; $150 for 3 years. Institutions—$85 for 1 year; $225 for 3 years. Subscribers outside the United States: Add $40 per year for delivery. To subscribe or change an address, contact *WSQ* Customer Service, The Feminist Press at the City University of New York, The Graduate Center, 365 Fifth Avenue, Suite 5406, New York, NY 10016; 212-817-7915; info@feministpress.org.

RIGHTS & PERMISSIONS
Fred Courtright, The Permissions Company, 570-839-7477; permdude@eclipse.net.

SUBMISSION INFORMATION
For the most up-to-date guidelines, calls for papers, and information concerning forthcoming issues, write to wsqeditorial@gmail.com or visit feministpress.org/wsq.

ADVERTISING
For information on display-ad sizes, rates, exchanges, and schedules, please write to *WSQ* Marketing, The Feminist Press at the City University of New York, The Graduate Center, 365 Fifth Avenue, Suite 5406, New York, NY 10016; 212-817-7918; sales@feministpress.org.

ELECTRONIC ACCESS AND SUBSCRIPTIONS
Access to electronic databases containing backlist issues of *WSQ* may be purchased through JSTOR at www.jstor.org. Access to electronic databases containing current issues of *WSQ* may be purchased through Project MUSE at muse.jhu.edu, muse@muse.jhu.edu; and ProQuest at www.il.proquest.com, info@il.proquest.com. Individual electronic subscriptions for *WSQ* may also be purchased through Project MUSE.

ISSN: 0732-1562   ISBN: 978-1-936932-92-4 $25.00

Contents

PART VIII. **ALERTS AND PROVOCATIONS**

Editors' Note

In recent years, more light has been shed on the politics of citation in re-inscribing power dynamics in the academy, especially in regard to gender and race. In a post on her academic blog *feministkilljoys*, Sara Ahmed argues that citational practices are a "rather successful reproductive technology, a way of reproducing the world around certain bodies" (2013). She goes on to observe that citational practices play a key role in creating hierarchies in the academy that delineate the contours of disciplines. These contours include what are considered canonical or germinal texts in the field, and define the center and periphery of a given discipline.

Attending to the centrality of citation in maintaining white, cishetero-male privilege in the academy, the movement Cite Black Women works toward making Black women's scholarship more visible. In order to do so, Cite Black Women "engages with social media and aesthetic representation (t-shirts) in order to push people to critically rethink the politics of knowledge production by engaging in a radical praxis of citation that acknowledges and honors Black women's transnational intellectual production" (Cite Black Women 2018). Christen A. Smith began the campaign at the 2017 meeting of the National Women's Studies Association in Baltimore, Maryland, by selling T-shirts that read "Cite Black Women" as a way to fundraise for the Winnie Mandela School in Salvador, Bahia, Brazil. Soon after, Smith joined with other Black scholars to form a collective who published their Cite Black Women resolutions with the following goals:

1) Read Black women's work;
2) Integrate Black women into the CORE of your syllabus;

WSQ: Women's Studies Quarterly 48: 1 & 2 (Spring/Summer 2020) © 2020 by Natalie Havlin and Jillian M. Báez. All rights reserved.

3) Acknowledge Black women's intellectual production;
4) Make space for Black women to speak; and
5) Give Black women the space and time to breathe. (Cite Black Women 2018)

These resolutions resulted in the creation of the hashtags #CiteBlackWomen and #CiteBlackWomenSunday. In 2018 the *Times Higher Education of London* published a feature story on Cite Black Women and, moving outside of the academy, *Essence* magazine listed the movement as one of the top ten issues in their April 2018 issue.

We foreground the work of the Cite Black Women collective in our introduction to this special issue of *WSQ Inheritance* in order to recognize and acknowledge Christen A. Smith's and the collective's important labor in centering the foundational intellectual and political role of Black women in feminist movements as well as in gender and women's studies. The #CiteBlackWomen collective focalizes key concerns that this special issue of *WSQ* and we, as general editors of *WSQ*, share: How does the transference of feminist knowledge production occur? Whose feminist scholarship is preserved, acknowledged, and passed on? How might feminist scholars grapple with the power dynamics of whose work is recognized and built upon in order to transform our scholarship and political practices?

Indeed, the forty-eight-year history of *WSQ* exemplifies both past and ongoing struggles to build a radical politics of citation and legacy of feminist of knowledge production. In 1972 Florence Howe and the Feminist Press launched the *Women's Studies Newsletter* to share information about new program developments, resources, and the emerging National Women's Studies Association. In 1981 the editorial board and Howe renamed the newsletter *Women's Studies Quarterly* and expanded the focus to feature scholarship and reviews of new publications. From 1975 to 1982, the National Women's Studies Association copublished the newsletter and subsequently *Women's Studies Quarterly*. From its beginnings, *WSQ* was committed to accessible writing for a larger audience (not just academics) and attending to the most urgent issues facing women. In particular, much space was devoted in the newsletter to pedagogy from preschool to the college classroom. The earliest issues of the *Women's Studies Newsletter* from 1972 to 1981 regularly featured bibliographies and reviews of U.S. and international women writers, as well as recent publications and feminist media for newsletter readers to incorporate into their newly launched women's studies courses in both high schools and universities. These early issues also published occasional articles and letters by women of color about the need to recover and acknowledge women of color's intellectual and political contributions to feminist politics, to the emerging field of women's studies, and to the formation of the National Women's Studies Association. From 1974 and 1980, the newsletter published articles by Barbara Smith, Erlinda Gonzáles-Berry, Michele Russell, Rita B. Dandridge, Maithreyi Krishnaraj, Alice Chai, Ellen Henle and Marlene Merrill, Angela Jorge, and Betsy Brinson discussing struggles to establish Black feminist and Latina feminist courses as well as strategies for teaching and recovering Black, Latina, Korean, and South Asian women's literature and history (*Women's Studies Quarterly*, CUNY Academic Works). Contributors such as Rayna Green, Nupur Chaudhuri, Leila Ahmed, and Krishna Lahiri discussed struggles to address racism and women of color's contributions within the National Women's Studies Association (*Women's Studies Quarterly*, CUNY Academic Works). Ann Cathey Carver (1980) analyzed the "realities" of "Building Coalitions between Women's Studies and Black Studies," and Tia Cross, Freada Klein, Barbara Smith, and Beverly Smith discussed the consciousness-raising format as a process for feminists to address "their own racist feelings and behaviors through the use of a uniquely feminist tool" (1980, 27). The newsletter also printed material related to the 1981 National Women's Studies Convention: Audre Lorde's convention keynote address, "The Uses of Anger," poetry by Mary E. Gibson, Antonia Quintana Pigno, and Joy Harjo, and reflections by Leila Ahmed and Krishna Lahiri. By revisiting the contributions and dialogue of women of color feminists in the first decade of *WSQ*, we recognize and recover the labor and critical intellectual contributions of women of color who persistently struggled to make *WSQ* and the field of women's studies spaces to grow anti-racist, anti-capitalist, and anti-imperialist feminist scholarship and political practice.

Inheritance offers us an opportunity to reflect on the histories that shaped *WSQ* and emergent scholarship. This issue marks the fiftieth anniversary of the Feminist Press, *WSQ*'s publisher since its inception as an academic journal. Jamia Wilson, the current executive director of the Feminist Press, honors the legacy of the Press in her Alerts and Provocations piece. Exploring the shifting political economy in feminist publishing and media—such as the recent closings of several feminist publications, both on- and offline—Wilson interrogates what it means to inherit feminist institutions, and how we might change them in this generation to advocate for more value for feminist media work and scholarship.

We thank guest editors Maria Rice Bellamy and Karen Weingarten for developing the issue and curating such timely scholarship, book reviews, and essays revisiting Marianne Hirsch's work on postmemory. We greatly appreciate Debra Priestly's willingness to allow us to feature her haunting art on the cover of this issue. We also extend thanks to *WSQ* poetry editor Patricia Smith for assembling such engaging reimaginations of feminist inheritance and the poets for sharing their work with us. *WSQ* prose editor Rosalie Morales Kearns also curated creative explorations of the meanings and histories that prompt rethinkings of inheritance. We thank Rosalie for her work on *Inheritance*, as well as on *WSQ* over the past three years, and look forward to reading future work by emerging women authors who she publishes through Shade Mountain Press.

We were very fortunate to benefit from the knowledge of the editorial board as well as previous general editors of *WSQ*. We extend gratitude and congratulations to our editorial assistant Elena Cohen. Since joining the staff at *WSQ*, Elena has been essential to maintaining the institutional memory of *WSQ* and guiding new general and guest editors through the production process. While assisting in the production of *Inheritance*, Elena completed her PhD in political science at the CUNY Graduate Center and launched her law firm, exemplifying a feminist commitment to producing new scholarship and enacting social justice. We also thank and congratulate editorial assistant Melina Moore. While completing a PhD in English, Melina coordinated and assisted in the publication of *WSQ* and worked as an instructor and communication fellow at Baruch College. Producing each issue of *WSQ* is also a true collaboration among the guest editors, editorial assistants, and general editors with the Feminist Press. We extend deep gratitude to Jamia Wilson, Lauren Rosemary Hook, Nick Whitney, Jisu Kim, Drew Stevens, Lucia Brown, and Dorsa Djalilzadeh at the Feminist Press.

At almost fifty years of existence, *WSQ* has taken multiple forms and been housed at various locations over the course of its history. In 1985 the Feminist Press and *WSQ* moved from Old Westbury College at the State University of New York to the City University of New York. The CUNY Graduate Center's inheritance of *WSQ* for the last fifteen years—something we reflect on as *WSQ* leaves the CUNY Graduate Center following the publication of this issue—has provided an opportunity for CUNY faculty and graduate students to help shape women's studies and the development of new and intersecting fields such as trans studies, LGBTQ studies, gender studies, sexuality studies, ethnic studies, and global studies. Thank you to the Office of the Provost at the CUNY Graduate Center for supporting the editorial assistant positions. We would also like to extend a very special thank you to Dr. Dána-Ain Davis and the Center for the Study of Women and Society (CSWS) staff for the opportunity to expand the collaboration between *WSQ* and CSWS in the past few years. Finally, we would like to recognize the generosity of the School of Arts and Sciences at Hunter College, and the Office of the Provost at LaGuardia Community College.

Natalie Havlin
Associate Professor of English
Department of English
LaGuardia Community College
City University of New York

Jillian M. Báez
Associate Professor of Africana
    and Puerto Rican/Latino Studies
Department of Africana
    and Puerto Rican/Latino Studies
Hunter College
City University of New York

Works Cited

Ahmed, Sara. 2013. "Making Feminist Points." *feministkilljoys* (blog), September 11, 2013. https://feministkilljoys.com/2013/09/11/making-feminist-points/.

Carver, Ann Cathey. 1980. "Building Coalitions between Women's Studies and Black Studies: What Are the Realities?" *Women's Studies Newsletter* 3, no. 3: 16–19. https://academicworks.cuny.edu/wsq/428.

Cite Black Women. 2018. "Our Story." Accessed January 3, 2019. https://www.citeblackwomencollective.org/our-story.html.

Cross, Tia, Freada Klein, Barbara Smith, and Beverly Smith. 1980. "Face-to-Face, Day-to-Day, Racism CR." *Women's Studies Newsletter* 3, no. 1: 27–28. https://academicworks.cuny.edu/wsq/468.

Women's Studies Quarterly. CUNY Academic Works. https://academicworks.cuny.edu/wsq.

Introduction: An Intersectional Inheritance

Karen Weingarten and Maria Rice Bellamy

In 1973, on a trip to Tanzania, Angela Davis noticed a group of Masai women balancing wooden boards on their heads because they were in the process of constructing new homes for their village (Davis 1981). Davis, intrigued by the central role women played in the building process, inquired further, and learned that because women in this community were responsible for all housework, building the actual homes—where they cooked their meals, raised their children, and lived their lives—was also their job. Davis notes that this labor—the job of creating a physical structure—positions them as critical and productive workers in the Masai economy. Davis records this experience as a demonstration of the value of work, and particularly of women's work. As scholars interested in the issue of inheritance, we begin with this reference because of how it literalizes the critical role of women in inheritance. Masai women are not just responsible for making a house a home but of actually building the home where the next generation will be created and reared, and where beliefs, customs, and traditions will be inculcated. Further, in addition to being the site where inheritable goods are created and housed, their homes are themselves objects to be passed down. In Masai society, women's role in world building is recognized, and thus their status is appropriately elevated. We open this issue of *WSQ* with the recognition and affirmation that inheritance is foremost a feminist issue.

In the most technical terms, inheritance implies the bequest of money or property from one person to another, usually from a parent to a child, to ensure that accumulated wealth is dispersed according to the wishes of the original possessor. Inheritance also relates to reproduction, specifically the

WSQ: Women's Studies Quarterly **48: 1 & 2 (Spring/Summer 2020)** © 2020 by Karen Weingarten and Maria Rice Bellamy. All rights reserved.

passing down of genes and family traits. Beyond these primary definitions of inheritance is a deeper understanding that inheritance is not simply the transference of a past but also the possibility of a future. Bequeathing the gains of one generation to selected recipients in the next necessarily means that some parties will be excluded from the benefits of the bequest and the possibilities that come with it. Inheritance should finally be recognized as a process that is frequently beyond the control of both the originator and the recipient. Inheritance, in its broadest sense, implies the passing down of material goods, possibilities, advantages, and entitlement as well as inequity, trauma, subjugation, disadvantage, and disenfranchisement. In other words, the negative implications of inheritance must be considered in any scholarly inquiry on the subject.

The feminist implications of inheritance are complex and multifaceted, and in our Western context particularly, inheritance can never be separated from issues of gender, race, ethnicity, sexuality, class, and national origin. Women play a complex, sometimes tension-ridden, role in inheritance. The female body (understood normatively) is often the primary site for generational transfer—even if women are frequently excluded from inheritance—yet women in positions of privilege can also be complicit in maintaining and participating in processes of exclusionary inheritance. In the aftermath of slavery, colonialism, war, and other experiences of subjugation, negative forms of inheritance are passed down through the generations and continue to limit the possibilities of descendants in contemporary society. Taken together, the collection of essays in this issue demonstrate that the study of inheritance demands the recognition of these negative resonances as well as the intersectional nature of inheritance.

We approach this special issue from a foundation of scholarly engagement exploring how contemporary society and individuals are shaped by their inheritance from previous generations and historical moments. Maria's first book (2016) extends Marianne Hirsch's paradigm of *postmemory* beyond its original focus on the descendants of Holocaust survivors to consider how female writers from diverse backgrounds represent the afterlife of inherited cultural and historical traumas in contemporary society. Maria recognizes, as a new genre of American literature, the preponderance of recent fiction representing negative inheritances related to marginalization and exclusion, cultural and collective trauma, war and exile, and sexual violence, among other atrocities. She argues that these narratives of postmemory function as efforts to repair the damages of traumatic legacies by representing them in cultural forms relevant to the inheritor's contemporary moment. These works then demonstrate the power of narrative and other forms of artistry to mediate and ameliorate the debilitating effects of negative inheritances. Maria's current research explores contemporary representations of and engagement with slavery by African American and European American individuals and institutions as a means of recognizing the critical role slavery has played in defining the United States' national identity, culture, and system of race-based inequities as well as deconstructing the racist worldview that undergirds these social structures.

Karen's first book (2014) tracks the cultural representation of abortion in early twentieth-century American novels, films, and other popular artifacts in order to demonstrate how the abortion debate, as we currently understand it, was inherited from an earlier moment in American history. Through her work, she shows how enmeshed arguments about abortion have been, and continue to be, in eugenics, economics, and new and emerging biopolitical systems where bodies are counted inasmuch as they can produce and reproduce. Her current work returns to the nineteenth and early twentieth centuries in order to understand how anxieties about disability, race, and sex have shaped theories of heredity and impacted the way women were viewed and treated during pregnancy. She links the theory of *maternal impression*—the belief that a woman's experiences and emotions during pregnancy shape the developing fetus—to eugenics, and to new reproductive technologies that emerged both to treat infertility and to monitor pregnancies more closely than ever. In doing this work, she shows how anxiety during pregnancy, which is so often the anxiety of inheritance, is culturally constructed, and has roots in theories regarding racialized motherhood *and* ableist motherhood that have told American women it is their imperative to produce healthy children for the advancement of their race.

Our research builds on generations of feminist and intersectional theory that has approached questions of inheritance as a means of critiquing systems of power. In her groundbreaking book *Women, Race & Class*, from which our opening anecdote derives, Angela Davis argues powerfully for connecting black women's material lives in the late twentieth century to a history of slavery and racism that created a system of inheritance—based on racial capitalism (a term coined by Cedric Robinson [1983] two years later)—that systematically marginalizes and excludes black women from the cultural and material benefits of their labor. Davis's book centers black women's experiences to create a genealogy that traces institutional inheritance through the accumulation of—and exclusion from—property, wealth, and status. In a parallel vein, Gayle Rubin, in her pioneering text "The Traffic in Women: Notes on the 'Political Economy' of Sex," centers sex in her Marxist and feminist analysis of systems of exchange and access to power. As Rubin argues in her essay, "Kinship systems do not merely exchange women. They exchange sexual access, genealogical statuses, lineage names and ancestors, rights *and* people—men, women, and children—in concrete systems of social relations" (1975, 177). Inheritance begins in kinship systems, centered on women's bodies and the home, and extends out into larger systems of social relations. These pioneering scholars suggest the intersectional nature of inheritance in ways that would reverberate with Kimberlé Crenshaw's (1991) coining of the term *intersectionality* more than a decade later.

From this critical foundation, we sought for this issue scholarship from interdisciplinary perspectives that would explore the full range of possibilities suggested by the concept of inheritance. The submissions we received reveal the mechanisms of inheritance within and across all meaningful human boundaries: gender, sexuality, race, ethnicity, nation of origin, citizenship status, and more. The essays selected for publication consistently concern the cultural and historical ramifications of inheritance, highlighting the importance of cultural, social, and institutional forces in shaping our lives and opportunities. As the essays in this issue show, inheritance is never *just* an economic imperative or system of exchange: it extends far beyond personal or even familial transfers to create broader cultural and historical legacies closely tied to systems of oppression, social hierarchies, and access to power.

Inheriting Bondage: In the Wake of Slavery and Colonialism

Our issue begins with two powerful essays that trace the impact of slavery and colonialism in the United States and Australia, and the rules of inheritance engendered by these systems. Brooke N. Newman's "Blood Fictions, Maternal Inheritance, and the Legacies of Colonial Slavery" traces the connection between the principle of blood inheritance and the statute of *partus sequitur ventrem*, the law that determined that a child's position in society would always follow the mother's. Newman shows how the meaning of "pure bloodlines" in the early modern era in the British, Spanish, Portuguese, French, and Caribbean colonial contexts affected the eventual decision to have the status of the enslaved person be transferred from the mother as if her tainted blood could only produce tainted off-spring. Blood—or early American conceptions of bloodlines—influenced how inheritance was defined in the United States, and continues to have ramifications for our present day. Macushla Robinson's "The Hidden Histories of Heirlooms: Slavery, Decorative Arts, and the Domestic Labor of Forgetting" examines the inheritance of heirlooms in white families and how the histories of slavery and violence that produced these heirlooms are erased and new narratives created through the process of preserving and caring for these items. Using her own familial history as a starting point, Robinson demonstrates how the domestic labor of white women fosters the forgetting of an object's provenance and how that forgetting obscures its connection to violent historical legacies. The section ends with Sohomjit Ray's review essay, "Afterlives of Slavery, Epistemologies of Race: Black Women and Wake Work," which reviews three contemporary scholarly and creative works that examine the modern inheritance of slavery from African American perspectives as well as the wake of violence and persisting inequity resulting from New World slavery.

Inheritance of Institutional Violence: Race, Gender, and Sexuality

The essays in this section consider the profound structural inequities we inherit from colonial and racist legacies, and how those negative inheritances affect life and opportunities generations later. In her essay, "Eugenic Housing: Redlining, Reproductive Regulation, and Suburban Development in the United States," Laura L. Lovett reveals the relationship between eugenics and housing to show how twentieth-century housing developments were designed to encourage "fitter" persons have larger families. Literalizing the principles of eugenics, these housing developments, many of which still exist, provided amenities to enable their residents to raise large families, while others were carefully excluded, primarily on the basis of race and nation of origin. Jasmine L. Harris turns to higher education in her essay, "Inheriting Educational Capital: Black College Students, Nonbelonging, and Ignored Legacies at Predominantly White Institutions." Her important essay asks us to consider the many ways black students at predominantly white institutions (PWIs) are marginalized, thereby ensuring they do not reap the same benefits from these universities as their white peers, and cannot pass those benefits on to their progeny. Harris argues that, although black students are attending community colleges, for-profit universities, and historically black colleges in increasing numbers, these institutions do not provide the same upward mobility as not-for-profit PWIs do for white students. Both Lovett's and Harris's essays demonstrate how institutions originally created for the benefit of white, Western Europeans continue to provide inheritable benefits for white people while denying them to black people, even if blacks are now able to enter those institutions. Finally, Ashley Currier and Keeley B. Gogul examine the colonial inheritance of antisodomy laws in Namibia in "African Antisodomy Laws as Unwanted Colonial Inheritances." Their essay demonstrates that, even as Namibia separates itself from the remnants of its colonial past, its leaders cling to antisodomy laws created during colonialism, passively carrying them forward with the effect of politicizing homophobia "to promote a heteronormative future" for the independent nation.

Finally, Jeannie Ludlow's review essay, "Reenvisioning Reproductive Labor," unpacks Laura Briggs's powerful argument that all politics are reproductive politics alongside Deirdre Cooper Owens's historical project to recover and name the disenfranchised women whose bodies were used to advance gynecological knowledge. As Ludlow shows, while Briggs argues that much of our contemporary society is built on the foundations left by racist, colonial, and sexist reproductive ideologies that have had far-reaching effects on policy and the current political climate, Owens's historical study of gynecology shows how those very histories were elided to credit white male doctors whose advancements were made possible by the abuse of black and Irish women.

Scholarly Inheritance: Revisiting Marianne Hirsch's "Family Pictures: *Maus*, Mourning, and Post-Memory"

This section revisits Marianne Hirsch's classic essay in which she first outlines the contours of her theoretical paradigm of *post-memory* (later rewritten by Hirsch as *postmemory*). Three scholars whose work has been influenced by the concept of postmemory reflect on the significance of Hirsch's essay and its contemporary resonances, and Hirsch, too, responds to her work almost three decades later. We chose this essay for this issue because it has been important to Maria's scholarship and relevant to understanding the negative inheritances of traumatic memory. A key emphasis in Hirsch's original essay is the photograph—a commonly inherited item which, in the context of the Holocaust, carries with it the unwieldy consequences of one of the most devastating events in recent memory. Hirsch argues that the Holocaust photograph captures "that which no longer exists, to suggest both the desire or the necessity and, at the same time, the difficulty or the impossibility of mourning in the face of massive public trauma" (1992–93, 7). To confront this fraught inheritance, Hirsch proposes the term *postmemory* as a means to connect the past and present when trauma has interfered to shatter the connection.

In her response to Hirsch's concept of postmemory, Caroline Kyungah Hong emphasizes how postmemory can be productive in its haunting and how memories, and postmemories, of violence, exclusion, and marginalization can be shared among unrelated parties to build community. Tahneer Oksman, who draws on Toni Morrison's work, explores how Hirsch's concept of postmemory teaches us that history lives in the bodies of second and third generations of inheritors, and how these inheritances can move us both to recognize and remember past traumas and to forge hopeful and ethical possibilities for the future. In her essay, Sonali Thakkar recognizes the negativity inherent in the theorization of postmemory, yet cites Hirsch's emphasis on the child as a means of holding open the future. As the child exercises agency and creativity in representing the traumatic past, postmemory, for Thakkar, offers a model for *reparative remembering*. This section concludes with Hirsch's own reflection on the continuously evolving and expanding conception and experience of postmemory, and particularly on the ways the other scholars' areas of inquiry coincide with Hirsch's own efforts to rethink and redefine this important paradigm.

Reclaiming Feminist, Queer, and Intersectional Inheritances

The next section of essays enacts the process of feminist historiography through the recovery and reconsideration of histories that center women and people of color. In "Recovering the 'Most Neglected Feminist Leader of the Twentieth Century': Crystal Eastman, Historical Memory, and the Bequest of an Intersectional Inheritance," Amy Aronson investigates why Crystal Eastman, whose work was instrumental to the founding of several feminist and anti-racist organizations, has largely been forgotten in feminist history. Aronson's feminist recovery of Eastman positions her as an early model of intersectionality. In "'Doing Josephine': The Radical Legacy of Josephine Baker's Banana Dance," K. Allison Hammer argues that Baker's banana dance challenged rather than confirmed masculine, racist, and colonialist discourse. Hammer characterizes Baker's dance as a performance of female phallicism through which she challenged negative representations of black women and asserted dominance for herself. Jalylah Burrell concludes this section with "'We Always Somebody Else': Inherited Roles and Innovative Strategies in Black Women's Stand-up Comedy." In this essay, Burrell provides an insightful history of black women's stand-up comedy, and outlines Marsha Warfield's engagement with her inheritance both from black female comedic pioneers and the 1970s black feminist movement.

Representing Marginalization and Contemporary Dis/inheritance
The last section of critical essays explores contemporary forms of disinheritance and what Stacie Selmon McCormick terms *perverse inheritance*. In her essay "Birthrights and Black Lives: Narrating and Disrupting Perverse Inheritances," McCormick characterizes as a perverse inheritance the denigration of black motherhood derived from slavery that has been perpetuated over time. She examines the genre of life-writing as it helps restore the voices of black mothers who have lost their sons to state-sponsored violence and who have thus suffered the negative inheritances of racial and gender oppression in their motherhood experiences. In "Queer Dis/inheritance and Refugee Futures," Ly Thuy Nguyen considers the inheritance of queer descendants of Vietnamese refugees, who are doubly displaced due to the inheritance of trauma and their family's rejection of their queerness. Nguyen defines and illustrates her original concept of *queer dis/inheritance* by examining artistic productions of queer descendants of Vietnamese refugees. Meghana Nayak's essay "The Politics of Disinheritance" grapples with the concept of disinheritance through a different lens. Her essay examines how women from cultures perceived as anti-feminist (in the United States) navigate their families' values and beliefs, and the complicated roles they play as spokeswomen for those cultures. More than any other essay in this collection, Nayak's takes a pedagogical approach to disinheritance as she relates stories of her students' struggles to claim feminism without disinheriting their families. Finally Rebecah Pulsifer's

essay, "More Than and Not Quite: Exploring the Concept of the Human" reviews two recent scholarly works that explore contemporary debates on the concept of *the human* and how cultural and scientific inheritances (and contemporary developments) affect our understanding of this concept in light of racialized others, nonhuman animals, artificial intelligence, and many other possibilities.

We proudly present the essays in this issue for the breadth and depth of their critical examination of the mechanisms of inheritance. Their efforts to recover feminist figures lost or devalued in historical records contribute to scholarly discourse on inheritance and the production of inheritable knowledge that creates new possibilities for understanding the future of inheritance. The issue is completed with a broad variety of creative works inspired by the many possibilities of the term *inheritance*.

We are profoundly honored to publish this collection during the year the Feminist Press celebrates its fiftieth anniversary. In light of this historic milestone, we are delighted to include in this special issue the reflections of Feminist Press Executive Director and Publisher Jamia Wilson. The Feminist Press, which has dedicated itself to reprinting feminist classics, has restored to the public access to texts that have been lost and without audience for years. This recovery work has been central to the feminist project of constructing a new genealogy—a new inheritance—for our cultural moment. The work of the Feminist Press and other publishing houses, alongside feminist scholars, librarians, and activists, have pushed educators to include more diverse authors—and more women writers— in K–12 through postsecondary classrooms. They have transformed the humanities and its legacy by changing the narrative of cultural production. As book critic Parul Sehgal recently emphasized in a 2019 *New York Times* review essay of newly discovered writing by women, "It's not enough to give thanks that these writers have been restored to us; we need to ask why they vanished in the first place." As literary scholars, our work has been profoundly shaped by this question, by this history and inheritance.

To close our introduction, we would like to discuss the cover of this issue, which features the work of artist Debra Priestly. We were particularly drawn to Priestly's work because it invokes the home space, as represented by the mason jar, a common fixture in many nineteenth-century and early twentieth-century American homes. Mason jars suggest the preservation and passing down of foods that nourish and build generations within a family. Priestly and the scholars whose work fill this issue, however, require their audiences to take a closer look at the mechanisms of inheritance, of things stored away and passed down. Priestly fills her mason jars with powerful images of enslaved men, women, and children, as well as schematic drawings of slave ships revealing captive Africans stuffed into the hold of ships and tax receipts for the sale of enslaved people. These images render the jars as repositories of both the memories of the people and the evidence of financial gain for exchange of these people. Priestly uses an everyday object to represent histories excluded from white, masculinist, mainstream U.S. history. These jars and these human lives, Priestly tells us, are our inheritance. In order to locate inheritances lost or denied, we must often look in unconventional places, follow unexpected trails, and reckon with the consequences of these losses and discoveries.

We'd like to thank Jillian M. Báez and Natalie Havlin, the departing general editors of *WSQ*. They have left the feminist readers of *WSQ* an impressive legacy that we hope to see continued. Thank you also to Elena Cohen, our editorial assistant, who helped with the laborious work of compiling this collection, including reaching out to the many peer reviewers whose efforts have strengthened the quality and cohesiveness of every piece in this issue. We thank Rosalie Morales Kearns and Patricia Smith for their efforts to curate and edit the beautiful poetry and prose pieces featured in this volume. We thank the Feminist Press for assistance and support. Thank you, Debra Priestly, for allowing us to use your provocative and moving artwork for our cover. Finally, our heartiest thanks go to all of the contributors who submitted their work to our special issue and worked so hard to produce such excellent and thought-provoking scholarship. Reading your work was a wonderful learning experience, and working with you to shape your individual contributions to this larger collection was a wonderfully enriching and satisfying process.

Karen Weingarten is an associate professor of English at Queens College, CUNY. Her first book was *Abortion in the American Imagination: Before Life and Choice, 1880–1940*. In addition to this issue of *WSQ*, she coedited a special issue on "disorienting disability" for *South Atlantic Quarterly*. She has written about reproduction, abortion, and disability in *Hypatia*, *Literature and Medicine*, and *College Literature*, among other places. You can find some of her recent public writing on maternal impressions, eugenics, and pregnancy on the collaborative blog *Nursing Clio*. She can be reached at karen.weingarten@qc.cuny.edu.

Maria Rice Bellamy is an associate professor of English and director of African and African Diaspora Studies at the College of Staten Island, CUNY. She is the author of *Bridges to Memory: Postmemory in Contemporary Ethnic American Women's Fiction*, and teaches African American, multiethnic American, and contemporary women's literature. Her current book project, "American Postmemory: Slavery in Black and White," explores contemporary representations of slavery in fiction, memoir, and popular culture from both African American and European American perspectives. She can be reached at maria.bellamy@csi.cuny.edu.

Works Cited

Bellamy, Maria Rice. 2016. *Bridges to Memory: Postmemory in Contemporary Ethnic American Women's Fiction.* Charlottesville: University of Virginia Press.

Crenshaw, Kimberlé. 1991. "Mapping the Margins: Intersectionality, Identity Politics, and Violence against Women of Color." *Stanford Law Review* 43, no. 6: 1241–99.

Davis, Angela Y. 1981. *Women, Race & Class.* New York: Random House.

Hirsch, Marianne. 1992–93. "Family Pictures, *Maus*, Mourning, and Post-Memory." *Discourse* 15, no. 2: 3–29.

Robinson, Cedric J. 1983. *Black Marxism: The Making of the Black Radical Tradition.* Chapel Hill: University of North Carolina Press.

Rubin, Gayle. 1975. "The Traffic in Women: Notes on the 'Political Economy' of Sex." In *Toward an Anthropology of Women*, edited by Rayna R. Reiter, 157–210. New York: Monthly Review Press.

Sehgal, Parul. 2019. "What Is a Book Critic's Responsibility When a Work Is Rediscovered?" *New York Times*, January 25, 2019. https://www.nytimes.com/2019/01/25/reader-center/sylvia-plath-story-discovered.html.

Weingarten, Karen. 2014. *Abortion in the American Imagination: Before Life and Choice, 1880–1940.* New Brunswick, NJ: Rutgers University Press.

PART I. **INHERITING BONDAGE**

IN THE WAKE OF SLAVERY AND COLONIALISM

Blood Fictions, Maternal Inheritance, and the Legacies of Colonial Slavery

Brooke N. Newman

Abstract: This article examines early modern European and colonial American understandings of racial and slave status as hereditary conditions rooted in blood. Focusing primarily on the Chesapeake and Caribbean colonies, I argue that notions of inheritable blood shaped the development of legal innovations and social practices linking African maternal ancestry to permanent commodification and marginalization. Across the Anglo-Atlantic world, unregulated sexual behaviors disrupted racial legal regimes increasingly undergirded by fictions of blood, leading to legal prohibitions against, and ongoing sociocultural concerns surrounding, interethnic mixture. **Keywords:** slavery; race; heredity; blood; sexuality

Introduction

On March 4, 1815, Thomas Jefferson sat at his desk and wrote a now-infamous letter to Francis Gray, a Massachusetts politician, in which he addressed Gray's query during a previous visit to Virginia: "What constitute[s] a mulatto by our law?" As he penned his response, Jefferson may have glanced through his study window at the landscaped grounds of Monticello, where hundreds of enslaved men, women, and children toiled on his behalf. Perhaps his thoughts turned to Sarah "Sally" Hemings, an enslaved woman of African and European ancestry who had served as his intimate companion for over three decades and bore at least six of his children (Gordon-Reed 2008). We will never know.

WSQ: Women's Studies Quarterly 48: 1 & 2 (Spring/Summer 2020) © 2020 by Brooke N. Newman.

A consummate man of science, Jefferson addressed Gray's inquiry with detached, methodical detail. Referring to a Virginia law of 1792, he clarified that "one-fourth of negro blood, mixed with any portion of white, constitutes the mulatto" (Jefferson 1815). To fully transmute black into white by mixing "the pure blood of the white" and "the pure blood of the negro," Jefferson elaborated, involved a variety of intricate combinations, similar to "the mixtures of different liquors or different metals," most conveniently expressed through algebraic equations:

> Let the first crossing be of a, pure negro, with A, pure white. The unit of blood of the issue being composed of the half of that of each parent, will be $a/2+A/2$, call it, for abbreviation, h (half-blood).

> Let the second crossing be of h and B, the blood of the issue will be $h/2+B/2$, or substituting for $h/2$ it's equivalent, it will be $a/4+A/4+B/2$, call it q (quarteroon) being ¼ negro blood.

> Let the third crossing be of q and C, their offspring will be $q/2+C/2$ $=a/8+A/8+B/4+C/2$, call this e (eighth) who having less than ¼ of a, or of pure negro blood, to wit ⅛ only, is no longer a mulatto, so that a third cross clears the blood. (Jefferson 1815)

Using the language of blood quantum to fix racial identity in a physical substance of the body, Jefferson simultaneously naturalized the legal construction of race and underscored the intrinsic malleability of "pure" bloodlines. If A and h "cohabit," as he put it, their offspring inherited traits in proportion to the degree of ancestral admixture in their blood. Legal "whitening" conformed to a fundamental principle of natural history, Jefferson argued: "That a fourth cross of one race of animals with another gives an issue equivalent for all sensible purposes to the original blood." Still, to "clear the blood" of African ancestry through intermixture with whites did not equate to liberation from bondage. For enslaved individuals, freedom depended "on the condition of the mother, the principle of the civil law, *partus sequitur ventrem*, being adopted here" (Jefferson 1815).

Jefferson's remarks to Gray capture two interrelated legal fictions inherited from the early modern era, both of which proved fundamental to the emergence and perpetuation of racial classifications and hereditary slavery in the colonial Atlantic and the antebellum United States. First, that racial identity inhered in blood and was thus not only innate and transmittable from one generation to the next but also subject to perceived improvement or degradation through mixture. And second, that slave status originated in the commodified wombs of the earliest generations of enslaved women, who, as (alleged) heathen captives of a "just" war, consigned their progeny to perpetual servitude—irrespective of paternal blood. Transmitted indefinitely along a tainted maternal line of descent, the stigma of hereditary bondage became a vehicle for the inheritance of what Colin Dayan calls "negative personhood" (2011, xii). Beginning officially in Virginia in 1662, though observed in the Spanish Americas, Brazil, and Barbados well before then (Dorsey 1994; Morris 1999; Handler 2016), Anglo-American lawmakers marked enslaved women as incapable of reproducing free, rights-bearing subjects. Formalizing a process of human commodification that for many African captives commenced en route to the European trade forts on the West African coast, English colonial authorities used legal instruments to stipulate which segments of the labor force would be accounted non-persons vulnerable to the demands of the market (Tomlins 2010; Smallwood 2007).

For women of African descent who were subjected to the law's twisted logic, whereby enslaved mothers conveyed nothing but bondage and a "reproducible kinlessness" to their children, "the *partus* act was hardly theoretical," emphasizes Jennifer L. Morgan (2018, 14, 16). Codifying hereditary slavery through the maternal line encouraged the appropriation, degradation, and monetization of enslaved women's bodies and bloodlines. As a number of scholars have demonstrated, gendered racial ideologies and reliance upon enslaved women's productive and reproductive labor underpinned British Atlantic slave regimes from the seventeenth century onward (Brown 1996; Morgan 2004; Berry 2017; Fuentes 2016; Turner 2017). However, despite recent exceptions, the connection between colonial racial constructs as a matter of blood inheritance and the principle of *partus sequitur ventrem* has received little sustained attention from historians of early American and Caribbean slavery (Newton 2013; Morgan 2018; Newman 2018). Though Jefferson, like other nineteenth-century Southern slaveholders, referenced the defining power of the *partus* act, he failed to acknowledge that the principle of hereditary maternal bondage was a colonial legal inheritance that emerged within an early modern Atlantic world framework.

Recent work has recognized the extent to which long-standing religious and cultural ideas about inheritable blood influenced colonial racial constructs, legislation, and sexual practices impacting the lives of enslaved and free people of African, Native, and multiple ancestries (Goetz 2012; Brewer 2017; Newman 2018). Building on this newer scholarship as well as Orlando Patterson's description of hereditary enslavement as a state of "genealogical isolation," this essay traces the transplantation and reformulation of early modern Spanish, French, and English concerns about inheritable blood to the Americas beginning in the sixteenth century (1982, 5). It shows how European ideas about blood purity and the mixture of Christian and heathen bloodlines informed English colonial statutes and social conventions intended to ban or discourage interracial fornication and marriage, consign the offspring of enslaved women to permanent bondage, and curtail the rights of free people descended from enslaved ancestors. Offering an overview of the regional variations that influenced localized racial regimes, I argue that colonial authorities deployed discourses of heritability to legitimize and sustain slave systems and racial hierarchies across the British Atlantic. Whether through customary practices or legal codes, English legislators fixed the taint of "blackness," illegitimacy, and servility in maternal bloodlines, influencing attitudes toward enslaved women and their descendants—both bound and free—for centuries to come.

Blood Purity: Early Modern Precedents

Purity is a slippery, misleading word with an etymology dating back to the thirteenth century.[1] From a modern perspective, purity is associated with sexual chastity and the absence of a contaminant; hence purity is typically represented as a static condition. But premodern thinkers cast purity in an altogether different light. Emerging descriptions of national identity in early modern England, for instance, acknowledged that a people could attain a state of collective purity (e.g., balanced and unpolluted) on account of previous mixtures with other ethnic groups. Indeed, polyethnic mixing played a prominent role in English national mythmaking. Political theorists and dramatists referred to the *gens Anglorum*, or race of English-speaking people, as the beneficiaries of centuries-old blood mixtures involving real and mythical populations: Romans, Angles, Saxons, Jutes, Danes, and Trojans, among others. The key was not to shun intermingling with other ethnic groups entirely but rather to prevent undesirable blood mixtures once a people had achieved an ideal level of collective equilibrium (Floyd-Wilson 2003; Ruddick 2013; Schmidgen 2013).

The development of Anglo-American and Caribbean slave regimes took place in a changing Atlantic world context in which ideas about inheritable blood had long shaped European concepts of national and religious identity, family honor, and eligibility for civic and political participation. Beginning in the late fifteenth century, on the eve of Iberian expansion to the Americas, *limpieza de sangre* ("purity of blood") statutes began to proliferate across Spain. These laws excluded *conversos* and *moriscos*—Jewish and Muslim converts generally known as New Christians—from holding positions of public trust and prestige, which were reserved for Old Christians with supposedly ancient, unblemished lineages. Although purity of blood statutes emerged in a specific geopolitical and religious context, over the course of the sixteenth century Spanish colonial officials transplanted the ideology of limpieza de sangre to the Americas. In colonial Mexico and elsewhere, the Spanish instituted a hierarchical *sistema de castas*, or race/caste system, that stigmatized and stripped rights from individuals of Native, African, and multiple ancestries whose bloodlines were deemed "tainted" as a result of non-Christian or mixed lineage (Martínez 2008; Carr 2009). By the seventeenth century, purity of blood regulations had also spread across Portugal and Portuguese territories overseas; for example, in colonial Brazil, a 1671 decree excluded New Christians and persons of African and Native descent from all religious and government offices (Klein and Vidal Luna 2010, 251). Connections between supposed genealogical purity and social status led to the legal and administrative privileging of whiteness in the colonies, yet official racial categories remained open to alterations over time. The Spanish Crown later permitted the sale of *cédulas de gracias al sacar*, or certificates of whiteness, enabling select members of lower, mixed-blood castes to purchase the professional and educational benefits associated with a "white" classification (Loveman 2014; Twinam 2015).

As the Spanish and Portuguese colonized the New World, English Protestant commentators linked Iberians' supposed degeneration in the Americas and propensity for non-Christian sexual partners to their religious, ethnic, and genealogical inferiority. Jeremy Taylor, a Church of England cleric appointed Bishop of Down and Connor in Ireland after the Stuart Restoration, for instance, claimed that Catholic purgatory was nothing more than "a device to make men be *Mulata's*, as the Spaniard calls, half Christians" (1664, 152). If sexual relations with Native peoples and Africans led to the perceived dilution of the purity of European Christian blood, the English considered Spanish Catholic lineage already compromised and therefore better suited for mixtures with heathen peoples.

"Spanish blood they say amalgamates better than British with African," remarked Captain J. E. Alexander during an 1833 visit to Trinidad in a statement that exemplified centuries of English, and ultimately British, understandings of the inherited characteristics transmitted to subsequent generations through blood (1833, 117).

A preoccupation with the old nobility's supposed purity of blood also permeated sixteenth-century France decades before such concerns migrated across the Atlantic, where they were grafted onto local conditions in contested frontier spaces. In early modern France, the term *race* originated as a means of distinguishing between nobles belonging to and descended from aristocratic houses of varying antiquity. While the French frowned upon marriages between the old nobility and more recently ennobled families, they strongly condemned matches between aristocrats and commoners as *mésalliances*, or unequal unions. Mésalliances diluted the purity of noble bloodlines, producing kin of successively lesser stock known as *métis* or mixed bloods. In the French Atlantic world, as interethnic marriages and sexual relationships between French colonists and Native and African peoples became condemned as the most dangerous mésalliances, maintaining the integrity of white French blood superseded former concerns about preserving the purity of the old nobility (Aubert 2004; Belmessous 2005). The sexual exploitation of enslaved women and mésalliances between white men and African-descended women nevertheless gave rise to people of mixed descent who fit uneasily into colonial racial hierarchies rooted in notions of blood purity, especially in major French slave colonies such as Louisiana and Saint-Domingue (Spear 2009; Garrigus 2006). "There was no law, nor custom, that allowed the privileges of a white person to any descendant from an African, however remote the origin," reflected the planter-historian Bryan Edwards in his survey of the revolution in Saint-Domingue. "The taint in the blood was incurable, and spread to the latest posterity" (Edwards 1797, 9).

The English Crown's break with the Roman Catholic Church under the Tudors, coupled with renewed attempts to colonize Ireland and plant permanent settlements in North America, also transformed English ideas about blood during the sixteenth century. While Protestant reformers objected that the Anglican Church was not sufficiently purified of Catholic trappings, anti-Catholicism bound divergent English Protestants together, facilitating their identification as a common people distinct from and superior to the Spanish, the Portuguese, the French, and the Irish (Pestana

2009; Duffy 2017). Late sixteenth-century English observers derided the contemporary descendants of the Anglo-Normans, who had invaded Ireland centuries before, for contaminating their bloodlines through sexual mixture with Irish women. The Old English had degenerated in Ireland, lamented one commentator, "because the blood of theire Irishe mothers, hath wasted away the naturall love they bare to their mother England" (Males 1598, 43). Proponents of English colonization in Ireland held that the inherited traits and cultural practices of the New English settlers would civilize the Irish in due course. The English nevertheless continued to suspect that mixture with the Irish would pollute their bloodlines, particularly if English infants imbibed the breast milk of Irish wet nurses (Downey 2005; Feerick 2010).

Blood Purity: Colonial Innovations

English expansion into mainland North America and the Caribbean, where multiple ethnic groups coexisted and competed for dominance, exacerbated apprehensions about maintaining the supposed purity and superiority of English bloodlines in foreign climes. According to Thomas Trapham, author of a late seventeenth-century text on Jamaica's suitability for English bodies, inherited characteristics determined the fate of different groups in the Americas—though sexual mixture held the power to alter a people's collective blood inheritance. "Hence the Black may well become naturally Slaves, and the vast Territories of the Indians be easily invaded and kept in subjection by inconsiderable force of the Spanish Tyranny," he speculated. "And even those Conquerors through mixture with these animal People, reap their infirmity of Body and Mind, and now lay them open to a newer and more hopeful conquest" (Trapham 1679, 117). In the 1750s, Benjamin Franklin railed against the increasing numbers of Germans and enslaved Africans pouring into British North America: "The number of purely white people in the world is proportionably very small," he wrote; "I could wish their numbers were increased" (1755, 10). The resilience of "whiteness," as Franklin narrowly defined it then, held grave significance for Anglo-Americans contemplating a future in which Africans, Continental Europeans, and people of multiple ancestries might attain demographic majorities in North America. Other comments from the same period suggest that American colonists of English origin did not define "whiteness" in abstract terms but rather associated white racial identity with Anglo-Saxon lineage, uncontaminated with the blood of "swarthy" or "black" populations. A decade after Franklin's statement, the lawyer James Otis proclaimed that Anglo-Americans were not a "compound mongrel mixture of *English, Indian* and *Negro*" as commonly supposed in Britain but "freeborn *British white* subjects" (1764, 36–37).

In seventeenth-century Virginia, English ideas of inheritable blood, interethnic mixture, and Protestant superiority overlapped with growing labor demands to influence the treatment and conceptualization of enslaved and free Africans and Native peoples. On September 17, 1630, for example, Virginia legislators ordered "Hugh Davis, to be soundly whipt, before an Assembly of Negroes and others for abusing himself to the dishonor of God and shame of Christians, by defiling his body in lying with a negro; which fault he is to acknowledge next Sabbath day" (Hening I 1823, 145–46). The punitive sentence pronounced for Davis marks the first recorded description of an illicit sexual encounter between an English man and a "negro" (Goetz 2012, 73). Much remains unknown about Davis and his supposed crime, however. What was his social standing in the community? Was the unnamed "negro" an enslaved African woman? The Davis case suggests that Christian religious strictures prohibiting sexual contact with nonbelievers proved troubling to colonial officials as English masters compelled greater numbers of enslaved African captives to work in close contact with English men and women (Morgan 2004, 333). Concerns about intermixture between Christians and "heathens" had arisen years earlier when John Rolfe wrote to Sir Thomas Dale, then deputy-governor of Jamestown, for permission to marry Metoaka, better known as Pocahontas, despite her status as an "unbelieving creature" (Rolfe 1615). Stigmatizing and attempting to prevent sexual relations between English and non-Christian laborers facilitated the social and legal process by which African ancestry became increasingly yoked to eligibility for permanent hereditary slavery. Although Richard Ligon—who published an eyewitness account of his time in Barbados from 1647 to 1650—criticized English masters for refusing to convert enslaved Africans to Christianity, he acknowledged that "there be a mark set upon these people, which will hardly ever be wip'd off" (Ligon 1657, 53).

In 1662, the Virginia Assembly exercised the full extent of its authority over enslaved women's bodies and the commodification of their future offspring by instituting the matrilineal transmission of slave status. Unprecedented legal action was warranted, the Burgesses claimed, because "some doubts have arisen whether children got by any Englishman upon a negro woman should be slave or free" (Hening II 1823, 438). The punishment of Davis years earlier for fornication with a "negro" had apparently made little impact on everyday sexual practices, and children of mixed parentage challenged the colony's division between bound/heathen and free/Christian. To discourage sexual contact between English settlers and enslaved people and to clarify whose children were eligible for permanent servitude, the Virginia Assembly declared that "all children borne in this country shall be held bond or free only according to the condition of the mother" and "any Christians who shall commit fornication with a negro man or woman" would be subject to fines (1823, 439). In 1667 Virginia legislators further clarified that Christian baptism would have no impact on the legal status of enslaved children, who, having sprung from commodified wombs, existed solely for the profit of free English subjects (1823, 260).

Inheritable Blood and Gendered Commodification

The partus act demonstrates how rapidly changing local circumstances could prompt English colonial authorities to adopt methods prevailing in other coerced labor systems in the Americas. While Virginia lawmakers urged colonists to avoid sexual relationships with enslaved laborers, they also recognized the need for statutory guidelines regarding the status of the offspring produced by such illicit unions. In 1656 Elizabeth Key, an indentured "Moletto" servant of English and African ancestry reclassified as a slave by the overseer of her late master's estate, sued for and won her freedom on the basis of English paternity and Christian baptism. The success of her suit, and other cases involving individuals of mixed parentage contesting their legal status, inspired the 1662 law transforming both slavery and freedom into inheritable states dependent upon the condition of the mother (partus sequitur ventrem), in contrast to the English common law principle of *partus sequitur partem*, which favored the paternal line. Virginia's partus act proved highly influential, later influencing legal definitions in New York, South Carolina, Delaware, and beyond (Gordon-Reed 2008; Banks 2008), but it also captured laws and customary practices prevalent throughout the Atlantic world. A century later, while writing about Britain's Atlantic empire, Bryan Edwards characterized the principle of partus sequitur ventrem as "prevailing in all our colonies" (1793, 17).

Singling out enslaved women as the bearers of servile blood in perpetuity mitigated the uncertainty associated with the offspring produced by sexual unions between English Christian subjects and commodified non-persons expected to serve their masters for life. By embedding hereditary slavery in the bloodlines of enslaved women, colonial lawmakers harnessed the sexually exploitative aspects of coerced labor to benefit propertied landowners, with profound and lasting implications for the development of slave regimes and gendered racial constructs (Morgan 2018, 5). By both law and custom, women of African descent and their issue were set apart, tainted—even if they attained freedom. In 1643 Virginia legislators created a legal distinction between African and English women laborers by levying a head tax on the former while exempting the latter (Brown 1996, 2). Beginning in 1668, all adult men and free "Negro women" in Virginia became tithable, or taxable, underscoring the continued marginalization of free women of African ancestry. "Negro women, though permitted to enjoy the Privilege of their Freedom, yet ought not in all Respects to be admitted to a full Fruition of the Exemptions and Immunities of the *English*," the assembly declared (An Act 1668). English colonial legislators discouraged the incorporation of free women of African descent into settler communities due to their potential to disrupt the boundary of whiteness separating free and unfree populations.

The responsiveness of colonial law to local conditions aided officials seeking to erect divisions between English subjects and enslaved laborers by negating possibilities for legitimate sexual or marital unions between peoples of differing ethnic and religious backgrounds. In mainland North America and in the Caribbean colonies, English legislators attempted to squelch the intermingling of English and African bloodlines by: banishing colonists who fornicated with the enslaved or their descendants, prohibiting interracial sex and/or marriage, and rendering offspring of multiple ancestries base, illegitimate, and subject to extraordinary labor restrictions. In 1644 Antigua banned "carnall coppulation" between Christians and heathens and relegated any resulting progeny to service until age twenty-one. When the law was reissued in 1672, the Antigua Assembly increased the punishment for mixed-blood offspring to lifetime servitude (An Act 1644; Newman 2018). In 1663 the Bermuda Assembly passed a law banishing settlers convicted of copulating with or marrying Africans or individuals of mixed ancestry, whether enslaved or free (Bernhard 1999, 92).

Attempts to retain control over human property and protect the supposed purity of English blood by preventing mixed marriages continually frustrated colonial lawmakers. In 1664, for example, members of the Maryland Assembly complained that "divers freeborne English women forgettful of their free Condicon and to the disgrace of our Nation doe intermarry with Negro Slaves by which also divers suites may arise touching the Issue of such women and a great damage doth befall the Masters of such Negroes" (Newman 2018, 81). In response, Maryland adopted the common-law rule of patrilineal descent to discourage English women from marrying enslaved African men. The law subjected English women who bound themselves to enslaved men in wedlock, as well as any legitimate offspring produced by the union, to lifetime service. Local labor conditions and gendered social behaviors shaped the character of regional slave regimes and official responses to relationships, both licit and illicit, forged between Europeans and Africans.

Partus Sequitur Ventrem and the Law of Nature

When the Virginia Assembly opted to privilege matrilineal heritability in sexual unions involving colonial population pools, it followed a precept inherited from Roman law and Christian just war theory, which had become pervasive throughout European territories in the Americas (Watson 1989; Dorsey 1994). For centuries, Christian theologians and legal theorists supported the maxim that offspring should follow the mother in matters relating to lowly, unsanctioned, and dishonorable births. Thomas Aquinas described slavery as "a condition of the body, since the slave is to the master a kind of instrument of working" (1922, 180). Accordingly, he wrote, "The seed received by the mother should be drawn to her condition," and her master appointed the beneficiary of the fruit of her womb (180).

Early modern Christian legal theorists generally agreed that the rules governing the treatment of non-Christian captives of war and their offspring differed from strictures applicable to free Christians. "Nor are they servants only themselves but also their posterity for ever," wrote Hugo Grotius, a Dutch jurist whose influential treatise on the law of nations was published in English in 1654. Grotius justified hereditary maternal slavery for war captives on the basis of two different arguments: first, the issue of captive enemies would never have existed if Christians had exercised their highest right; and second, children born of "servile copulations were neither regulated by Law nor by certain custody, so that no sufficient presumption could shew the Father" (1654, 567). Thus, "*The Law of Nature is this, that he which is born without lawfull Matrimony, should follow the Moth-er*" (569; italics original). Other experts on natural law concurred. Samuel Puffendorf, for instance, observed that "it is every where allow'd, that the *Progeny* of Parents who are Bondmen, are also in a *Servile State*, and belong as Slaves to the Owner of their Mother" (1691, 240).

By the late seventeenth century, colonial authorities had set legal and customary restraints in place throughout the British Atlantic to curb and delegitimize sexual relations between free English settlers and men and women of African descent. In an attempt to preserve the labor capac-ity and bloodlines of English women, officials condemned sexual contact between female indentured servants and enslaved African men (Tomlins 2010, 402; Fischer 2002, 100–101). Lawmakers across the Chesapeake nevertheless discovered scattered instances of marriages and illicit unions between lower-status English serving women and enslaved men. For co-lonial laborers denied the privileges of elite landowners, racial constructs and prohibitions against intermixture between Christians and persons of foreign, heathen ancestry may have mattered, but so did other consider-ations. Because the concerns of propertied white men dominate the colo-nial archive, what motivated English women to marry or engage in illicit relations with enslaved men remains unclear. But their common objec-tification by and shared sexual vulnerability to English men might have played a role (Foster 2019).

In 1681 the Maryland Assembly fined ministers who performed inter-racial marriage ceremonies as well as masters and mistresses who sought to augment their labor force by granting female servants permission to wed enslaved men (An Act 1681). Nine years later, lawmakers reiterated the unlawfulness of interracial marriage by relegating free men of African descent to lifetime slavery for marrying white women. Marital unions and intimate relations that threatened the institution of slavery and white male patriarchal control over the bodies and future offspring of enslaved and free women were criminalized. Sexual encounters inevitably led to the birth of offspring whose existence blurred emerging social and legal dis-tinctions between English colonists of "pure" blood and marginalized ra-cial groups, including persons of African, Native, and multiple ancestries. As the Virginia Burgesses clarified in 1691, it was incumbent upon colo-nial authorities to prevent "that abominable Mixture, and spurious Issue, which hereafter may increase in this Dominion, as well by Negroes, Mulat-toes, and Indians, intermarrying with English or other White Women, as by their unlawful accompanying one another" (Hening III 1823, 86–87).

By the early eighteenth century, attempts to interfere in the sexual lives of British settler populations in mainland North America had spread well beyond Virginia and Maryland to Pennsylvania, New Jersey, Massachusetts Bay, and North Carolina. Authorities enacted statutory restrictions designed to monitor and control sexual practices and generate racial divisions. Some measures were extreme. A Pennsylvania act of 1700 introduced castration as a penalty for enslaved men convicted of having attempted to ravish or have "carnal knowledge of any White Woman, Maid, or Child." New Jersey followed suit in 1704 with its own castration provision for the same sexual behavior. However, the Crown subsequently overturned both statutes due to the unprecedented severity of castration as a punishment for rape. Whipping, branding, and sale remained permissible. In 1705 Massachusetts authorities outlined a number of penalties for white persons who engaged in sexual relations with African or mixed-descent partners. In practice, colonial officials prosecuted only white women and black men. In North Carolina, a 1715 statute banned intermarriage between whites and "any Negro, Mulattoe or Indyan," suggesting shared concerns across Anglo-America for the preservation of a racialized social order dependent on the existence of legal and cultural barriers based on bloodlines (An Act 1705, 747–48; Tomlins 2010, 413).

Blood Legacies

In the colonial British Atlantic, the discretionary power of local officials to enact provincial statutes, or adopt customary practices, outside English legal traditions proved fundamental to the development of slave regimes and racial classifications. Anglo-American and Caribbean legislators operated within a broader transatlantic constitution characterized by permissible legal divergence, so long as colonial laws were not "repugnant" to English legal norms (Bilder 2004, 2). Matthew Bacon, the prominent common law attorney, argued that the permissibility of provincial statutes and customs depended on both the nature of the divergent practices and specific local conditions: "Of such Customs as are against the Rules of the Common Law, yet not being unreasonable in themselves are good, and from the Conveniency of them bind in particular places" (1736, 671).

Bacon's explanation is telling. While Thomas Jefferson, early modern Christian legal theorists, and colonial lawmakers referenced tainted bloodlines and natural law to justify the maternal transmission of slave status and permanent racial subordination, Bacon offered a straightforward rationale: convenience. The British Crown and its advisory body, the Privy Council, let divergent colonial laws or customs stand if they appeared reasonable and suited to local conditions. The legal fiction ascribing the transmission of hereditary slave status to the wombs of enslaved women was one such custom; racial identity as a maternal blood inheritance was another. Moreover, both of these inherited principles, which stemmed from early modern notions of blood purity, dramatically influenced American racial constructs. Jefferson admitted as much when he remarked that mathematical formulas conveniently expressed what he and previous generations of Virginia legislators took for granted: that bloodlines governed racial identity, eligibility for freedom, and the full liberties of citizenship (Jefferson 1815).

The 1662 partus act had made certain that the mixture of blood between enslavers and those whom they held in bondage would not result in the loss of valuable human property. Blood lineage proved determinative in assigning status and conveying rights, but it remained subject to the rule of law. "Slaveholders have ordained, and by law established, that the children of slave women shall in all cases follow the condition of their mothers," wrote the prominent African-American abolitionist Frederick Douglass in 1845 (1845, 3). To Douglass, colonial officials' motive for instituting partus sequitur ventrem to designate slave status was obvious: "To administer to their own lusts, and make a gratification of their wicked desires profitable as well as pleasurable; for by this cunning arrangement, the slaveholder, in cases not a few, sustains to his slaves the double relation of master and father" (1845, 4). The blood of white fathers could never transform enslaved Africans into free citizens, he concluded. "And then who *are* Africans?" questioned the former enslaved fugitive and autobiographer, Harriet Jacobs. "Who can measure the amount of Anglo-Saxon blood coursing in the veins of American slaves?" (1861, 69). Ultimately, inherited blood metaphors both naturalized human commodification and offered an evocative means by which the dispossessed could articulate personhood.

Brooke N. Newman is associate professor of history and interim director of the Humanities Research Center at Virginia Commonwealth University. She is the author of *A Dark Inheritance: Blood, Race, and Sex in Colonial Jamaica*. She can be reached at bnewman@vcu.edu.

Notes

1. According to the Oxford English Dictionary, *purity* stems from Anglo-Norman, Old French, and Latin origins and was first used in reference to freedom from moral pollution. By the fifteenth century, purity also designated a lack of bodily contamination, a meaning which assumed sexual connotations just as England began colonizing Virginia.

Works Cited

"An Act against Carnall Coppulation between Christian & Heathen, November 20, 1644, Antigua." Leeward Islands, Acts. The British National Archives, Kew. CO 154/1, f. 55.

"An Act concerning Negroes and Slaves, September 1681." Maryland. 1889. William Hand Browne. *Archives of Maryland: Proceedings and Acts*. Volume 7. Baltimore: Maryland Historical Society.

"An Act Continuing the Tax on Negro Women, September 17, 1668." Virginia. Orders and Minutes of Assembly, 1660–1682. Board of Trade and Secretaries of State: America and the West Indies, Original Correspondence. The British National Archives, Kew. CO 5/1376.

"An Act for the Better Preventing of a Spurious and Mixt issue, October 24, 1705." 1814. *The Charters and General Laws of the Colony and Province of Massachusetts Bay*. Boston: T.B. Wait and Co.

Alexander, Captain J. E. 1833. *Transatlantic Sketches, Comprising Visits to the Most Interesting Scenes in North and South America, and the West Indies*. Philadelphia: Key and Biddle.

Aquinas, Thomas. 1922. *The Summa Theologica*, 3rd Part, Supplement, translated by the Dominican Fathers. New York.

Aubert, Guillaume. 2004. "'The Blood of France': Race and Purity of Blood in the French Atlantic World." *William and Mary Quarterly* 61, no. 3: 439–78.

Bacon, Matthew. 1736. *A New Abridgment of the Law*. Volume I. London.

Banks, Taunya Lovell. 2008. "Dangerous Woman: Elizabeth Key's Freedom Suit—Subjecthood and Racialized Identity in Seventeenth Century Colonial Virginia." *Akron Law Review* 41, no. 3: 799–837.

Belmessous, Saliha. 2005. "Assimilation and Racialism in Seventeenth and Eighteenth Century French Colonial Policy." *American Historical Review* 110, no. 2: 322–49.

Bernhard, Virginia. 1999. *Slaves and Slaveholders in Bermuda, 1616–1782*. Columbia: University of Missouri Press.

Berry, Daina Ramey. 2017. *The Price for Their Pound of Flesh: The Value of the Enslaved, from Womb to Grave, in the Building of a Nation*. Boston: Beacon Press.

Bilder, Mary Sarah. 2004. *The Transatlantic Constitution: Colonial Legal Culture and the Empire*. Cambridge, MA: Harvard University Press.

Brewer, Holly. 2017. "Slavery, Sovereignty, and 'Inheritable Blood': Reconsidering John Locke and the Origins of American Slavery." *American Historical Review* 122, no. 4: 1038–78.

Brown, Kathleen. 1996. *Good Wives, Nasty Wenches, and Anxious Patriarchs: Gender, Race, and Power in Colonial Virginia*. Chapel Hill: University of North Carolina Press.

Carr, Matthew. 2009. *Blood and Faith: The Purging of Muslim Spain*. New York: The New Press.

A Collection of All the Acts of Assembly, Now in Force, in the Colony of Virginia. 1733. Williamsburg, VA.

Dayan, Colin. 2011. *The Law Is a White Dog: How Legal Rituals Make and Unmake Persons*. Princeton, NJ: Princeton University Press.

Dorsey, Joseph C. 1994. "Women Without History: Slavery, Jurisprudence, and the International Politics of Partus Sequitur Ventrem in the Spanish Caribbean." *Journal of Caribbean History* 28, no. 2: 165–207.

Douglass, Frederick. 1845. *Narrative of the Life of Frederick Douglass, An American Slave, Written by Himself*. Boston: The Anti-Slavery Office.

Downey, Declan. 2005. "Purity of Blood and Purity of Faith in Early Modern Ireland." In *The Origins of Sectarianism in Early Modern Ireland*, edited by Alan Ford and John McCafferty, 216–28. Cambridge: Cambridge University Press.

Duffy, Eamon. 2017. *Reformation Divided: Catholics, Protestants and the Conversion of England*. London: Bloomsbury.

Edwards, Bryan. 1793. *The History, Civil and Commercial, of the British West Indies*. Volume II. London.

———. 1797. *An Historical Survey of the French Colony in the Island of St. Domingo*. London.

Feerick, Jean. 2010. *Strangers in Blood: Relocating Race in the Renaissance*. Toronto: University of Toronto Press.

Fischer, Kirsten. 2002. *Suspect Relations: Sex, Race, and Resistance in Colonial North Carolina*. Ithaca, NY: Cornell University Press.

Floyd-Wilson, Mary. 2003. *English Ethnicity and Race in Early Modern Drama*. Cambridge: Cambridge University Press.

Foster, Thomas A. 2019. *Rethinking Rufus: Sexual Violations of Enslaved Men*. Athens: University of Georgia Press.

Franklin, Benjamin. 1755. "Observations Concerning the Increase of Mankind,

Peopling of Countries, &c." In William Clarke. *Observations on the Late and Present Conduct of the French, with Regard to their Encroachments upon the British Colonies in North America*. London: S. Kneeland.

Fuentes, Marisa J. 2016. *Dispossessed Lives: Enslaved Women, Violence, and the Archive*. Philadelphia: University of Pennsylvania Press.

Garrigus, John. 2006. *Before Haiti: Race and Citizenship in French Saint-Domingue*. New York: Palgrave Macmillan.

Goetz, Rebecca Anne. 2012. *The Baptism of Early Virginia: How Christianity Created Race*. Baltimore: John Hopkins University Press.

Gordon-Reed, Annette. 2008. *The Hemingses of Monticello: An American Family*. New York: W. W. Norton and Company.

Grotius, Hugo. 1654. *The Illustrious Hugo Grotius of the Law of Warre and Peace*. London.

Handler, Jerome S. 2016. "Custom and Law: The Status of Enslaved Africans in Seventeenth-Century Barbados." *Slavery & Abolition* 37, no. 2: 233–255.

Hening, W. W. 1823. *The Statutes at Large; Being a Collection of all the Laws of Virginia, from the First Session of the Legislature, in the Year 1619*. Volume I–III. New York.

Jacobs, Harriet Ann. 1861. *Incidents in the Life of a Slave Girl*. Boston: L. Maria Child.

Klein, Herberts, and Francisco Vidal Luna. 2010. *Slavery in Brazil*. Cambridge: Cambridge University Press.

Ligon, Richard. 1657. *A True & Exact History of the Island of Barbadoes*. London.

Loveman, Mara. 2014. *National Colors: Racial Classification and the State in Latin America*. Oxford: Oxford University Press.

Males, W. 1995. "The Supplication of the Blood of the English most Lamentably Murdered in Ireland Crying out of the Yearth for Revenge, 1598." *Analecta Hibernica* 36. Dublin.

Martínez, María Elena. 2008. *Genealogical Fictions: Limpieza de Sangre, Religion, and Gender in Colonial Mexico*. Stanford, CA: Stanford University Press.

Morgan, Jennifer L. 2004. *Laboring Women: Reproduction and Gender in New World Slavery*. Philadelphia: University of Pennsylvania Press.

———. 2018. "*Partus sequitur ventrem*: Law, Race, and Reproduction in Colonial Slavery." *Small Axe* 22, no. 1: 1–17.

Morris, Thomas D. 1999. *Southern Slavery and the Law, 1619–1860*. Chapel Hill: University of North Carolina Press.

Newman, Brooke N. 2018. *A Dark Inheritance: Blood, Race, and Sex in Colonial Jamaica*. New Haven, CT: Yale University Press.

Newton, Melanie J. 2013. "Returns to a Native Land: Indigeneity and Decolonization in the Anglophone Caribbean." *Small Axe* 17, no. 2: 108–122.

Otis, James. 1764. *The Rights of the British Colonies Asserted and Proved*. London.

Oxford English Dictionary. n.d. "purity." Accessed February 9, 2019. http://www.oed.com.proxy.library.vcu.edu/view/Entry/154916?redirectedFrom=purity&.

Patterson, Orlando. 1982. *Slavery and Social Death: A Comparative Study*. Cambridge, MA: Harvard University Press.

Pestana, Carla Gardina. 2009. *Protestant Empire: Religion and the Making of the British Atlantic World*. Philadelphia: University of Pennsylvania Press.

Puffendorf, Samuel. 1691. *The Whole Duty of Man According to the Law of Nature*. London.

Rolfe, John. 1615. "The Copy of the Gentleman's Letters to Sir Thomas Dale." *American Journeys*. http://www.americanjourneys.org/pdf/AJ-079.pdf.

Ruddick, Andrea. 2013. *English Identity and Political Culture in the Fourteenth Century*. Cambridge: Cambridge University Press.

Schmidgen, Wolfram. 2013. *Exquisite Mixture: The Virtues of Impurity in Early Modern England*. Philadelphia: University of Pennsylvania Press.

Smallwood, Stephanie E. 2007. *Saltwater Slavery: A Middle Passage from Africa to American Diaspora*. Cambridge, MA: Harvard University Press.

Spear, Jennifer M. 2009. *Race, Sex, and Social Order in Early New Orleans*. Baltimore: Johns Hopkins University Press.

Taylor, Jeremy. 1664. *A Dissuasive from Popery, by Jeremy, Lord Bishop of Down*. London.

Thomas Jefferson to Francis C. Gray. March 4, 1815. Manuscript/Mixed Material. Library of Congress. https://www.loc.gov/item/mtjbib021963/.

Tomlins, Christopher. 2010. *Freedom Bound: Law, Labor, and Civic Identity in Colonizing English America, 1580–1865*. Cambridge: Cambridge University Press.

Trapham, Thomas. 1679. *A Discourse of the State of Health in the Island of Jamaica*. London.

Turner, Sasha. 2017. *Contested Bodies: Pregnancy, Childrearing, and Slavery in Jamaica*. Philadelphia: University of Pennsylvania Press.

Twinam, Ann. 2015. *Purchasing Whiteness: Pardos, Mulattos, and the Quest for Social Mobility in the Spanish Indies*. Stanford, CA: Stanford University Press.

Watson, Alan. 1989. *Slave Law in the Americas*. Athens: University of Georgia Press.

The Hidden Histories of Heirlooms: Slavery, Decorative Arts, and the Domestic Labor of Forgetting

Macushla Robinson

Abstract: In many white colonial and transatlantic families, heirlooms store wealth generated by, and at the expense of, the enslaved. Disconnected from their violent origins, such objects make wealth palatable, transmitting it down generations. This paper lays bare the domestic practices of inheritance, which encompass the keeping of and caring for objects, and selective remembering and silencing that endows heirlooms with filial significance. This intergenerational labor has largely been enacted by white women, and thus this paper argues that this labor of forgetting is a female technology—even if in service of a patrilineal genealogy. **Keywords:** heirlooms; inheritance; slavery; reproductive labor; decorative arts; family

In *Incidents in the Life of a Slave Girl*, Harriet Jacobs describes a transaction between her grandmother and her grandmother's owner. Her grandmother had loaned her owner $300, with which she purchased a silver candelabra. Upon the owner's death, Jacobs's grandmother applied to the estate's executor to be repaid, but was told that the estate was insolvent. Instead, the executor *sold* Jacobs's grandmother to pay other debts. Jacobs noted that this did not "prohibit him from retaining the silver candelabra, which had been purchased with that money. I presume [it] will be handed down in the family, from generation to generation" (Jacobs 1987, 20). The executor sacrificed Jacobs's grandmother's freedom, and the labor by which she had somehow accumulated hundreds of dollars, for the wealth of white descendants. Janet Neary writes that "by showing how slaves are distributed along with other objects, such as family heirlooms, Jacobs

WSQ: Women's Studies Quarterly 48: 1 & 2 (Spring/Summer 2020) © 2020 by Macushla Robinson.

reveals the workings of the chattel principle and the genealogical disavow-al upon which racial slavery is based" (2016, 159). It is likely that this piece of silverware is still out there, stored in someone's cupboard or displayed on a sideboard, silent and long since disconnected from this origin story. It would be only one of many domestic objects purchased with fortunes made from slavery and passed down generations.[1] Such family heirlooms sequester capital generated by, and at the expense of, the enslaved. Neary argues that these "mementos of the past and literal bearers of value for the future" implicate "private family keepsakes in a regime of racial terror" (2016, 159). Their provenance not only throws cherished objects into a new light that elicits filial shame; it also challenges the innocence and le-gitimacy of the privilege that these objects embody. The stakes are high: the revelation of an object's violent origins demands that we recognize the privileges that heirlooms transmit.

Neary's call to (re)connect sentimental heirlooms to slavery is a first step. But in order to reveal the violent origins of such objects, we need to understand the practices that have concealed that violence, since the operations of concealment are extensions of that violence. In this essay, I will examine some of the techniques by which the family heirloom nat-uralizes the wealth of white families—a circular operation of sentiment, which incentivizes and is engendered by historical amnesia. *To forget* is a verb—and the act of *forgetting* is a constant, if unconscious, labor that eras-es and thus inoculates the object from its implication in regimes of terror. Caring for heirlooms entails iterative domestic labors of cleaning, storing, and storytelling that are ongoing processes that maintain both their senti-mental and fiscal value. The domestic sphere conceals the implications of inheritance in heirlooms that often reside in the dining room. In this paper, I bring discourses on domestic (feminized) labor into conversation with theories of historical memory and silencing.

This analysis relies upon my personal experience as a daughter, grand-daughter, and niece within a postcolonial family in Australia.[2] As Ashley Barnwell writes, "Intimate family practices channel and conduct political currents, as two colonial processes—dispossession and transportation—reverberate across generations" (2018, 448). This encompasses manifold strategies of organizing and endowing objects with meaning. But it is only by "tracing family practices of both narration and silence [that we can ex-amine] how the legacy of colonial narratives and discriminations can also be seen to meander into the intimate sphere, in the stories we tell both within and about families" (Barnwell 2018, 448). This is intimate knowledge, traceable through lived, personal experience. We cannot unravel filial strategies of both narration and silence from the outside, as though we are neutral bystanders. The position of neutrality is a fiction that shelters us from our own implication in the layered violence that we study. I will not hold myself apart from this history. Rather, I will excavate it from within. Throughout this essay I use the first-person plural pronoun *we*. This *we* refers to the descendants of perpetrators—specifically of those who enslaved or profited from the enslavement of people kidnapped in West Africa. I am part of white postcolonial family—a subject position that I simultaneously inhabit and seek to interrogate.

The Secret Life of Heirlooms

The heirloom is a particular kind of object. It exists at the threshold of public and private systems of value. The term *priceless heirloom* is a commonplace that denotes the irreplaceable nature of objects imbued with sentimental value.[3] Following Arjun Appadurai, we might understand heirlooms as "ex-commodities"—that is, as things "retrieved, either temporarily or permanently, from the commodity state and placed in some other state" (1986, 16). The financial value of family heirlooms is complicated by the accrual of sentimental and historical value. But seemingly noneconomic, personal forms of value (which only become visible when someone dies and filial procedures of inheritance take hold) are entangled with economic value. Igor Kopytoff insists that an object's nonsalability gives it an aura that sets it apart from ordinary things (1986, 69). However, the distinction between the "common" exchangeable object and the rare, unique object is never really hard and fast. Indeed, they overlap: sentimental value wrests economically valuable things from the world of finance—the liquidity of which also poses a threat to the family as a transgenerational organization of wealth. Sentiment tacitly prohibits the sale of objects for personal enrichment that might be frittered away in the daily survival of an individual. The stories we tell about objects—those auratic material resonances that heirlooms carry—capture and retain value in the object precisely because it cannot be exchanged for anything else. To mark an economically valuable object as a sentimental heirloom is to sequester it: we imbue objects with private sentiment by telling stories that inscribe them with filial significance. Thus, the heirloom secures intergenerational wealth. This seemingly intimate exchange of sentiment is in fact an operation of power, which," Kopytoff writes, "asserts itself symbolically precisely by insisting on its right to singularize an object, or a set or class of objects" (1986, 73). Taken out of circulation on the open market, the object participates in a slow arc of circulation over generations. Outlasting the individuals who own it, the object conducts the conditions of its own inheritance.

Much labor has gone into disconnecting heirlooms from their less palatable implications. We should not think of the heirloom as a static object but as a spur to and product of active social and material practices. A trace of this remains in an earlier instantiation of the term *heirloom*—the fifteenth-century Middle English term *ayre lome*, meaning "inherited tool or implement."[4] While the word has come to refer to any item of financial, historical, or sentimental significance, an heirloom in the original sense of the term is a tool—an object with a purpose—implying and eliciting particular techniques, skills, and strategies. As "special" objects, heirlooms are rarely used. The reifying process that transforms *tool* into *heirloom* might divest objects of their original functionality, but only to have them take on different, psychosocial functions of sequestering wealth and expunging their origins. The heirloom is at once an object that must be maintained as well as the very techniques by which it is maintained. The object and the habits surrounding it are mutually sustaining and thus inseparable.

This requires a shift in how we understand the object, one that aligns with current theories of material agency, object-oriented ontology, and thing theory, which all hold, in varying degrees, that we ought to revise our anthropocentric account of the world and acknowledge the liveliness of the material world in which we are entangled. Thinking of the object as having agency, though, does not require that we divest human agents (in this case, the colonizing plantocracy) of their culpability.[5] There is no innate reason that recognizing material agency should eclipse the agency and responsibility of human actors. Instead, we should take an assemblage approach in which human and object agencies are entwined. We might venture further than this, to Bill Brown's thing theory, which resists the discursive sublimation of the thing into the object: "Although the *object* was asked to join philosophy's dance, things may still lurk in the shadows of the ballroom and continue to lurk there after the subject and object have done their thing, long after the party is over" (Brown 2001, 3). In some ways, my work on heirlooms is spurred by the stubborn unassimilable thingness of heirlooms. Nevertheless, this is not a work of thing theory outside or beyond human culture, but rather a reckoning at the confluence of culture and things—materiality and meanings. My research remains invested in the social and human practices surrounding objects. At the same time, it also invests in material agency inasmuch as it glimpses a scenario in which the object's agency disrupts the strategies of silencing at work in filial inheritance. In this sense, we should understand the maintenance of heirlooms as an attempt by families to control and subdue the agency of an object that might tell inconvenient truths.

The Kitchen, the Dining Room, and the Cabinet

My grandmother would keep me entertained in the summer holidays by going through the objects in her house and telling me where they came from, who owned them, and what they meant to our family. In my grandmother's show-and-tell of heirlooms, there was an implicit appeal to my childhood greed: if I polished up the candlesticks or arcane flatware enough, I might one day inherit them. There was a cabinet in the dining room that contained many things we never used: teacups and crystal glasses, Spode Blue Italian decorative plates, silver and brass candlesticks. We would sit on the floor and take things out one by one, holding them as she told me stories about their origins. She would animate this motley collection of things, knitting them together into a larger narrative of the family that seemed, at the time, remarkably whole. Each thing had unique properties, and each thing connected to this cast of characters from the past. Each story gave its object meaning, and with meaning, sentimental value (which is never wholly separable from financial value). The stories were part of the inheritance; their repetition strengthened a specific object's meaning for me. That meaning belonged not to me alone, but to a family—a group of people connected by a constellation that can include a name, a hierarchy, entrenched norms, social and bodily codes and choreographies, legal bonds, and shared sets of experience. Once a thing's story had stuck, it would do the work of memory almost on its own. Objects reproduced memory—filial narrative—with every encounter.

In my grandmother's house, each object's location disclosed a tacit hierarchy, but one that was not necessarily organized around historical periods. Rather, the hierarchy was an inscription of "private" significance: things that were kept in the trunk in her bedroom were precious, whereas those that were kept in my grandfather's workshop (a converted garage) were less so. This arrangement of objects within the household, which Judy Attfield (2000) calls the "domestic ecology of things," created surprising juxtapositions. Attfield contends that by holding things from different eras together, the domestic ecology of things collapses historical periodization, which necessarily occludes the provenance of the objects contained within. Inside the domestic sphere, history drags and eras bleed into one another. Such unruly arrangements might reveal the ways in which the past is not neatly cauterized and contained within historical narrative.

The cabinet in my grandmother's dining room had a large hole in the top that accommodated a ceramic basin (now lost) which would be filled with soapy water to wash the "good" china. The object's design tacitly asserted that the things stored in that cabinet were too precious to be trusted with (possibly inattentive) servants. This reveals an important fact about the domestic labor of cleaning: the Victorian housewife (a product of the colonial era even if she never left Britain) would devote herself to domestic service, but as the head of a household staff, she did not do a lot of the hands-on work herself. Since, as Dorothy Roberts writes, "the Victorian ideal of womanhood arose in part out of the institution of slavery," she might be likened to an "overseer" within the domestic sphere (1997, 59). In my family, generations hence, the "help" has disappeared, but the hierarchy of objects remains entrenched—a division of labor and value passed from parent to child in a series of informal and intimate exchanges. The hands-on work (literally the work of touching) has been charged with significance. It entrenches a hierarchy of care that continues to index the preciousness of the object.

Learning how to take care of objects is not an abstract process; we pick up the techniques of polishing, washing, and storing things precisely by polishing, washing, and storing them—informal and repetitive gestures undertaken often under the guidance of a mother, aunt, or grandmother. That is, we learn by practice. We cannot always separate the labor of caring for things from the sensual and sentimental experience of holding things. In performing the everyday care of objects, we reperform the stories that we have been told about them. Such domestic labors are mechanisms of inheritance that metabolize violence. The care of heirlooms reproduces a bundle of silences that protect the attachment of whiteness to wealth. This attachment requires constant maintenance. It is a ritual enactment of a promise to keep heirlooms safe for the future.

The Complexities of Reproductive Labor

There is a growing literature on the reproductive labor, maintenance, and care work of generations of middle-class white women sequestered in the home, and within that literature a few scholars gesture toward themes of race and the history of slavery.[6] Maria Mies ([1986] 2014) frames white women as the victims of a white male patriarchy in much the same way that the enslaved were victims of European colonizing forces. She writes that "the weak Victorian women of the nineteenth century were the products of the terror methods by which this class had moulded and shaped 'female nature' according to its interests" (Mies 2014, 88). Furthermore, that "the bourgeois class domesticated its 'own' women into pure, monogamous breeders of their heirs, excluded them from work outside their house and from property" (2014, 90). This is an important observation; however, it is equally important that we attend to Mies's conflation of the treatment of European women—their economic and social transformation into the subjugated category of the housewife—with the treatment of enslaved women. Mies sees these two different subjugations as forming the basis of transcontinental solidarity and shared resistance to the same oppressive forces. But we might also see it as a bargain made by white women at the expense of the enslaved. Mies's explanation of the mechanisms of capitalist accumulation, though accurate in its description of subjugated white women, glosses over the interfemale racial divisions that sustain forms of oppression necessary to and emergent from slavery. Mies effectively lets white women off the hook for their extensive role in, and benefit from, slavery as a system.

In fact, archival records show that some white women did very well out of slavery, both as the financial beneficiaries of fortunes built on plantation slavery, and as slave owners in their own right.[7] Hilary Beckles (1999) has shown the extent to which British women in the Caribbean became independent slave owners, often "leasing" enslaved women to urban colonial administrators under the euphemism of "housekeepers." Stephanie E. Jones-Rogers's (2019) book *They Were Her Property: White Women as Slave Owners in the American South* similarly documents the extent to which white women participated in slavery as independent economic agents. The lineage of these seemingly independent women rests upon the subjugation of blackness and its attendant formation of whiteness. While Mies's assessment of "housewifization" as a tool of European patriarchal structures of domination is important and helpful, we need to complicate our understanding of reproductive labor to account for the trade-offs, complicities, and bargains that shaped and continue to shape the domestic sphere.

To Forget Is a Verb

While the construction of history has conventionally been a masculine territory, women have typically been tasked with maintaining the more sentimental domain of filial memory, and with that, the work of forgetting. Forgetting depends upon selective remembering. We cannot remember everything: if we did, we would be overwhelmed by a great wash of information that would render the past incoherent and unassimilable. Inasmuch as memory is made possible by strategic omissions, it is coterminous with forgetting—foregrounding some elements of history while diminishing or entirely concealing others. But the selection and consolidation of some memories at the expense of others is no mere neurological necessity. For descendants of perpetrators, some memories are profoundly uncomfortable, and this discomfort, entwined with sentimental attachments, is a powerful motivator for forgetting. If, as Jack Halberstam asserts, women are the repositories of generational logics, then we also have to acknowledge the alliances that many women have made in becoming the agents of such generational logics (2011, 70).

The dialectic of memory and forgetting is a tool of the powerful that might, following Michel-Rolph Trouillot, be called *silencing*. In his historical study of power and memory in the Haitian Revolution, Trouillot defines silencing as "an active and transitive process" deployed by the victorious: "Mentions and silences are thus active, dialectical counterparts of which history is the synthesis" (1995, 48). Trouillot likens these active processes to the embodied, iterative routine of tying a shoe, a species of memory so ingrained that it does not involve explicit recall (1995, 14). Friedrich Nietzsche, too, gives an account of forgetfulness as an active rather than passive process. In the second essay of *The Genealogy of Morality*, he writes that forgetfulness makes room for the noble functions of ruling (Nietzsche 2000, 494). This forgetfulness is "not merely a vis inertiae" but rather "an active capability to repress, something positive in the strongest sense" (2000, 494). While active—something we *do*—it is not conscious. Just as Trouillot uses an everyday routine to explain how forgetting becomes habitual, Nietzsche likens it to digestion, a "thousandfold process" which is the very instrument of our survival and the most funda-mental of physical functions. Mental digestion (*Einverseelung*) is a means of absorption, just as inheritance is a naturalization that incorporates that which is absorbed into the filial body. Unconscious, extractive forgetting is not the discarding of what we do not want to remember, but rather the incorporation of it such that it seems so natural that we do not think about it at all.

Historical amnesia is perhaps better described as an operation of suppression rather than of forgetting, by which things are hidden but never really disappeared. Adapting the concept of the *unthought known* from Christopher Bollas and repurposing it to understand her status as a post-Holocaust German citizen, Gabriele Schwab (2010, 7) writes that silencing "constitutes a dimension of the unconscious that emerges from experiences that have been lived but never fully known."[8] Within this (post)psychoanalytic frame, he conceives of both the self and the moth-er as *objects*—but not as *static*. This slippage between object and agent (which holds potential for theories of object-oriented ontology) posits the mother-object as a transformative process (Bollas 2017). In Schwab's for-mulation, the unthought known is a species of memory that has not been lived firsthand—memory that has been harbored and suppressed across generations—a kind of anti-inheritance, the absent center that constitutes inheritance. Knowledge that is *unthought* lives "in the back the mind," as if the mind were a theater with actors waiting in the wings to deliver their lines.

The family transmits its lore through a chain of intergenerational con-versations. It only takes one parent to omit the crime of slavery to break that chain—to stop declaring complicity and allowing a silence to settle around difficult histories. Thus the crimes of our ancestors are silenced and metabolized. They become second-, third-, and fourth-generation memories. But they do not go away: they remain as unthought hauntings, subsonic presences detectable through objects.[9] Not wanting to surrender the heirloom, we habitually hold its implications at bay. Having evolved nuanced forms of silencing, we fill such silences with stories, little mythoi of the family that deflect by sharing memories that eclipse the gaps in which uncomfortable questions lurk. The objects that we inherit carry these stories, and as such they help us to metabolize and conceal the (often violent) conditions of their existence. But, since memory is inseparable from what it forgets, they also hold open the possibility of rupture.

The Promise to Reproduce

Decades after my time on the dining-room floor with my grandmother, her death and the attendant procedures of inheritance troubled my understanding of the family's narrative. It is often only at the moment of death, which is also the moment of legal inheritance, that heirlooms may be dislodged from their "proper" place. In sorting through them, photographing and inventorying each object, we disrupted and recalibrated the domestic ecology of things. The process uncovered things that, until that moment, I did not know existed, or to which I had paid no attention. The project of dividing up heirlooms disturbed the order in which they had existed; things previously neglected, ignored, and kept in the places that suggested their unimportance were listed alongside the heirlooms that I had been looking at, hearing about, and caring for over many years. This did not lead to a transparent rearrangement of the hierarchy based on financial value. The negotiation of inheritance was a pas de deux between different forms of value; we were debating not the *inheritance* of capital—that much was easy—but its entanglement with sentiment and identity. Having inventoried and categorized all my grandmother's belongings, descendants laid claim to an inheritance, pulling it into their own hierarchies of knowledge, signification, and ownership.

Legally and customarily, inheritance follows patrilineal lines—notwithstanding Hortense Spillers's (1987) important essay "Mama's Baby, Papa's Maybe," which details the reversal of this norm within slavery, where the condition of the child followed that of its mother. The patrilineal lines of inheritance within white families are, however, complicated by sentimental economies of inheritance over which women have often had dominion; objects such as jewelry and decorative arts—the silver candelabra in Jacobs's slave narrative—are typically passed along matrilineal lines and as such might be understood as a bargaining chip in the covenant of patrilineal white inheritance.

Inheritance is a privilege that comes tethered to reproductive responsibility: the conventional language of a last will and testament will bequeath something to someone in a longer chain of inheritance, to the "lawful heirs of his/her body." Indeed, on a more informal scale, the inheritance of some of my grandmother's belongings was conditional; in the very moment that they were offered, I was asked for reassurance that they would stay in the family. Since I do not plan on having children, I needed to allay the concern that the things I inherited would disappear with me by nominating someone in the family to whom I would pass these things when I die. This offhand, casual question made the logic of inheritance and its ties to an implicit responsibility to reproduce (a child, a genealogical future, a filial narrative) explicit. Biological reproduction, which is necessary to the maintenance of a family across time, is closely bound up with cultural reproduction of filial narratives, the creation of a constituency to whom the stories might be told. The abstraction of the unborn child is the other half of the transgenerational gift exchange that is inheritance. Being within a family is itself a form of responsibility, a lineage that we are expected to uphold. Families impose responsibility from one generation to the next: take care of the things you inherit, and have children so that there may be future custodians of this inheritance. Born as the fulfillment of a generational promise, we also take up that promise to reproduce in a transgenerational cycle by which we occlude the crimes of our ancestors and transmit the wealth begotten from them. As such, we are also born accountable in a call-and-response with histories large and small. If we did not understand ourselves to be part of a family, and entitled to its sequestered wealth, then we might plausibly argue that we were not responsible for those structures that brought us into being. If we were radically severed from this history and did not hold that which was born out of it in our hands, then we might be able to assert our innocence. But we are not.

The Paradox That Produces a Possibility

The heirloom is a paradox at the heart of forgetting. At once a conduit of memory and forgetting, heirlooms are not only material objects but also the practices that surround them and secure their sentimental value. Filial memory attaches some stories to objects and masks others. Stories are catalyzed by and catalysts for care. This is a Möbius strip by which the family traps wealth in seemingly innocuous forms and cloaks the violence of slavery and colonization in sentiment.

At the same time, such objects hold potential for a very different engagement with their difficult histories as triggers for uncomfortable questions. At the very moment of inheritance, they might also call out for a reckoning with their own histories. Thus inheritance presents a choice: either carry on the labor of forgetting, or attempt to rupture the material and conceptual norms of putting things in drawers and cabinets that engineer selective and coherent narratives. As an anchor for the unthought known, the heirloom is also a vector by which the past crashes into the present. It belongs both to the past and to the future. It is waiting.

My purpose in this paper is to reveal the violence tethered to ornamental, delicate dining implements and decorative arts. This is not a "prescription for repair" to borrow Halberstam's formulation from their introduction to Stefano Harney and Fred Moten's *The Undercommons* (Harney and Moten 2013, 5). But it is nevertheless a site of possibility: to show that the spoils of chattel slavery are in our midst, and that by dissecting the anatomy of generational inheritance that extends the pernicious logic of enslavement, we might—just might—acknowledge a call to decolonize the dining room.

Macushla Robinson is a writer, curator, and doctoral student in the Politics Department at the New School. Formerly an assistant curator of Contemporary International Art at the Art Gallery of New South Wales in Sydney, Australia, Robinson furthers her work on the fractures, tensions, and subtle impossibilities of material practices through research, while continuing to push her curatorial practice. She can be reached at macushla.robinson@gmail.com.

Notes

1. See James Walvin's *Slavery in Small Things* for evidence of the conspicuous consumption of the plantocracy.
2. Like anybody else, my family is a collage of different social classes and conditions, but the branch of the family that I consider in this research is an upper-middle-class Australian one of Scottish and English descent. It is overall highly educated and erudite—no doubt because of the fortunes its members made from slavery—but has retained not much liquid cash from its various colonial exploits. Indeed, my grandparents were so ostentatiously frugal and waste-conscious (partly out of their environmentalist commitments) that I grew up thinking we were poor, if not working class. Their thrifty habits are in fact common among "old money" families—those that retain arcane inheritances but not necessarily "usable" wealth. It's worth noting that the conditions of my own childhood were more substantially shaped by my parents' decision to live an alternative lifestyle, subsisting on unemployment benefits in various and chaotic commune-style arrangements. The connections between postcolonial families and back-to-the-land "hippie" movements will be the subject of future research.
3. Consider, for example, the trope of someone who, desperate to flee a war-torn country or feed their children, sells or exchanges some precious family

heirloom. This is often used to mark the gravity of their situation, a painful breaking of some unspoken agreement about sentiment and filial rights and obligations.

4. The ultimate origins of the suffix *loom* are unknown, but the term drags past meanings that resonate within the broader history of slavery that I am exploring. Its northern European antecedent was a nautical term meaning "slow-moving ships" (Liberman 2016). This etymology and its implications are outside the scope of this essay and will be the subject of more in-depth analysis elsewhere.

5. In *Vibrant Matter: The Political Ecology of Things*, Jane Bennett (2009) suggests that the failures of the electrical grid have to be attributable beyond company directors to nonhuman or intrahuman assemblages, and that the cost of this theory is the solid culpability of human actors.

6. There are several important critiques of Marxist feminist discourse and its shortcomings when it comes to race, among them bell hooks's (1984) *Feminist Theory: From Margin to Center* and Angela Davis's (1981) *Women, Race & Class*.

7. The privilege of white women often hinged on matrimony, a theme that I will develop elsewhere. Suffice to say that marriage was one important mechanism by which white women benefited from slavery, and as many narratives of brutal mistresses in the U.S. South attest, this privileged status was fiercely defended. See Freeman 2002 for a further discussion of how the institution of marriage is closely tied to regimes of citizenship and endows its members with rights pertaining to the collective social body, the accumulation of property, and the nation itself.

8. I am citing Christopher Bollas via Gabriele Schwab because she is one of the few voices writing from the perspective of the children of perpetrators. However, I want to stress the historical specificity of slavery and its impact on subsequent generations, its way of living in the present.

9. For an analysis of this process through photographs see Tina M. Campt's (2017) *Listening to Images*, which might be productively applied to objects.

Works Cited

Appadurai, Arjun. 1986. "Introduction: Commodities and the Politics of Value." In *The Social Life of Things: Commodities in Cultural Perspective*, edited by Arjun Appadurai, 3–63. Cambridge: Cambridge University Press.

Attfield, Judy. 2000. *Wild Things: The Material Culture of Everyday Life*. London: Bloomsbury.

Barnwell, Ashley. 2018. "Hidden Heirlooms: Keeping Family Secrets across Generations." *Journal of Sociology* 54, no. 3: 446–60.

Beckles, Hilary. 1999. *Centering Women: Gender Discourses in Caribbean Slave Society*. Oxford: James Currey Publishers.

Bennett, Jane. 2009. *Vibrant Matter: A Political Ecology of Things*. Durham, NC: Duke University Press.

Bollas, Christopher. 2017. *The Shadow of the Object: Psychoanalysis of the Unthought Known* (anniversary edition). New York: Columbia University Press.

Brown, Bill. 2001. "Thing Theory." *Critical Inquiry* 28, no. 1: 1–22.

Campt, Tina M. 2017. *Listening to Images*. Durham, NC: Duke University Press.

Davis, Angela Y. 1981. *Women, Race & Class*. New York: Random House.

Freeman, Elizabeth. 2002. *The Wedding Complex: Forms of Belonging in Modern American Culture*. Durham, NC: Duke University Press.

Halberstam, J. Jack. 2011. *The Queer Art of Failure*. Durham, NC: Duke University Press.

Harney, Stefano, and Fred Moten. 2013. *The Undercommons: Fugitive Planning and Black Study*. Wivenhoe, UK: Minor Compositions.

hooks, bell. 1984. *Feminist Theory: From Margin to Center*. Cambridge, MA: South End Press.

Jacobs, Harriet. 1987. *Incidents in the Life of a Slave Girl: Written by Herself*. Cambridge, MA: Harvard University Press.

Jones-Rogers, Stephanie E. 2019. *They Were Her Property: White Women as Slave Owners in the American South*. New Haven, CT: Yale University Press.

Kopytoff, Igor. 1986. "The Cultural Biography of Things: Commoditization as Process." In *The Social Life of Things: Commodities in Cultural Perspective*, edited by Arjun Appadurai, 64–91. Cambridge: Cambridge University Press.

Liberman, Anatoly. 2016. "Looming, looming, looming: Part 2." *OUPblog* (blog), Oxford University Press. December 28, 2016. https://blog.oup.com/2016/12/looming-word-origin/.

Mies, Maria. (1986) 2014. *Patriarchy and Accumulation on a World Scale: Women in the International Division of Labour*. London: Zed Books.

Neary, Janet. 2016. *Fugitive Testimony: On the Visual Logic of Slave Narratives*. New York: Fordham University Press.

Nietzsche, Friedrich. 2000. *Basic Writings of Nietzsche*. Translated by Walter Kaufmann. New York: Random House.

Roberts, Dorothy E. 1997. "Spiritual and Menial Housework." *Yale Journal of Law and Feminism* 9: 51–80.

Schwab, Gabriele. 2010. *Haunting Legacies: Violent Histories and Transgenerational Trauma*. New York: Columbia University Press.

Spillers, Hortense J. 1987. "Mama's Baby, Papa's Maybe: An American Grammar Book." *Diacritics* 17, no. 2: 64–81.

Trouillot, Michel-Rolph. 1995. *Silencing the Past: Power and the Production of History*. Boston: Beacon Press.

Walvin, James. 2017. *Slavery in Small Things: Slavery and Modern Cultural Habits*. West Sussex: Wiley Blackwell.

Afterlives of Slavery, Epistemologies of Race:
Black Women and Wake Work

Kimberly Juanita Brown's *The Repeating Body: Slavery's Visual Resonance in the Contemporary*, Durham, NC: Duke University Press, 2015

Christina Sharpe's *In the Wake: On Blackness and Being*, Durham, NC: Duke University Press, 2016

Natasha Trethewey's *Monument: Poems New and Selected*, Boston: Houghton Mifflin Harcourt, 2018

Sohomjit Ray

The discernible connection shared by all three books under consideration here—two academic texts and one collection of poems—is that they all offer insightful meditations on the long afterlives of transatlantic slavery and the epistemological emergence of the category of race. In the second chapter of *In the Wake*, Christina Sharpe observes that "the question for theory is how to live in the wake of slavery, in slavery's afterlives, the afterlife of property, how, in short, to inhabit and rupture this episteme with their, with our, knowable lives" (2016, 50). The *their* in this sentence refers to Africans like those aboard the slave ship *Zong*, which set sail in 1781 from West Africa with twice the allowed "cargo" toward Jamaica, entering those abducted into the violent "racial calculus" (Hartman 2007, 6) of the slave trade in which human beings became property; the *our* in this sentence includes several generations of the African diaspora whose lives follow in the wake of slavery, like the unnamed girl-child described in Sharpe's book, with the single word *Ship* attached in tape to her forehead, waiting to be rescued after the disastrous earthquake in Haiti in 2010. Sharpe's early refusal of the lie that slavery and its scaffolded logics are a matter of the past clears the ground for what she terms "wake work": the simultaneous inhabiting and rupturing of epistemological bases derived from slavery. In taking the knowability of these lived truths for granted, Sharpe is left free to not merely offer evidence of "our abjection from the realm of the human" but also to ask what survives the "ontological negation" of black lives in the diaspora (2016, 14). The most significant theoretical interventions in response to the second imperative are given in the last two

WSQ: Women's Studies Quarterly **48: 1 & 2 (Spring/Summer 2020)** © 2020 by Sohomjit Ray. All rights reserved.

chapters, where Sharpe formulates three interlinked concepts and pedagogies: anagrammatical blackness, black redaction, and black annotation.

After presenting the example of Glenda Moore—who was denied shelter on Staten Island during Hurricane Sandy in 2012 and condemned as an unfit mother after this act of cruelty resulted in the death of her two young sons—Sharpe asks what semiotic process scrambles meaning when blackness is seen to qualify otherwise stable categories of "human." Building on Fred Moten's observation that blackness effectively functions as "an ongoing irruption that anarranges every line" and "pressures the assumption of the equivalence of personhood" (Moten 2003, 1), Sharpe arrives at her description of *anagrammatical blackness* as "blackness's signifying surplus: the ways that meaning slides, signification slips, when words like *child*, *girl*, *mother*, and *boy* abut blackness" (2016, 80). It's this signifying surplus that explains how *girl* may not mean *girl*, but *prostitute*, or how *mother* suddenly becomes synonym for "birther of terror" (77). Black annotation and black redaction are explained as tools of resistant praxis, where the signifying surplus is redacted while annotation with care brings the black child into view as a child again.

Despite Sharpe's commitment to this ethic of care, a few blind spots remain in a short text of such expansive scope. Sharpe's frame is steadfastly ontological, leaving her early promise of a more materialist critique largely unfulfilled. Sharpe includes the African continent—its present and past colonization, and contemporary migrations from Africa under duress of global capital flows—in the history that has seen black lives annotated and redacted. But this parenthetical inclusion of Africa, although thrilling in its promise of a pan-African solidarity, highlights instead that Sharpe's engagement with the continent in doing wake work remains contingent on whether it fits her self-imposed framework that is more ontological than materialist. Incorporating Africa as a conditional afterthought contradicts Sharpe's call to care as a guiding premise of doing wake work.

Published a year before *In the Wake*, Kimberly Juanita Brown's *The Repeating Body* attempts to restore the primacy of black women's visibility as an afterimage of slavery through careful examinations of slavery's visual resonances. Brown tracks the repetitions of black women's bodies across an impressive archive that spans literary classics like Toni Morrison's *Beloved*, Octavia E. Butler's *Kindred*, and Jamaica Kincaid's *The Autobiography of My Mother*; visual texts and artwork like Betye Saar's mixed-media assemblages, Carrie Mae Weems's photography, María Magdalena Campos-Pons's installations and images, Faith Ringgold's thangka prints; and films like Carlos Diegues's *Xica da Silva*. Through engagement with these artists' works, Brown seeks to address "the impossible duality between black women's representations and slavery's memory," tracking how black women's images and afterimages become "visual vessels" for the history of the black Atlantic, but simultaneously function as "a logistical inconvenience" (2015, 3, 4).

What emerges in the four chapters that follow are various instances in which black women are simultaneously unseen and yet visually necessary—that is, how black women emerge as "ghost[s] of representation" (Brown 2015, 4). Factored into this dynamic, black women's bodies repeat as afterimage across time, "waiting to have their stories told" (2015, 6). Using the repeating figurations of Margaret Garner, Sally Hemings, and Chica da Silva, the first chapter establishes the theoretical premises of seeing the "repeating body" as an afterimage. The second chapter focuses on the fragmented figurations of the slave mother, tracing the inherent paradoxes situated in the bodies of enslaved women tasked with reproducing capital and modernity while balancing the inherently opposed categories of "slave" and "mother." The third chapter begins with a critique of Elaine Scarry's central thesis in *The Body in Pain*, where black women remain inexplicably unseen, and features two brilliant sections on the armed, armored, and indestructible body in memorializations of Harriet Tubman, and on the conflicted afterimages of the bound and broken body of Blessed Anastácia in Brazilian popular imaginary. The fourth chapter excavates representations in which black women are envisioned as entities beyond death, such as the Afro-Brazilian deity Yemayá. Brown concludes her diverse archival explorations with Carrie Mae Weems's masterworks of gaze-reversing photography in *Roaming* and *The Louisiana Project*. In taking the very form of photography as emancipatory of the repeating dynamic she has examined at length, Brown concludes that it is in this space that we might locate "the possibility of freedom" for the black female body haunted by the long afterlife of slavery (2015, 194).

Reading the poems selected from Natasha Trethewey's *Bellocq's Ophelia* in her career-spanning anthology *Monument*, however, might be reason to attenuate Brown's optimism of photography as inherently emancipatory. Inspired by the photographs taken by E. J. Bellocq in 1912 of a sex worker who was a white-skinned black woman, Trethewey names her Ophelia and imagines her story in a series of interconnected lyrics. The reader is warned by the Susan Sontag epigraph that "the camera's rendering of reality must always hide more than it discloses," before Trethewey's Ophelia unsentimentally explains her role in the creative process: "I'm not so foolish / that I don't know this photograph *we* make / will bear the stamp of his name, not mine" (2018, 42). The occlusion of public history is evident here as a condition of post-slavery life in the black diaspora. In presenting a representative selection of her impressive canon in *Monument*, Trethewey lets us see the full project of intimate memorialization that has been her life's work. Her mastery of the lyric form is revealed in a new light in this anthology, and the interweaving of personal tragedy and deep erudition effect a breathtaking expansion of the poet's "I" as she uses her knowable life to examine the frequently overlooked corners of all we take for granted: the unseen and invisible labor of black women, the hierarchical basis of race ideology, the inheritance of racial exclusion in Enlightenment and the Western epistemological traditions, the embodiment of blackness as otherness in art and life, and the reluctance to acknowledge both the past history of black freedom and the contemporary devaluation of black life and livability. In the poem from which this anthology derives its name, Trethewey notes the ceaseless industry of a group of ants in this "world made by displacement" (2018, 98). She concludes the poem by reflecting on what she has *not* done—but the reader, holding this carefully hewn and quietly elegant monument of words, images, and rhythm, is left with the proof of her fierce attention to detail.

Sohomjit Ray is an assistant professor of English at the College of Staten Island, CUNY. He has published on South Asian literature, translation, and the cultural politics of neoliberalism in *The Translator* and *South Asian Review*. He can be reached at sohomjit.ray@csi.cuny.edu.

Works Cited

Hartman, Saidiya. 2007. *Lose Your Mother: A Journey Along the Atlantic Slave Route*. New York: Farrar, Straus and Giroux.

Moten, Fred. 2003. *In the Break: The Aesthetics of the Black Radical Tradition*. Minneapolis: University of Minnesota Press.

PART II. **INHERITANCE OF INSTITUTIONAL VIOLENCE**

RACE, GENDER, AND SEXUALITY

Eugenic Housing: Redlining, Reproductive Regulation, and Suburban Development in the United States

Laura L. Lovett

Abstract: American eugenicists in the 1930s saw housing programs as a vehicle for a new form of reproductive regulation promoting large families for the so-called fit while limiting family size among the so-called unfit. Housing developers, federal agencies, and real-estate associations used a eugenically informed racial hierarchy to justify redlining and preferential home loans that discriminated against African Americans and immigrants. Reframing this history from a feminist perspective, I argue that these practices were intended as a form of eugenic regulation that enforced women's role as reproducers. This reproductive agenda contributed to a legacy of race-based discrimination in housing, and disparities in wealth that resulted from those differences. **Keywords:** eugenics; housing; reproductive regulation; redlining

Racial and reproductive politics lay at the heart of the history of housing policy in the United States. From restrictive zoning policies to preferential home-loan programs and "redlined" neighborhoods, federal programs justified racial discrimination from the 1930s until well into the postwar period (Freund 2007; Nightingale 2012; Rothstein 2017). These housing policies need to be understood as a form of coercive reproductive regulation, because the eugenicists who promoted them intentionally designed them as tools for discriminatory reproductive control. Though often discussed by housing scholars as creating opportunities for white families, or as discrimination against nonwhite families, these histories are typically framed in terms of home ownership and its economic consequences. I argue that these housing policies constituted a form of reproductive politics, specifically a pronatalist politics. To the eugenicists who promoted them at the time, housing developments and preferential home loans were

WSQ: Women's Studies Quarterly 48: 1 & 2 (Spring/Summer 2020) © 2020 by Laura L. Lovett. All rights reserved.

forms of reproductive incentive, which they hoped would increase birth rates among those who qualified for home loans and discourage large families among those they deemed less fit.

Historians have offered powerful evidence of how racial discrimination informed housing segregation in the United States (Freund 2007; Hoff 2008; Light 2010; Nightingale 2012; Rothstein 2017). Redlining, for instance, graded neighborhoods using a racial and ethnic hierarchy, among other criteria, and then used those grades as justification to deny home loans in "low grade" neighborhoods, which were outlined in red on residential maps. Richard Rothstein's (2017) history of redlining practices in Baltimore reveals how this form of discrimination was enacted, yet his work says surprisingly little about the roots of the racism that informed redlining. In their respective works, David M. P. Freund and Jennifer Light point to the influence of eugenic thinking on zoning and redlining practices, but acknowledge that the topic has received "limited" treatment (Freund 2007, 54–55; Light 2010). In my previous scholarship, I described the interest of the American Eugenics Society in housing.[1] In this article, my goal in articulating the eugenic roots of redlining is not to merely fill in a gap in our understanding of racist reasoning in the United States but to refigure our understanding of housing as a site of reproductive regulation.

Housing reform and the planning of "family communities" were understood by American eugenicists as essential actions needed to encourage the reproduction of those they considered to be the "most fit" (Lovett 2007a). Eugenic housing advocates promoted developments and policies that would encourage large families, while stressing the importance of selective screening of residents using eugenic standards, which relied heavily on a racist hierarchy. The conjunction of their efforts with those of regional planners and new governmental housing agencies informed the rise of American suburbs and reinforced the systematic exclusion of racial and ethnic minorities. The resulting racial inequities in home ownership and in housing segregation were motivated by reproductive concerns among an influential group of policy makers and planners sympathetic to eugenic thinking.

"Urban Sterilization"

Anxieties about the impact of urbanization on the population of the United States in the early twentieth century framed early social-science ideas and policies. Indeed, many American eugenicists idealized what they saw as the vanishing northern and western European rural families. Taking their cues from sociologist Edward A. Ross, one of the originators of the concept of *social control*, they celebrated the farmer and castigated "the deteriorating influences of the city and factory" (Ross 1905, 385). Ross's rural orientation led him to link the "frontier experience" to the creation of those features of Anglo-Saxon Americans that he admired (Ross 1905, 360–63). As Ross put it, "The hardships of the pioneer life pitilessly screened out the weak and debilitated, leaving only the hardy and vigorous" (1904, 1061). As alluring as this nostalgic vision of the past seemed to him, Ross realized that the frontier was closed and the same selective processes were no longer at work. Instead, the "simple life" was being thrown over by young Americans for the "great glittering cities." But, the cities, in Ross's imagination, threatened to "run down" what two centuries of selection had created. He warned that "with shortened lives, bachelorhood, late and childless marriages, and small families, the cities constitute so many blast furnaces where the talented rise and become incandescent, to be sure, but for all that are incinerated without due replacement" (Ross 1904, 1063). To Ross's mind, the idealized eugenic countryside had been replaced by the "urban sterilization" inherent in city life for the white, native-born European Americans (Lovett 2007a).

At about the same time, Ross coined the term *race suicide* to frame the statistical discussion of "differential birth rates" between what he called "less civilized" races with higher reproduction rates and the declining rates among the "more civilized" races. The resulting public campaign to urge white, "native-born" women to reproduce more rapidly—pitting them against the fecund women of supposedly "inferior" races—has been seen as an anti-feminist response to changing expectations and opportunities for women after the Civil War. As women began attending colleges and universities as regular students or leaving farms for factories, their reproductive choices became the targets of arguments aimed at "correcting" the perceived demographic crisis caused by declining birth rates (Gordon 1990; Bederman 1995; Horowitz 1993). Indeed, Dorothy Roberts cites Theodore Roosevelt's condemnation of the "willful sterility" of white native-born American women as one of the centerpieces of the theoretical framework for eugenic thinking in America, featuring a racist anxiety about being "replaced" by immigrant or African American numbers as Roosevelt popularized Ross's "race suicide" fears from his "bully pulpit" (Roberts 1997, 61).

Ross's worries of rural depopulation and urban sterilization influenced the major eugenics text, Paul Popenoe and Roswell Hill Johnson's *Applied Eugenics*, for which he wrote the preface (Popenoe and Johnson 1918). Popenoe edited the *Journal of Heredity* from 1913 to 1918 (Klein 2001; Ladd-Taylor 2001; Stern 2005), while Johnson used his training from Charles Davenport's Station for Experimental Evolution at Cold Spring Harbor to launch a eugenics and social-hygiene program at the University of Pittsburgh in 1912 (Slavishak 2009; Schaffner 2010). Unlike more genetically oriented books such as Davenport's *Heredity in Relation to Eugenics*, Popenoe and Johnson's *Applied Eugenics* argued for a fruitful exchange between eugenic emphasis on heredity and euthenics' emphasis on the environment, built or otherwise (Davenport 1913; Popenoe and Johnson 1918). As Kyla Schuller (2018) has noted, this emphasis on the role of the environment in heredity has deep roots in the nineteenth century with continuing influence on actions taken in the name of inheritance.

Echoing Ross and others, Popenoe and Johnson argued that a "Back to the Farm" movement should be a significant site of eugenic action, forecasting eugenic interest in American suburban development in the decades that followed. Popenoe and Johnson worried that the movement of "the best representatives" of country families to the cities would be dysgenic because "the best" would then reproduce at a lower urban birth rate. Citing agronomist and former Liberia College president Orator Fuller Cook Jr.'s article on "Eugenics and Agriculture," they argued for the need to reverse this trend and keep "superior members of our race" on the land (Popenoe and Johnson 1918, 357; Cook 1916). By "our race," Cook, and by extension Popenoe and Johnson, meant "Anglo-Saxons," the "white race," or what eugenicists sometimes called the "American race." For Popenoe and Johnson, farm life had to be made more attractive to "energetic and capable young people," who were of European descent (Popenoe and Johnson 1918, 359). Of course, white city dwellers could be persuaded to have more children, but the rural environment was seen as more generally favorable to children than urban apartment houses. Moreover, many of the new city apartment buildings constructed to accommodate the urban migration did not allow children, forcing urban-dwelling couples to delay having children (Popenoe and Johnson 1918, 377).

Popenoe and Johnson's vision for a more expansive eugenics, which included rural-like, child-friendly housing, laid the foundation for later American eugenicists' housing efforts and for the most famous explicitly eugenic housing development in Europe, Alfred Dachert's village in

France (Dachert 1931). The houses of the Jardins Ungemach, now sur-rounding the European Parliament building in Strasbourg, France, were designed and created by Dachert beginning in 1921. Starting with 140 homes, Dachert designed Jardins Ungemach to encourage larger families by incorporating a labor-saving layout that allowed mothers to more easily incorporate childcare into other household tasks. Regular food deliveries and community childcare were also intended to make mothering easier. Because families had been carefully selected using eugenic criteria, if they did not eventually have children, they were asked to leave (Dachert 1931).

Significantly, Dachert credits *Applied Eugenics* with inspiring him to create his village, a fact that Popenoe and Johnson note approvingly in their second edition, where urban sterilization is considered "evil" and a "prime factor in racial decay" (Popenoe and Johnson 1933, 339; Dachert 1931; see also Currell 2010, 276). For an American implementation, the New Deal suburban "experiments" like Radburn, New Jersey, offered the eugenicists' hope. A model for postwar development, the New Deal com-munity was planned "with the interests of children in mind." Playgrounds, community nurseries, good schools, and affordable homes made this com-muter suburb the answer to Popenoe and Johnson's worries.

Eugenic Housing in the United States

From its incorporation in 1926, leaders of the American Eugenics Society (AES) expressed interest in a range of reforms promoting reproduction and large families among those they considered to be "superior" people. Unlike eugenics efforts focused on biological heredity, the American Eu-genics Society became as concerned with improving the environment as with improving an individual's biological inheritance. This broader under-standing extended the domain of eugenic reform to living conditions, nu-trition, home life, and social life generally associated with female gendered roles (Lovett 2007a; Schuller 2018).

Ellsworth Huntington and Leon Whitney sought to popularize the eugenic pronatalism agenda of the AES in their 1927 book, *The Builders of America*, which used the idea of a group of "builders" to delineate who should be reproducing. Whitney, a veterinarian and the enthusiastic sec-retary of the AES, penned the first draft, and Huntington, a professor of geography at Yale, doubled its length with his revisions. In addition to including race, immigration status, ethnicity, and class in the population they hoped to increase, they also identified ability and disability as a focus of eugenic efforts. These builders were men and women whose "brains are well balanced, well directed, and active; people of fine temperament, fine intelligence, and fine health" (Huntington and Whitney 1927, 1). The most "obvious starting point" for detecting these builders was the Army Intelligence test (Huntington and Whitney 1927, 11; Martin 1973; Stern 2005; Lovett 2007a).

During the First World War, the U.S. Army administered mental tests to hundreds of thousands of recruits. Huntington and Whitney adopted the resulting grading scheme for these intelligence tests as the foundation for their eugenic system without recognizing any racial or cultural bias in these tests. They interpreted these "grades of mentality" ranked A to E as human types: the A grade corresponded to the "very superior type," while the E grade corresponded to the "very inferior type" (Huntington and Whitney 1927, 290).

As fond as they were of eugenic sterilization as a means of eliminating "lower-grade" individuals from future generations, Huntington and Whitney knew that their proposed transformation of the American population required more. In particular, they understood that the size of their "higher-grade" families had to increase. As president of the AES from 1934 to 1938, Huntington articulated a program that he hoped would "produce actual results measurable in the number and quality of children" (Huntington 1934, Lovett 2007a). Huntington's advocacy of what the he called a four-child family norm grew from AES secretary Frederick Osborn's "practical steps" to promote larger families, which included the "elimination of city slums," raising economic standards on farms, encouraging "endowment and dowry systems," and supporting marriage and childbearing among college students. Bolstered by these practical steps, Osborn hoped that a four-child ideal of the family would replace the "dysgenic" Small-Family Ideal (Osborn 1934).

As president of the AES, Huntington transformed this advice into a proposal for eugenic housing. Starting with the assumption that urbanization lowers birth rates, he proposed forming a housing corporation to design communities for the kinds of young couples who might take out eugenic insurance to pay for the birth of their children. The key element of these communities would be their rural-like character, "which seem(s) to be favorable not only to the growth of children themselves, but to the production of comparatively large families," as well as communal facilities such as laundries, cooperative nurseries, and playgrounds for the hordes of supposedly superior children (Huntington 1934).

The AES had long been concerned with the effects of urban living as they called for slum clearance and an end to low urban birth rates. Their concerns with slums focused on high birth rates and poor conditions in buildings that housed African Americans and new immigrants, while white and highly educated city dwellers lived in better conditions but chose to have fewer children. Huntington's renewed enthusiasm for housing reflected New Deal spending on housing and community development. Huntington followed these governmental programs closely and wished to put federal funds in service of a "eugenic ideal" of housing (American Eugenics Society 1926; Conkin 1976; Lovett 2007a).

Criteria for family selection in federal housing programs during the 1930s were often explicitly eugenic insofar as they incorporated screening for hereditary diseases. For instance, in his 1937 USDA report on family selection, John Holt notes that health was a selection criterion for all of the housing, farm, and reclamation settlement programs sponsored by the U.S. government. The New Deal Rural Resettlement program refined the health criteria to make hereditary disease an explicit criterion. Including selection on the basis of hereditary disease was directly eugenic, even if it was not labeled as such. In addition, the selection board for the Subsistence Homestead program required that all applicants either have children or be of childbearing age. While this is not definitive evidence that these New Deal programs were shaped by the efforts of American eugenicists, eugenic and New Deal housing ideals were mutually reinforcing. Race-based selection criteria for residents suggests that there may be an even stronger connection, where eugenic ideals of hereditary quality informed how families were chosen for housing programs (Currell 2017, 497).

Race-based selection criteria were explicitly incorporated into housing policies and real-estate practices during the 1930s. For American eugenicists during the early twentieth century, race had become a proxy for eugenic value embodied in a "Nordic scale," a racial hierarchy that placed "Anglo-Saxons" at the top and African Americans from the South at the bottom based on results of the Army Intelligence tests (Stern 2005). This hierarchy would become part of the selection criteria for home loans administered by the Home Owner Loan Corporation (HOLC).

The National Housing Act of 1934 established the Federal Housing Administration (FHA) and the Home Owner Loan Corporation, which helped secure loans for housing (Hillier 2003; Rothstein 2017). HOLC standards for awarding loans graded properties: grade-A properties were described as the "best" because of their "homogeneous" population of "American business and professional men," while grade-C housing was "definitely declining" and marked by "infiltration of lower grade populations" (Jackson 1985). The resulting FHA Underwriting Manual recommended preventing financial risk by rejecting "incompatible racial elements" (Hillier 2003). Kenneth T. Jackson and many other historians after him note that African American neighborhoods were invariably rated D on the grading scale: "Detrimental influences. Undesirable population. Mostly rented homes with poor maintenance, vandalism, unstable families. This is the red area" (as cited in Jackson 1985).

Despite their shared fondness for grading humans, the none of HOLC's documents explicitly reference eugenics. That said, Homer Hoyt, who became the chief economist at the FHA in 1934, created the system of valuing real estate by ethnicity in such a way that it re-created the racial hierarchy espoused by American eugenicists. According to Hoyt, "Certain racial and national groups, because of their lower economic status and their lower standards of living, pay less rent themselves and cause a greater physical deterioration of property than groups higher in the social and economic scale" (1933, 314). This system rested on a racial scale, in which Hoyt placed the English, Germans, and Scandinavians at the top; northern Italians, Poles, and Lithuanians in the middle; and southern Italians, African Americans, and Mexicans at the bottom (Hoyt 1933, 317). Hoyt's racial scale reflects the scale proposed by Carl Brigham in his 1923 book, *A Study of American Intelligence,* based on results from the Army Intelligence tests that were interpreted by Brigham as demonstrating the intellectual superiority of northern Europeans over southern Europeans, and African Americans (Brigham 1923, 146–47). Hoyt admitted that his racial hierarchy may not have been scientific: he differentiated between northern and southern Italians, for instance, where Brigham ranked all Italians as third from the bottom of his scale. Hoyt's scale was not meant to be scientific though—he notes that it reflects only prejudices that effect land values. That Hoyt knew enough to realize that his racial scale differed from the so-called scientific ranking, however, reveals that he was aware of and influenced by eugenic racial rankings.[2]

While eugenicists do not seem to have commented on Holt's HOLC standards, Huntington, as a geographer, had written extensively on the relationships between race and place (Huntington 1925). In *The Builders of America*, Huntington and Whitney approvingly invoke Ernest Burgess's analysis of urban zones in Chicago, and agree with Burgess's estimation of suburbs as "zones of restricted development" where "the American of our native traditions feel somewhat secure from the tide of immigrant invasion" (Huntington and Whitney 1927, 91). Even before the HOLC had codified its racial scale, Huntington understood that racial restrictions made suburban development a site of eugenic action.

Huntington first promoted a eugenic housing idea in his 1936 essay, "A Family Community" for the *Atlantic Monthly*'s Million Dollar Community Contest. Huntington's ideal community promoted child bearing by "enabling high-grade parents to have families of reasonable size without lowering their standard of living." The keys to this community were four-fold: "(1) young parents, (2) suburban homes, (3) co-operative enterprises, and (4) expert trustees" (Huntington n.d.). Subsidized health care and scholarships would lighten the economic cost of child rearing, while communal laundries, garages, groundskeeping, health services, and housekeeping would make parenting easier and discourage excess individualism. The family-oriented community that Huntington imagined would supposedly create a model city while physically improving its population (Lovett 2007a).

Family thinking had always been an important feature of the American eugenics movement. In 1937 and 1938, Dr. Willystine Goodsell, a professor at the Teacher's College of Columbia University and vice president of the AES, organized several "outreach conferences" seeking to build connections to recreation experts, housing planners, religious leaders, "family relations" experts, birth-control advocates, educators, nurses, physicians, and publicists; all with the aim of promoting larger and fitter families. Goodsell was particularly engaged with the connections between eugenics and housing (Goodsell 1937; Lovett 2007a, 2007b).

In 1938 Goodsell organized an AES-sponsored housing conference in New York City (Anonymous 1938). This conference attempted to articulate and strengthen the relationship between eugenics and community planners. Many of the presenters at the Conference became some of the most important postwar housing-policy advocates. Warren S. Thompson of the Scripps Foundation for Research in Population Problems connected the need for housing subsidies to increased family size. He argued that housing put a direct limit on decisions about family size because they imposed "competing choices in family budgets" (1938a, 1). He urged that "the cost of adequate housing" be considered in terms of its effect "in determining the number of children that will be raised in many families" (1938a, 1). For Thompson, publisher of the most widely used textbook on demography until the 1960s and a long-standing member of the AES, the "city-village-rural differentials in reproduction" should frame U.S. housing considerations. With the rural birth rate higher than the urban birth rate, city-based subsidies were not enough. In his words, "even if housing in cities is greatly improved and cheapened for the moderate sized family, it is quite uncertain whether this alone will have any very marked effect on the birth rate of the urban population." Location mattered. Thompson argued that high birth rates would only be achieved by moving people from congested cities to "rural and semi-rural areas." In a published version of his comments, Thompson claimed even more emphatically that housing programs must encourage the "propagation of sound stock and discouraging those which are harmful biologically" (Thompson 1938b). Thompson, like Huntington and others, grasped the eugenic implications of suburban development and believed that eugenics had to be considered as new communities were planned (Lovett 2007a).

Suburban development—with its promise of redistributing population away from city centers in ways that could be regulated for race, ethnicity, and socioeconomic factors—promised to encourage the birth rate in what came to be called *bedroom communities*. In his presentation at the AES Housing Conference, Russell Black, president of what would be eventually be called the American Planning Association, agreed that suburban development was the best solution to population redistribution away from urban centers. As a developer of the famous New Deal Suburb of Radburn, New Jersey, Black had been involved in the planning of the model greenbelt community. Reluctant to claim that suburbs would wholly arrest declining white native-born population trends, Black *did* embrace eugenic ideology, arguing, in his words, "We have great mutual concern that the quality of the American people shall not be forced out by degrading and unhealthful environment nor bred out by unfortunate inheritance" (1938, 2). For Black, the planner for the Philadelphia tristate regional plan and Princeton, New Jersey, urged other "housers" to shape the environment to "make the most of whatever human material is at hand" (Black 1938, 2; Lovett 2007a).

Housing activist Edith Elmer Wood was more willing than Black to find direct eugenic implications in housing. Wood had been advocating slum clearance and redevelopment since at least 1931 when she urged giving "every American child something like an even break to show the stuff that was in him" (Wood 1931, 296). As a member of the Regional Planning Association of America, she helped redefine residential neighborhoods and influenced the Greenbelt developments of the federal Resettlement Administration (Hayden 2004, 125–26). At the AES Housing Conference, she recognized that the issues that concerned her and other planners were better described as "eugenics and euthenics." Of particular concern for Wood was the nature of governmental support for housing. She advocated for limiting spending on public housing, which would limit dwelling size and thus limit the size of families that could healthily inhabit those quarters. Wood argued that the population effects of spending limitations in the Wagner-Steagall Act (the national housing act that supported low-income housing and slum clearance) were understood and referred to in the congressional debate as the "race suicide amendment" (1938, 4). Without more government support, Wood feared that housing for larger families would not be possible.

Nevertheless, Wood claimed that the private-housing system should be under the influence of organizations such as the AES. It was up to eugenicists, Wood claimed, to "change the ideology and family-size habits" of those who could afford to use the FHA system (1938, 5). Wood herself advocated a "three-bed-room standard as a family norm" for both its social and eugenic consequences (Wood 1938). In her words, "Houses are also like factories. Their output is children—the citizens of tomorrow" (Wood 1940; Lovett 2007a).

Woods's eugenics concerns were also shared by Robert Cook, the managing editor of the *Journal of Heredity*. In 1937 Cook published an article in that journal titled "Eugenics at Greenbelt," where he notes that the government programs to create new communities by the Resettlement Administration of the U.S. Department of Agriculture were not claimed to be "eugenic experiments," but that they certainly had eugenic implications because of their selection criteria. The Greenbelt development was a suburban community in Maryland created for low-income residents. It was one of many such communities developed under the New Deal's resettlement program. Each family that wanted to live in Greenbelt had to go through a selection process where their finances, "personality, intelligence, and cooperative spirit" were all evaluated. The result of this selection process could be a group of families that were more desirable from a eugenic point of view. However, Greenbelt shared the same problem as many other federal housing programs, in that most of the housing had two or three bedrooms. This was interpreted by Cook to mean that the housing was appropriate for two-child families, instead of the four- or five-child families that the AES recommended for the eugenically select. So, on the one hand, if the residents of Greenbelt really were eugenically superior, their new housing would in fact have the dysgenic effect of limiting their family size (Cook 1937). On the other hand, however, if their lower income was an indicator of their eugenic undesirability, then the Greenbelt's small number of rooms would have a eugenic effect as it encouraged smaller family size among its residents.

From both Cook's and Wood's perspectives, the eugenic message in favor of housing that promoted a three- or four-child family was not really getting through to federal housing planners. Federal housing advocates were happy to advocate family-friendly features of their developments and selectively admit those who they thought were appropriate to their new communities, but to Cook and Wood they did not fully embrace a shared eugenic vision for their communities and the number of rooms in their ideal homes seemed to favor a two-child norm rather than a four-child norm.

Conclusion

Eugenicists deliberately embraced suburban development in the 1930s. Suburban communities embodied their ideal of a child-friendly rural environment that was affordable and close to the benefits of the city. These bedroom communities, they hoped, would allow families to have more children, at least four, but according to eugenicists, these families had to be selected. Racially restrictive practices, such as redlining based on a eugenically organized racial hierarchy, constituted a form of eugenic discrimination. Like direct interventions, such as eugenic sterilization, housing practices thus became a form of reproductive regulation intended to encourage selected families to have more children, while discriminating against African Americans and many immigrant groups in order to deny them housing that would make it easier for their families to grow. Indeed, the eugenicists' ideal of the four-child family came to fruition in the postwar "baby boom" with its average family of 3.5 children often housed in these segregated suburban communities.

While urban historians have noted the parallels between the history of racially discriminatory housing policies and the history of eugenics in the United States, appeals to shared nativist racism do not capture the extent to which these histories were intertwined. Eugenicists, such as Ellsworth Huntington, understood housing to be an important site of eugenic action and deliberately steered the American Eugenics Society toward suburban development as a form of eugenic intervention. Huntington and other members of the AES were happy to start with eugenic selection based on a racist hierarchy "validated" by the Army Intelligence tests but understood that more extensive selection and greater emphasis on family size were essential for their ends. In this context, Homer Hoyt's adoption of the same racial hierarchy advocated by eugenicists can be read, at minimum, as an acknowledgment of the compatibility of racially and ethnically informed housing discrimination and eugenic ideals in the 1930s. But evidence for a more substantial relationship between housing and eugenics does not have to rest on Hoyt and the HOLC. Other real-estate developers and planners were openly sympathetic to the demographic and eugenic concerns of the American Eugenics Society. Restrictive suburbs, such as Radburn, New Jersey, were not merely white enclaves, they were sites of eugenically informed reproductive regulation.

The consequences of eugenically informed housing practices have been profound. Access to housing, whether through governmentally sponsored communities or through governmentally guaranteed loans, became a major source of durable wealth for a vast number of Americans in the postwar period (Yinger 2001; Briggs 2018). Without access to these loans, many African Americans were excluded from access to higher quality schools and concentrated in certain neighborhoods, where home values were depressed. The wealth differential between white Americans who received housing assistance and African Americans and Latinos who did not was estimated to reach $600 billion nationwide in 1994 (Yinger 1995). More recently, these historic practices of residential segregation set the stage for "reverse redlining" where loan companies targeted neighborhoods that had previously been excluded from low-rate home loans. Far from being a reparation for the past, these loans were predatory: charging high fees, trapping owners at very high levels of debt, and costing owners their home and savings when they could not meet repayment (Taylor 2019). A 2006 report notes that African American and Latina women were especially targeted for these subprime loans (Fishbein and Woodall

2006). The resulting default rate was much higher for these loans with the effect of draining even more wealth from these previously redlined neighborhoods. These loans contributed significantly to the collapse of the housing market in the United States in 2007. The resulting inherited disparities in home ownership are rooted not just in racial discrimination per se. They are the legacy of the reproductive politics of American eugenics that sought to alter women's reproductive decisions by any means available, including housing.

Laura L. Lovett is an associate professor in the Department of History at the University of Massachusetts, Amherst. Her current research program focuses on African American feminism and the women's movement. She can be reached at lovett@history.umass.edu.

Notes
1. Some portions of this essay are drawn from Lovett 2007a and 2007b. They are marked with parenthetical references.
2. Hoyt acknowledges that his racial hierarchy was created by John Usher Smythe, a fellow Chicago real-estate broker and insurance underwriter. Jennifer Light has used quantitative methods to confirm the importance of these ethnic divisions in the HOLC grades assigned for Chicago (Light 2010).

Works Cited

American Eugenics Society. 1926. "Report of the President of the American Eugenics Society," June 26, 1926, p. 14. American Eugenics Society Papers, American Philosophical Society, Philadelphia, PA.

Anonymous. "Conference on Eugenics Aspects of Housing," April 1, 1938. Ellsworth Huntington Papers, Classified Subject File, Group 1; S *Recent Trends in American Housing*, series IV, box 27, folder 280. Yale University Library, New Haven, CT.

Bederman, Gail. 1995. *Manliness and Civilization: A Cultural History of Gender and Race in the United States, 1880–1917*. Chicago: University of Chicago Press.

Black, Russell. 1938. "Planning for Housing-Slum Reclamation, Garden Cities and Greenbelt Areas," Conference on Eugenics Aspects of Housing, April 1, 1938. Box 67, folder 20. Edith Elmer Wood Papers, Columbia University Library, New York, NY.

Briggs, Laura. 2018. *How All Politics Became Reproductive Politics: From Welfare Reform to Foreclosure to Trump*. Berkeley: University of California Press.

Brigham, Carl. 1923. *A Study of American Intelligence*. Princeton, NJ: Princeton University Press.

Conkin, Paul Keith. 1976. *Tomorrow a New World: The New Deal Community Program*. Ithaca, NY: Cornell University Press.

Cook, O. F. 1916. "Eugenics and Agriculture." *Journal of Heredity* 7, no. 6: 249–54.

Cook, Robert C. 1937. "Eugenics at Greenbelt." *Journal of Heredity* 28, no. 10: 339–44.

Currell, Sue. 2017. "You Haven't Seen Their Faces: Eugenic National Housekeeping and Documentary Photography in 1930s America." *Journal of American Studies* 51, no. 2: 481–511.

Currell, Susan. 2010. "Breeding Better Babies in the Eugenic Garden City: 'Municipal Darwinism' and the (Anti)Cosmopolitan Utopia in the Early Twentieth Century." *Modernist Cultures* 5, no. 2: 267–90.

Dachert Alfred. 1931. "Positive Eugenics in Practice: An Account of the First Positive Eugenic Experiment." *Eugenics Review* 23: 15–18.

Davenport, Charles. 1913. *Heredity in Relation to Eugenics*. New York: Henry Holt & Co.

Fishbein, Allen J., and Patrick Woodall. 2006. "Women Are Prime Targets for Subprime Lending: Women Are Disproportionately Represented in High-Cost Mortgage Market." Consumer Federation of America Report. Accessed September 14, 2019. https://consumerfed.org/pdfs/WomenPrimeTargetsStudy120606.pdf.

Freund, David M. P. 2007. *Colored Property: State Policy and White Racial Politics in Suburban America*. Chicago: University of Chicago Press.

Goodsell, Willystine. 1937. "Housing and the Birth Rate in Sweden." *American Sociological Review* 2, no. 6: 850–59.

Gordon, Linda. 1990. *Woman's Body, Woman's Right: Birth Control in America*. New York: Penguin Books.

Hayden, Dolores. 2004. *Building Suburbia: Green Fields and Urban Growth, 1820–2000*. New York: Vintage Books.

Hillier, Amy E. 2003. "Redlining and the Home Owners' Loan Corporation." *Journal of Urban History* 29, no. 4: 394–420.

Hoff, Derek S. 2008. "The Original Housing Crisis: Suburbanization, Segregation, and the State in Postwar America." *Reviews in American History* 36, no. 2: 259–69.

Horowitz, Helen L. 1993. *Alma Mater: Design and Experience in the Women's Colleges from Their Nineteenth-Century Beginnings to the 1930s*. Amherst: University of Massachusetts Press.

Hoyt, Homer. 1933. *One Hundred Years of Land Values in Chicago*. New York: Arno Press.

Huntington, Ellsworth. n.d. "A Family Community." Ellsworth Huntington Papers, Classified Subject File, group 1, series IV, box 27, folder 277. Yale University Library, New Haven, CT.

———. 1925. *The Character of Races: As Influenced by Physical Environment, Natural Selection and Historical Development*. New York: Charles Scribner's Sons.

———. 1934. "Tentative Suggestions as to Future Policies of the American Eugenics Society." Ellsworth Huntington Papers, Classified Subject File, group 1, series IV, box 29, folder 293. Yale University Library, New Haven, CT.

Huntington, Ellsworth, and Leon Whitney. 1927. *The Builders of America*. New York: William Morrow & Co.

Jackson, Kenneth T. 1985. *Crabgrass Frontier: The Suburbanization of America*. New York: Oxford University Press.

Klein, Wendy. 2001. *Building a Better Race: Gender, Sexuality, and Eugenics from the Turn of the Century to the Baby Boom*. Berkeley: University of California Press.

Ladd-Taylor, Molly. 2001. "Eugenics, Sterilisation and Modern Marriage in the USA: The Strange Career of Paul Popenoe." *Gender & History* 13, no. 2: 298–327.

Light, Jennifer. 2010. "Nationality and Neighborhood Risk at the Origins of FHA Underwriting." *Journal of Urban History* 36, no. 5: 634–71.

Lovett, Laura L. 2007a. *Conceiving the Future: Pronatalism, Reproduction, and the Family in the United States, 1890–1938*. Chapel Hill: University of North Carolina Press.

———. 2007b. "'Fitter Families for Future Firesides': Florence Sherbon and Popular Eugenics." *Public Historian* 29, no. 3: 69–85.

Martin, Geoffrey. 1973. *Ellsworth Huntington: His Life and Thought*. Hamden, CT: Archon Books.

Nightingale, Carl H. 2012. *Segregation: A Global History of Divided Cities*. Chicago: University of Chicago Press.

Osborn, Frederick. 1934. "Notes for Eugenic Program," Ellsworth Huntington Papers, Classified Subject File, group 1, series IV, box 73, folder 2815. Yale University Library, New Haven, CT.

Popenoe, Paul, and Roswell H. Johnson. 1918. *Applied Eugenics*. New York: Macmillan.

———. 1933. Applied Eugenics. Second Edition. New York: Macmillan.

Roberts, Dorothy. 1997. *Killing the Black Body: Race, Reproduction, and the Meaning of Liberty*. New York: Pantheon Books.

Ross, Edward A. 1904. "The Value Rank of the American People," *The Independent*, November 10, 1904.

———. 1905. "Causes of Race Superiority" In *Foundations of Sociology*, 353–85. New York: Macmillan.

Rothstein, Richard. 2017. *The Color of Law: A Forgotten History of How Our Government Segregated America*. New York: W. W. Norton & Company.

Schaffner, Karen J. 2010. "A Link in U.S.-Japan Eugenics Connections—Roswell Hill Johnson." *International Culture* 24: 121–45.

Schuller, Kyla. 2018. *The Biopolitics of Feeling: Race, Sex, and Science in the Nineteenth Century*. Durham, NC: Duke University Press.

Slavishak, Edward. 2009. "From Nation to Family: Two Careers in the Recasting of Eugenics." *Journal of Family History* 34, no. 1: 89–115.

Stern, Alexandra Minna. 2005. *Eugenic Nation: Faults and Frontiers of Better Breeding in Modern America*. Berkeley: University of California Press.

Taylor, Keeanga-Yamahtta. 2019. *Race for Profit: How Banks and the Real Estate Industry Undermined Black Homeownership*. Chapel Hill: University of North Carolina Press.

Thompson, Warren S. 1938a. "Eugenic Aspects of the Housing Program." Conference on Eugenics Aspects of Housing, April 1, 1938. Box 67, folder 20. Edith Elmer Wood Papers, Columbia University Library, New York, NY.

———. 1938b. "The Effect of Housing Upon Population Growth." *The Milbank Memorial Fund Quarterly* 16: 359–68.

Wood, Edith Elmer. 1931. *Recent Trends in American Housing, etc.* New York: Macmillan.

———. 1938. "The Scope and Methods of Modern Housing." Conference on Eugenics Aspects of Housing, April 1, 1938. Edith Elmer Wood Papers, Columbia University Library, New York, NY.

———. 1940. "That 'One Third of a Nation.'" *Survey Graphic* 29, no. 2: 83–88.

Yinger, John. 1995. *Closed Doors, Opportunities Lost: The Continuing Costs of Housing Discrimination*. New York: Russell Sage Foundation.

———. 2001. "Housing Discrimination and Residential Segregation as Causes of Poverty." In *Understanding Poverty*, edited by Sheldon H. Danziger and Robert H. Haveman, 359–91. Cambridge, MA: Harvard University Press.

Inheriting Educational Capital: Black College Students, Nonbelonging, and Ignored Legacies at Predominantly White Institutions

Jasmine L. Harris

Abstract: Admission to college in the United States, and subsequent access to job opportunities, networks, and wealth accumulation, are all mechanisms of educational capital in graduates' lifetimes, providing (or inhibiting) generational capital accessible to their children. However, since the United States is built on a foundation of racialized inheritance, Black college graduates do not accumulate and pass down educational capital in the same ways as their white peers. This paper explores belonging and educational capital accrual for Black students at predominantly white institutions (PWIs) to unpack the concept of inheritance as a presumed right in higher education. The connections between race and gender, education, inheritance, and capital are defined via cultures of exclusion, and structural policies limiting Black students access to, and ability to inherit capital from, prestigious PWIs. **Keywords:** race; higher education; belonging; gender; inheritance

The United States is built on a foundation of racialized and gendered inheritance. The origins of inheritance as a concept include the development of structural policies and cultural beliefs enabling entire empires to be passed down via family ties (Ditz 2014, 26). White settlers in the United States used inheritance to improve the economic potential of their children (Shammas 1987, 145–63). The indigenous people whose land they co-opted as well as the enslaved Black people forced into bondage to build infrastructure on that land, however, were prohibited from building similar livelihoods (Rasmussen 2010, 203). Over time, higher education, along with property ownership, became mechanisms racializing access to upward social mobility, thereby limiting access to generational wealth and status to white men and their progeny.

WSQ: Women's Studies Quarterly 48: 1 & 2 (Spring/Summer 2020) © 2020 by Jasmine L. Harris.

Patricia Hill Collins, theorizing on the state of education, race, and citizenship, identifies schools as the main public sites where students learn acceptable social interaction, and how perceptions of "citizenship" impact interpersonal behavior (Collins 2009, 2–3). In this way, Collins argues, "Schools do more than teach. They control access to jobs, sort people into groups by race and gender, attempt to control what we think and say, and attach privilege to some and not others" (2009, 4). This occurs via a critical mass of mundane behavioral expectations in the classroom, and the rewards or sanctions with which they are met. The connections between education, race, and inheritance make school, especially higher education, the setting where educational attainment and accrued capital are offered (or restricted) with lasting generational effects. Schools are inherently political spaces because their main function is preparing the next generation of citizens actively engaged in the social world (Collins 2009, 6). Black people and white women are no longer abjectly excluded from education, but their inclusion offers only entrance, not necessarily *belonging* on campuses. The institutional doors may be more widely open now, but engagement for nonwhite students is often superficial. Schools, and the teachers (across race, gender, and class lines) who facilitate cultural ideology there, maintain exclusionary ideals and social hierarchies (Collins 2009, 25).

Historic access to higher education was based so heavily on race and gender that structural access continues to be limited for Black people even as explicit policies restricting such access are long gone. Stagnant intergenerational mobility in Black communities is maintained as college degrees become more important to middle-class lifestyles (Rasmussen 2010, 202), a consequence of Black people's short legacy in higher education, and difficulty accruing educational capital from these institutions. This paper explores inheritable educational capital available to Black students at predominantly white institutions (PWIs) via the construction of racial hierarchies on campus.

Separate and Unequal

The prohibition of college education for white women and Black people historically has had lasting impacts on *who* can accumulate valuable educational capital in their lifetimes, and then subsequently pass it down. In 2019 income and wealth disparities persist for Black degree holders, men and women, and so, too, do poorer outcomes in health, wellness, and education (Hardy, Logan, and Parman 2018). Limited access to the country's most prestigious and predominantly white schools directly impacts the potential livelihoods of its Black graduates. As higher education was constructed in the United States, Black students were prohibited from attending schools with valuable educational capital. Simultaneously, universities opened specifically for Black students were blocked from manifesting educational capital of comparable value, and therefore the ability to pass down that value to Black graduates and their families. For Black people in higher education, there is and has been very little to inherit.

The first wave of expanded access to higher education focused on white women's educational inequality starting in 1837 with the opening of all-women's colleges, two hundred years after the first colleges began admitting white men (Perkins 1998). It would be another hundred years before PWIs begin openly admitted Black students, albeit in small numbers. Some institutions allowed Black student participation in courses, but barred them from living on campus or participating in campus activities—a clear signal that they didn't really *belong* there (Perkins 1998, 105). The early focus on white women's access to higher education positioned them in closer proximity to educated white men, and therefore privy to inheritable educational capital. The Seven Sisters colleges, opened from 1837 to 1889, were the beginning of an institutional focus on equal educational capital for white women. Their affiliations (official and social) and exclusive admissions imbued these institutions with prestige reserved explicitly for white women.

By contrast, unable to gain access to Ivy League schools, the Seven Sisters, or most of the public land grant colleges, Black people (especially in the South) almost exclusively attended Historically Black Colleges and Universities (HBCUs) starting in the mid-1960s (Gasman 2013). Through most of the twentieth century, these schools were founded by Southern states under federal law requiring them to establish separate colleges for Black students where existing higher education institutions were for white students only (Freeman and Cohen 2001, 589–92). Though often preferred because of their promise of cultural support and protection, the amount of educational capital potentially accrued from attendance at HBCUs was, and remains, substantially less valuable than for prestigious PWIs in majority white, mainstream America (Noel 2016, 1).

This is not to say that HBCU alumni do not pass down educational capital, but that the long history of devaluing credentials earned at HBCUs weakens the economic capital available via alumni membership (Noel 2016, 1). Social capital at these institutions works a bit differently, though. While still undervalued compared to PWIs, there is inheritable social status to be gained and passed down, if only in Black communities (Noel 2016, 1; Albritton 2012, 315; Freeman and Cohen 2001, 589–92). These schools offer an innate perception of belonging, and membership in an institutional "family" often unavailable to Black students at PWIs.

Part of the Family

As public education became a benefit to the labor market alongside U.S. industrialization, the "new economic order posed the danger of loosening family ties, with the school replacing the home as the source of instruction" (Viswanathan 1993, 90). As a result, modern conceptions of higher education are built on the premise of universities as extended families, where alumni status (and with it, access to elite social networks imbued with the university name) is among the most precious thing to pass down and share with children and grandchildren. Family membership on these campuses is cemented in the raced and gender focus of the institution, but only PWIs have been historically imbued with highly valued social and economic capital.

If student and alumni networks at universities are constructed as families, then campuses should be home, yet most PWIs were founded on the exclusion of Black students. This historical exclusion is one in a myriad of retellings perpetuating fictive notions of family and lineage on college campuses where Black people, in the minority as students, faculty, and staff, are not "family" at all. Instead, colleges and universities, like the businesses they model, are deeply invested in the maintenance of race, and subsequently class-based, inequalities under the guise of familial connection (Prendergast and Abelmann 2006, 42). At prestigious PWIs "family" is predominantly white, but also predominantly upper-class. This shared class membership is not incidental: belonging in the "family," in this context, has prerequisites not everyone can fill.

The connections between education, inheritance, and capital are racially constructed and defined via admissions guidelines and legacy policies that outline belonging in educational spaces. Black attendance at the country's top colleges is perpetually low; Black students make up 9 percent of Ivy League first-year students, which has been about the same percentage since 1980 (Ashkenas, Park, and Pearce 2017, 1–5). Despite Black students entering college every year in record numbers (*Journal of Blacks in Higher Education* 2012), Black students are unable to access prestigious institutions with any sustained success. University structures, policies, and campus cultures deny Black students access to mentoring and support networks afforded white classmates. As a result, perceived nonbelonging among Black students on college campuses is high, increasing as does the racial disparity of the campus population (Warikoo and Foley 2018, 1).

In an interview about familial connections to Vassar College, one of the Seven Sisters, a white woman alumnus—the parent of a Vassar student and the descendant of two generations of Vassar alumni herself—referred to the school as her "ancestral home" (Winum 2001). Vassar didn't admit its first Black student until 1941, and since then the percentage of Black students on campus has never reached double digits. On elite campuses, mental and physical fatigue makes degree completion difficult for Black students. And after graduation, for the fewer than 10 percent of Black students who obtain college degrees nationwide, the value of their alumni status, and therefore the value of that status to their children, is less than that of whites graduating from the same schools.

Not unlike connections perpetuated in the Vassar example, one-third of students admitted to Harvard University's class of 2021 were legacy students (Flanagan and Xie 2017)—which means they were admitted in part because of a previous family member's attendance. The admittance of these wealthy white students preserves racial hierarchies in American education. Their possession of the institution's name in perpetuity maintains the white supremacist hold over capital derived from attendance, preventing Black students from similar intangible possession of institutional membership. As college degrees become increasingly vital to potential wealth accumulation, affiliation with prestigious PWIs is even more significant to educational capital accrual than in previous decades.

Inheritance and Capital

Inheritance often involves the passing of prestige from one person, place, or thing to another. In fact, the value of an inheritance is in part dependent on the prestige imbued within it. Land, money, and titles are worth more or less depending on how others perceive what is being inherited and the value of that perception. Take, for example, owning a town house in New

York City's Upper East Side: though smaller in livable square footage and lot size, and without features like yards, driveways, or garages, they are nevertheless worth more than a house twice the size in Minneapolis. This is true not just because the two homes are in areas where the cost difference of housing is wide, but also because we, the collective appraisers of American society, have decided that the *opportunity* to live on the Upper East Side of Manhattan is inherently more valuable than the opportunity to live in Minneapolis. The value of the inheritance is based on the social status and access attached to it.

That valuation is comprised of a complex mix of access to restaurants, bars, museums, and shops, the neighborhood's walkability, school quality, and the prestige of owning a home in an expensive, and therefore exclusive, area. Someone inheriting ownership of a Manhattan townhouse, even if they're a long-lost relative who'd never otherwise be able to afford such a home, suddenly inherits not just the house itself but the prestige of the address as well. The property alone might not lend prestige, but additional status is gained via long-term engagement with the now accessible high-status neighbors. In this way, what is gained through inheritance is not just that which is tangible (the house itself), but also that which is given social definition.

School is one institution through which social status and generational access are passed down, though in a less tangible form. Patricia Hill Collins argues, "Elite groups manipulate education to convince the American public to view social inequalities . . . as natural, normal, and inevitable" (2009, 7), a reminder that the value of educational capital is determined by the valuation of the institution itself. The institution's value is based, in part, on who society assumes is there: the assumed race, gender, sexuality, religion, and increasingly, political identities, of students, faculty, and staff encourages or prevents imbued capital in these spaces. Prestigious PWIs provide the highest amount of educational capital in mainstream society because they are attended by mostly upper-class white students, inheriting centuries of connections and networks accessible as a result of their attendance.

By contrast, for-profit institutions, community colleges, and HBCUs hold the lowest amounts of capital because Black students are disproportionately represented there. Limiting inheritable capital accumulated by degree attainment to almost zero at these "less valuable" schools ensures Black students leave no educational legacy to pass on to future generations, even as economic labor markets force them into higher education. Difficulties accessing PWIs (because of cost, and questions of "readiness") lead Black people to for-profit institutions where the available educational capital to accumulate is minimal and decided along race and gender lines. In 2014, 31 percent of Black women graduate students attended for-profit institutions compared to 13 percent of white women (Smith 2017, 1). These institutions "exist in response to the reality that millions of prospective students exist outside the social machinery that delivers people to college" (Cottom 2017, 125), but the increasing economic importance of college degrees forces them there. Black students, who are more likely to receive degrees from less prestigious institutions, are particularly hurt because the cost of attendance necessitates large student loans with high interest rates, often without the potential for valuable capital after graduation (Baylor 2016). This trajectory to higher degree status is sometimes worse than not attending college at all as evidenced by higher rates of default of loans from these schools (Lynch, Engle, and Cruz 2010, 2; Cottom 2017, 37). Black students end up going to college anyway, often at predatory institutions, because college and assumptions of class status promised after attaining a college degree are too difficult to pass up.

This system of inheritance, capital conversion, and additional value accumulation primarily benefits white men because they are more likely than other groups to inherit something of value, more easily assume legal possession of their inheritance, and more regularly convert their inheritance into even more prestige (Jones 2017, 1). White graduates, from college acceptance to entrance into the labor market, benefit from educational capital at PWIs in ways that Black students simply cannot.

Relationship between Race and Education

Limiting access to prestigious PWIs also serves to maintain social narratives of Black people as disinterested in or unable to intellectually grasp advanced education. Low rates of Black matriculation become, as a result, the expectation rather than the rule. And so, generations of white men have benefited and continue to benefit from the capital derived from elite education, not just as a function of the education itself, but in the perceived value of the institution. Historical narratives of Black college students position them as anomalies, not as evidence of Black achievement but as a result of "unusual" individual work ethic, an intended consequence of their typical exclusion from prestigious institutions. Black students cannot just gain higher education membership through attendance the way property ownership buys membership into the "right" neighborhood, and they subsequently cannot pass down educational capital in the same way as white graduates. The structural and cultural foundations of educational inheritance limit how Black graduates are viewed, and subsequently suppress upward economic trajectories for Black people via educational achievement.

This is not merely a case of bad decision-making or lack of financial literacy. The value of educational capital by race is built on historic foundations of Black "diseducation" in the United States. As Black people were forced to build American infrastructure, they were simultaneously prohibited from learning (Wilder 2013, 107–9). Restricting education is a method of domination meant to block the potential for social, economic, or psychological freedom, and has historically prevented the same educational inheritances afforded to white graduates. These restrictions began a century of educational lag in Black communities, a perpetual sense of nonbelonging in educational institutions, and an inability to inherit or pass on educational capital for Black students. These inequities exacerbate along intersecting lines of race, gender, and class. White women's education was prioritized over that of Black people (not unlike voting rights) underscoring the value of gender when attached to whiteness. Black women, by comparison, were the last group to gain entrance to prestigious institutions.

The deep wealth disparities are, in part, a result of a century of minimal structural supports aimed at improving Black Americans lives, unlike the institutional supports provided to white people to jumpstart legacies of wealth and prosperity (Darity Jr. et al. 2018, 13). President Roosevelt's 1944 GI Bill, for example, sent hundreds of thousands of World War II veterans to college, but by 1946 only five thousand Black veterans were registered students. Stories from Black GIs repeatedly included being turned away at the college doors (Luders-Manuel 2017, 1). In the seventy-five years since, Black students remained more likely to attend poorly funded schools, further limiting the potential to access the resources and cultural prestige of PWIs. The lower average SAT scores, lower retention rates for first-year students, and higher student-faculty ratios are all reflections of that poor funding, and directly contributes to Black students' inability to accrue and pass down educational capital (Libassi 2018). By contrast, a larger percentage of white students attend private, nonprofit, four-year colleges and universities with more valuable credentials (Tate 2017, 1), compounding their educational inheritance and position atop the social and economic hierarchies. This accrual of educational capital has ramifications long past the education itself.

College degrees improve an individual's annual income by $17,500 on average (Caumont 2014), but Black college graduates earn 20 percent less in annual income than white graduates do (Carnevale, Rose, and Cheah 2011, 12). Attendance at prestigious institutions improves annual income, but Black graduates still fall way behind, indicating a racialization of incomes across professions. College degrees, then, are a gatekeeping tool preserving access to a racialized middle- and upper-class membership (Torche 2011, 772). A minimal likelihood of attendance at prestigious PWIs for Black students facilitates their nonbelonging on campus if they *do* attend, and ensures they are unable to access the "ancestral" resources hinted at by the Vassar alumnus earlier.

Stripping degree attainment of the same social capital afforded white graduates continued the racialization of derivable educational capital by race. There are countless stories of Black doctors, lawyers, judges, and professors presumed incompetent in public and professional settings despite their degree credentials. These experiences encourage internalized feelings of nonbelonging in higher education, even after leaving campus, and limit Black graduates' ability or desire to pass down those feelings to their progeny. Educational inheritance requires a sense of perpetual belonging not afforded to Black students or Black graduates. Belonging in educational settings includes a sense of safety with and connection to others in the same space. It requires familiarity with the institutional structure and culture to be successful (Harris, unpublished manuscript, 2019b, 10). Black people—often unfamiliar with the structures and cultures of PWIs—are boxed into perpetual nonbelonging there.

Black students continue to document experiences of racism and discrimination at PWIs, both at the hands of individual students, and the institutions' administrations. For example, in April 2019, Alexander McNab, a Black student at Columbia University, was physically and aggressively stopped from entering the Barnard College library (to which Columbia students have access) by campus security (Jaschik 2019, 1). In this example, nonbelonging isn't restricted to social boundaries: McNab's physical safety was at risk, and all because he didn't *look* like he belonged.

Both Barnard College, another of the Seven Sisters, and Columbia University, an Ivy League institution, are founded on the idea that Black people inherently do not belong. As such, Black students' presence in campus spaces can always be questioned, making incidents like these habitual. Zora Neale Hurston, the first Black woman to attend Barnard, described herself as the "sacred Black cow"—accepted, but distinctly out of place (Kaplan 2005, 41). More than ninety years after her attendance, Black students still remain outsiders on campuses where they *should* belong.

Racism on Campus

Black *diseducation*—the structural and cultural quarantine of Black people from all facets of school—does not just increase Black students' uncertainty about belonging, it also limits imagery of Black people across educational culture (Harris, unpublished manuscript, 2019a, 5). The process of diseducation is a concerted effort to strengthen a more concrete incompatibility between Black people and the culture of higher education; not just in the classroom, but among extracurricular activities tasked with engaging them. Their race has more salience than their education, unlike their white peers, who get to be students first and only. Schools are foundational settings of socialization, they teach us how to act, walk, talk, and think in a narrow white supremacist and heteronormative framing (Collins 2009, 100–101). Black students learn their nonbelonging early.

In particular, Black students learn their nonbelonging in school via interactions with white teachers and peers, as well as through witnessing interactions between white students and teachers. Experiences of racism in academic spaces, like the incident at Columbia and Barnard, are one way to remind Black students they do not belong. Racism at the hands of teachers and coaches is another. Sylvia Hatchell, the women's basketball coach at UNC Chapel Hill, resigned in April 2019 after players, a majority of whom were Black, claimed she threated to hang them by a noose if their game did not improve (Holcombe 2019). Greek life, too, especially at PWIs, has a long history of racism against Black students. In July 2019 white members of the Kappa Alpha fraternity at Ole Miss posed in front of Emmett Till's memorial armed with shot guns and assault rifles (Farzan 2019). The photos clearly antagonize the idea of Black safety in the South, especially for Black students attending the same university.

Well-maintained perceptions of nonbelonging for Black students make space, and the ability to identify and occupy spaces on campus deemed "safe" are vitally important to long-term survival, and success on campus because racial stereotypes of Black people perpetually threatens their physical safety and mental health. For white students, all spaces are those where they perpetually, and unquestionably, belong. If they are legacy students, it is likely that connection goes even deeper. They have heard stories about the buildings on campus. White students' sense of safety, as a result, is relatively unthreatened at PWIs. White supremacist foundations of college campuses mean processes of integration are tenuous for Black students, but hyper-surveillance and overregulation by campus administrators make success more difficult. These are not students who arrive with the same internalized feelings of campus belonging as many of their white peers do.

When Black students' safety is threatened, their nonbelonging on campus is confirmed. There is a totality to Black students' nonbelonging that spans all facets of higher education culture: academic, Greek life, and athletics. If colleges are racialized institutions (Ray 2019, 29), because they legitimate the unequal distribution of resources by race and gender, diminish the agency of Black students, perpetuate weak credentialing for Black graduates, and deviate in the practice of formal institutional policies like academic dishonesty and behavioral discipline along racial lines, then the educational capital derived from college attendance is also racialized. Through these institutional routines and practices, PWIs teach Black people's second-class citizenship as social fact, and therefore maintain the cultures and structures that do the work of their social degradation.

Inheriting Supports

The unique orientation of Black people to higher education, particularly to active and continuing practice of diseducation, limits the usefulness of educational inheritance for Black college alumni because a suspension of disbelief is required, most people are unwilling to engage in. Legacy policies are one mechanism by which white privilege in higher education is perpetuated (Wilder 2013, 150). If one-third of an entire Harvard class has legacy status, then attendance at Harvard is inheritable. But three hundred years of Black prohibition in formal systems of education means whiteness is likely required to achieve that status. Legacy students, then, can accumulate additional social and economic capital as a result of their attendance, perpetuating already disproportionate income and wealth accumulation along racial lines.

In 2014 sixty Black undergraduate students at Harvard participated in *I, Too, Am Harvard*, a multimedia project and campaign to bring the experiences and images of Black Harvard students to the fore (Butler 2014), capturing the diversity of what Harvard students *are*, beyond the expected white students. The project gained national attention in part because it problematized *who* belongs at prestigious institutions and also because the participants' personal narratives revealed patterns of nonbelonging on campus. Their experiences weren't new or unique to Harvard, just finally demanding public attention.

Harvard graduates report median family household incomes triple the national average, and are more employable than non-Harvard graduates even in down economies (Flanagan and Xie 2017). Their ability to invoke the Harvard name in job interviews, at networking events, and on professional social media sites make their attendance at the school invaluable. Ignoring the historical contexts under which relationships with U.S. colleges and universities were originally derived racializes educational inheritance and leaves little chance for Black people to gain similar access. Black graduates may on average have more money than their peers who did not attend college, but still earn and accumulate less wealth, and have to publicly assert their connections to prestigious institutions in ways white graduates do not (Reeves and Guyot 2017). This is true at Harvard and all other prestigious PWIs.

The admittance of Black students at PWIs improves institutional appearances of increased diversity but is seldom evidence of engagement and perceived belonging within the insitution. On modern American campuses, the belonging of white students, regardless of class or gender, is never in question, as revealed by the *I, Too, Am Harvard* project. By contrast, Black students have to work harder to shed their inherently conspicuous presence. They perceive themselves as existing outside of the institution itself, identifying people, places, and times where they feel unsafe, unwanted, and disconnected from the campus culture (Harris, unpublished manuscript 2019b, 2, 9). Black students in PWIs develop a distinctive consciousness rooted in their disempowerment on campus and reflecting the details of their oppressions (Collins 2009, 76–77). This alternative consciousness development includes all behavioral adjustments necessary to maintain access, if not belonging, at PWIs for Black students.

Instead, Black students have to reconstruct campus culture to more accurately reflect cultural communities in which they feel comfortable (Jack 2019, 57–58). One Black woman interview participant in Anthony Abraham Jack's research on the experiences of lower-income Black and Latinx students at prestigious PWIs, explained, "Sometimes, I feel like I go to an HBCU, except when I'm in class. My social scene is an HBCU scene" (2019, 58). This is where HBCUs hold considerably more cultural capital than do PWIs, regardless of level of observable prestige. HBCUs offer safety and protection in familiar environments that PWIs cannot promise, but with much less educational capital in the mainstream. Likewise, though this student found comfort and safety in a Black campus community, her overall perception of belonging has not improved in settings she has less control over and that are likely predominantly white, like the classroom.

Minimizing the presence of Black students in higher education limits available narratives of Black success in college. Black people are increasingly more educated, but rather than being conditioned to higher education achievement at a young age, the continuous erasure of Black successes in higher education perpetuates the inability to accumulate and pass on associated educational capital. Anecdotes about experiences of racism at school are not meant to essentialize those experiences as normal, and instead serve as evidence of patterns of educational inheritance as racialized. Black diseducation is not just about who is not in school, it is about making sure those who are remember their place, and are unable to benefit from attendance in the same ways as white students do.

It is not just higher education attendance that cannot be passed down. Very few academic successes can be held, publicly acknowledged, and passed down by Black people because they are unexpected and unwanted in academic spaces. Low rates of Black students in advanced placement courses (Solórzano and Ornelas 2004, 19–21) and college honors programs (Tyson 2011, 129), and generally lower standardized test scores (Jencks and Phillips 1998, 8; Soares 2011, 17), perpetually stunts Black students' success in higher education, but is positioned as a difference in hard work and intellect between Black and white students. Acceptance of naturalized social deficits damage the ability to successfully integrate into higher education, and multiple generations of perpetuating Black people as uneducated and unable to be educated continues to economically depress Black communities. Black middle-class children are already more downwardly mobile than children of other racial demographics (Reeves and Guyot 2017), and the nullification of educational capital as a mechanism for intergenerational mobility perpetuates this social fact.

Black graduates of PWIs do still pass down an alternative form of educational capital to descendants, as well as the art of performing belonging in higher education and the tools to help extend that performance beyond graduation to maintain institutional connections. Often what they share and pass down to one another, then, are survival mechanisms, expectation setting, and access to racialized support systems (Jack 2019). Black students gravitate toward one another at PWIs because their racial identity impacts everything that happens to them, so respite is often only found in the formal (and informal) Black spaces they manage to carve out (Jack 2019). Structuring PWIs around the needs of white men, and increasingly white women, teaches students that these racial hierarchies are natural, and a foundation for performative citizenship in the United States.

For Black college students, the most important form of educational capital is student-to-student. The spaces they create on campus, then, become the things passed down—not to biological family, but to the next generation of Black students who join the campus community. This isn't true of every PWI community, but those with a steady enrollment of Black students are likely to have identified spaces on campus where they feel safe. The protection of these boundaries, along with explanations of potential advocates, racial adversaries, and general patterns of cultural racism on campus have immediate and invaluable capital, access to which can drastically improve the experiences of Black students on campus, contribute to their academic success in the present, and provide longer-term social networks that may continue to improve outcomes via shared access to resources and opportunities. It is inheritable capital, if not the economic kind.

Conclusion

This system is not fair, of course. Black students inherit a kind of capital with high value in the present—improving their on-campus experiences and perceptions of safety and connection—but this cannot be used to accumulate economic capital after graduation. Even Black legacy students are less likely to be admitted to their parents' or grandparents' alma maters than white legacy students, evidence that attendance at PWIs isn't the root of educational inheritance, race is. For Black people at prestigious institutions, college is not "a safe haven in which secure safe passage to an upper-middle class future" (Prendergast and Abelmann 2006, 41), because that class membership is less accessible to them.

Degrees from PWIs provide less value to Black students than to their white peers because assumptions of intellect and capability are mapped on to Black students regardless of their tangible achievements. Alternative institutions, like state schools, HBCUs, community colleges, and for-profit institutions are positioned as "less valuable" than prestigious PWIs in the higher education marketplace, and Black students are more likely than white students to attend all four of the aforementioned types of major alternative types of higher education institutions, expanding the chasm of educational capital between PWIs and alternative types of higher education. This structure of higher education ensures Black students' inability to extract capital from education is a perpetual byproduct of institutional discrimination from the very first day of school. White students, and white teachers' behaviors toward Black students, together with policies explicitly excluding them from admittance, and then achievement, normalizes questions of their belonging in the classroom. Minimal penalties for discrimination they experience reinforce Black students' nonbelonging and encourages lag in educational attainment, annual income, and accumulated wealth, all symptoms of the disease of inheritable education.

Educational inheritance, then, can perhaps never exist for Black people in the same way as white people. Attendance at prestigious PWIs is never assumed of Black people because Black diseducation is too ingrained in the institution itself to provide space for beneficial connections and access to similar rates of upward social mobility. In this way, inheritance is racist; and racism is both cultural and incorporated into the structure and practice of higher education membership.

Jasmine L. Harris is an assistant professor of sociology at Ursinus College. She completed her PhD at the University of Minnesota, and was previously a visiting professor at Wake Forest University. At Ursinus, she teaches courses on race, gender, class, and the institutional construction of identity, broadly defined. She can be reached at jharris@ursinus.edu.

Works Cited

Albritton, Travis J. 2012. "Educating Our Own: The Historical Legacy of HBCUs and Their Relevance for Educating a New Generation of Leaders." *Urban Review* 44, no. 3: 311–31.

Ashkenas, Jeremy, Haeyoun Park, and Adam Pearce. 2017. "Even with Affirmative Action, Blacks and Hispanics Are More Underrepresented at Top Colleges Than 35 Years Ago." *New York Times*, August 24, 2017. https://www.nytimes.com/interactive/2017/08/24/us/affirmative-action.html.

Baylor, Elizabeth. 2016. "The Unlikely Area in Which For-Profit Colleges Are Doing Just Fine." Center for American Progress (website), December 1, 2016. https://www.americanprogress.org/issues/education-postsecondary/news/2016/12/01/291656/the-unlikely-area-in-which-for-profit-colleges-are-doing-just-fine/.

Butler, Bethonie. 2014. "'I, Too, Am Harvard': Black Students Show They Belong." *Washington Post*, March 5, 2014. https://www.washingtonpost.com/blogs/she-the-people/wp/2014/03/05/i-too-am-harvard-black-students-show-they-belong/.

Carnevale, Anthony P., Stephen J. Rose, and Ban Cheah. 2011. "The College Payoff: Education, Occupations, Lifetime Earnings." A Report for the Georgetown University Center on Education and the Workforce, Washington, DC.

Caumont, Andrea. 2014. "6 Key Findings about Going to College." Pew Research Center FactTank (website), February 11, 2014. https://www.pewresearch.org/fact-tank/2014/02/11/6-key-findings-about-going-to-college/.

Collins, Patricia Hill. 2009. *Another Kind of Public Education: Race, Schools, the Media, and Democratic Possibilities*. Boston: Beacon Press.

Cottom, Tressie McMillan. 2017. *Lower Ed: The Troubling Rise of For-Profit Colleges in the New Economy*. New York: The New Press.

Darity Jr., William, Darrick Hamilton, Mark Paul, Alan Aja, Anne Price, Antonio Moore, and Caterina Chiopris. 2018. "What We Get Wrong About Closing the Racial Wealth Gap." A Report by the Insight Center for Community Economic Development, Samuel DuBois Cook Center on Social Equity. https://socialequity.duke.edu/sites/socialequity.duke.edu/files/site-images/FINAL%20COMPLETE%20REPORT_.pdf.

Ditz, Toby L. 1986. *Property and Kinship: Inheritance in Early Connecticut, 1750–1820*. Princeton, NJ: Princeton University Press.

Farzan, Antonia Noori. 2019. "Ole Miss Frat Brothers Brought Guns to an Emmett Till Memorial. They're Not the First." *Washington Post*, July 26, 2019. https://www.washingtonpost.com/nation/2019/07/26/ole-miss-emmitt-till-guns-kappa-alpha-fraternity/.

Flanagan, William S., and Michael E. Xie. 2017. "Median Family Income for Harvard Undergrads Triple National Average, Study Finds." *Harvard Crimson*, January 25, 2017. https://www.thecrimson.com/article/2017/1/25/harvard-income-percentile/.

Freeman, Kassie, and Rodney T. Cohen. 2001. "Bridging the gap between economic development and cultural empowerment: HBCUs' challenges for the future." *Urban Education* 36: 585–596.

Gasman, Marybeth. 2013. "The Changing Face of Historically Black Colleges and Universities." A Report by the Center for Minority Serving Institutions, University of Pennsylvania, Philadelphia.

Hardy, Bradley L., Trevon D. Logan, and John Parman. 2018. "The Historical Role of Race and Policy for Regional Inequality," The Hamilton Project. Brookings Institute Report. https://www.hamiltonproject.org/assets/files/PBP_HardyLoganParman_1009.pdf.

Harris, Jasmine. 2019a. "Blackademics: The Disturbing Education of Black Girls in Predominantly White Schools." Unpublished manuscript, last modified December 3, 2019. Microsoft Word file.

———. 2019b. "The Evolution of Belonging: Space, Identity, and Culture for Marginalized Students on College Campuses." Unpublished manuscript, last modified May 2, 2019. Microsoft Word file.

Holcombe, Madeline. 2019. "UNC Women's Basketball Coach Resigns after Review Finds She Made 'Racially Insensitive' Remarks." CNN.com, April 19, 2019. https://www.cnn.com/2019/04/19/us/unc-womens-basketball-sylvia-hatchell-resigns/index.html.

Kaplan, Carla. 2002. *Zora Neale Hurston: A Life in Letters*. New York: Anchor Books.

Jack, Anthony Abraham. 2019. *The Privileged Poor: How Elite Colleges Are Failing Disadvantaged Students*. Cambridge, MA: Harvard University Press.

Jaschik, Scott. 2019. "Entering Campus Building While Black." *Inside Higher Ed*, April 15, 2019. https://www.insidehighered.com/news/2019/04/15/barnard-suspends-police-officers-after-incident-black-student.

Jencks, Christopher, and Meredith Phillips. 1998. *The Black-White Test Score Gap*. Washington, DC: Brookings Institution Press.

Jones, Janelle. 2017. "Receiving an Inheritance Helps White Families More Than Black Families." Economic Policy Institute (website), February 17, 2017. https://www.epi.org/publication/receiving-an-inheritance-helps-white-families-more-than-black-families/.

Journal of Blacks in Higher Education. 2012. "Black Student College Graduation Rates Remain Low, But Modest Progress Begins to Show." http://www.jbhe.com/features/50_blackstudent_gradrates.html.

Libassi, CJ. 2018. "The Neglected College Race Gap: Racial Disparities among College Completers." Center for American Progress (website), May 23, 2018. https://www.americanprogress.org/issues/education-postsecondary/reports/2018/05/23/451186/neglected-college-race-gap-racial-disparities-among-college-completers/.

Luders-Manuel, Shannon. 2017. "The Inequality Hidden within the Race-Neutral G.I. Bill." *JSTOR Daily*, September 18, 2017. https://daily.jstor.org/the-inequality-hidden-within-the-race-neutral-g-i-bill/.

Lynch, Mamie, Jennifer Engle, and José L. Cruz. 2010. "Subprime Opportunity: The Unfulfilled Promise of For-Profit Colleges and Universities." A Report by the Education Trust.

Noel, Marcus. 2016. "ROI on HBCUs: The Role of Historically Black Colleges in the 21st Century." Forbes.com, May 2, 2016. https://www.forbes.com/sites/under30network/2016/05/02/roi-on-hbcus-the-role-of-historically-black-colleges-in-the-21st-century/#a6aa798720be.

Perkins, Linda M. 1998. "The Racial Integration of the Seven Sister Colleges." *Journal of Blacks in Higher Education* 19: 104–8.

Prendergast, Catherine, and Nancy Abelmann. 2006. "Alma Mater: College, Kinship, and the Pursuit of Diversity." *Social Text* 24, no. 1: 37–53.

Rasmussen, Birgit Brander. 2010. "'Attended with Great Inconveniences': Slave Literacy and the 1740 Carolina Negro Act." *PMLA* 125, no. 1: 201–3.

Ray, Victor. 2019. "A Theory of Racialized Organizations." *American Sociological Review* 84, no. 1: 26–53.

Reeves, Richard V., and Katherine Guyot. 2017. "Black Women Are Earning More College Degrees, But That Alone Won't Close Race Gaps." Brookings (website), December 4, 2017. https://www.brookings.edu/blog/social-mobility-memos/2017/12/04/black-women-are-earning-more-college-degrees-but-that-alone-wont-close-race-gaps/.

Shammas, Carole. 1987. "English Inheritance Law and Its Transfer to the Colonies." *American Journal of Legal History* 31, no. 2: 145–63.

Smith, Ashley A. 2017. "For-Profit Graduate Schools Popular with Black Women." *Inside Higher Ed*, July 25, 2017. https://www.insidehighered.com/news/2017/07/25/black-women-graduate-students-enroll-higher-numbers-profits.

Soares, Joseph A. 2011. *SAT Wars: The Case for Test-Optional College Admissions.* New York: Teachers College Press.

Solórzano, Daniel G., and Armida Ornelas. 2004. "A Critical Race Analysis of Latina/o and African American Advanced Placement Enrollment in Public High Schools." *High School Journal* 87, no. 3: 15–26.

Tate, Emily. 2017. "Graduation Rates and Race." *Insider Higher Ed*, April 26, 2017. https://www.insidehighered.com/news/2017/04/26/college-completion-rates-vary-race-and-ethnicity-report-finds.

Torche, Florencia. 2011. "Is a College Degree Still the Great Equalizer? Intergenerational Mobility across Levels of Schooling in the United States." *American Journal of Sociology* 117, no. 3: 763–807.

Tyson, Karolyn. 2011. *Integration Interrupted: Tracking, Black Students, and Acting White After* Brown. New York: Oxford University Press.

Viswanathan, Gauri. 1993. "The Naming of Yale College: British Imperialism and American Higher Education." In *Cultures of United States Imperialism,* edited by Amy Kaplan and Donald E. Pease, 85–108. Durham, NC: Duke University Press.

Warikoo, Natasha, and Nadirah Farah Foley. 2018. "How Elite Schools Stay So White." *New York Times,* July 24, 2018. https://www.nytimes.com/2018/07/24/opinion/affirmative-action-new-york-harvard.html.

Wilder, Craig Steven. 2013. *Ebony and Ivy: Race, Slavery, and the Troubled History of America's Universities.* New York: Bloomsbury Press.

Winum, Jessica. 2001. "Family Ties: Vassar Legacies." *Vassar Quarterly* 97, no. 4.

African Antisodomy Laws as Unwanted Colonial Inheritances

Ashley Currier and Keeley B. Gogul

Abstract: Across the African continent, antisodomy laws are increasingly being repealed. Yet uneven support for the rescission of antisodomy laws in other African countries remains. In this essay, we treat the retention of antisodomy laws in Namibia as an unwanted colonial legacy that serves as a reminder of the unfinished business of decolonization. We explore how politicized homophobia in Namibia functions as a state tool by continually reinscribing inherited antisodomy laws to promote a heteronormative future. We explore why these laws remain on the books in spite of the government's policy of nonenforcement and consider their impact on the male prison population. Finally, we consider decolonization as a potential tool for collective mobilization in Namibia. **Keywords:** antisodomy laws; decolonization; inheritance; legacy; heteronormative futurity; Namibia; social movements

In 2019 Angola and Botswana joined Mozambique and South Africa as southern African countries that have decriminalized same-sex sex. In contrast, Malawi and Namibia have retained colonial-era antisodomy laws. Namibia's antisodomy law was part of Roman-Dutch common law, which is a form of "law developed through successive court cases instead of being stated in legislation" (Hubbard 2007, 120).[1] After independence, Namibia "inherited" this law, which dates back to 1927; the Combating of Immoral Practices Act of 1980 strengthened it (Other Foundation 2017, 7).[2] In contemporary Namibia, the common-law crime of sodomy applies to anal sex between men, and "unnatural sexual offences" covers mutual masturbation and "other unspecified sexual activity between men," such as oral sex (Hubbard 2007, 120). The law does not apply to sex between women,

WSQ: Women's Studies Quarterly 48: 1 & 2 (Spring/Summer 2020) © 2020 by Ashley Currier and Keeley B. Gogul.

103

generating legal invisibility for lesbian and bisexual women (Frank and Khaxas 1996).

As in other postcolonial countries in the Global South (Puri 2016), Namibian politicians exploit antisodomy statutes to justify homophobic rhetoric in their deployment of "politicized homophobia." A form of propaganda that fuels anti-colonial sentiment, politicized homophobia depicts same-sex sex as an unwanted colonial import and lesbian, gay, bisexual, and transgender (LGBT) rights as continuing Western imperialism (Currier 2019). Politicized homophobia resolves the paradox between antisodomy laws as a colonial inheritance and the contemporary nationalist construct of LGBT rights as ongoing Western imperialism, and mobilizes both concepts in service of the state. In a 2008 report tracing the colonial origins of antisodomy laws, Human Rights Watch noted how "judges, public figures, and political leaders have, in recent decades, defended those laws as citadels of nationhood and cultural authenticity. Homosexuality, they now claim, comes from the colonizing West. They forget the West brought in the first laws enabling government to forbid and repress it" (2008, 8). Given the government's investment in politicized homophobia, it is notable that Namibian authorities seem disinterested in enforcing the antisodomy law. According to the Namibian Legal Assistance Centre, "There are no reported court cases involving prosecution for consensual sodomy or unnatural sexual offences between adult males since Namibian independence" (2015, 67).[3]

The Namibian government's unofficial moratorium on the antisodomy law and simultaneous deployment of politicized homophobia over the past twenty years seems to indicate ambivalence about the role of gender and sexual diversity in the newly liberated nation. On one hand, the moratorium indicates an unwillingness to prosecute people who engage in nonnormative sex acts. On the other hand, state leaders' use of politicized homophobia demonstrates that they can police gender and sexual diversity more ruthlessly and forcefully than former colonizers who now champion LGBT rights. In this regard, both sexual minority women and men experience the negative effects of a universalized anti-homosexual prejudice that proponents of politicized homophobia deploy when they defend the antisodomy law's continued existence. However, we explore a more calculated reason for the moratorium, one that protects inherited antisodomy laws as a way to fortify the state's anti-LGBT agenda. Arresting and prosecuting offenders would expose these colonial-era laws to "penal code modernization" through the Namibian court system (Frank and Moss 2017, 954). Such exposure risks changes to these laws that would, in turn, disempower politicized homophobia as a tool the state can use to advance its narrative of a heteronormative future. Thus, state leaders choose to keep these laws and *intentionally* fail to arrest and prosecute offenders. While this would seem to mitigate the impact of antisodomy laws, state leaders invoke antisodomy laws in nonprosecutorial ways that simultaneously violate the rights of Namibian citizens—both gay and straight—and, ironically, threaten the future of all Namibians.

The state mobilizes antisodomy laws to justify denying incarcerated people access to condoms, using the argument that because sodomy is illegal, prisoners have no legal right to condoms. Incarcerated men who have sex with men (MSM) are at risk of contracting HIV due to the lack of safer-sex technologies available in prisons. Approximately 27 percent of MSM in Namibia are HIV positive, whereas about 13.8 percent of the Namibian population are HIV positive (Fay et al. 2011). Furthermore, a meta-analysis of prisons worldwide found that recent incarceration is associated with an 81 percent increase in HIV risk (Stone et al. 2018). Upon their release, prisoners rejoin the population at large, thus exponentially increasing the chances of HIV transmission outside of prison walls.

In this essay, we treat the retention of antisodomy laws in Namibia as an unwanted inheritance from colonial occupiers, evidence of the unfinished business of decolonization. We explore why these laws are unenforced and examine how they affect the Namibian prison population. Finally, we discuss how and why Namibian social movements and lawmakers have not treated the repeal of colonial-era antisodomy laws as part of the nation's continuing commitment to decolonization.

Inheritance, Legacy, and Heteronormative Futurity

We deploy the terms *inheritance*, *legacy*, and *futurity* to understand how postcolonial African governments *inherited* laws that remained in place at the time of independence. In many cases, lawmakers and constitutional architects changed or repealed these laws as countries struggled to shake off the last vestiges of colonial rule. However, laws that remain unchanged—like the antisodomy law in Namibia—have affected multiple generations, thus becoming lasting *legacies* of colonial rule. This generational multiplicity imparts a temporal futurity to these laws, as future generations inherit the social and cultural effects of these legacies. As Jack Halberstam explains,

> The time of inheritance refers to an overview of generational time within which values, wealth, goods, and morals are passed through family ties from one generation to the next. It also connects the family to the historical past of the nation, and glances ahead to connect the family to the future of both familial and national stability. (2005, 5)

Importantly, this connection between history and futurity, and family and the state, inscribes inherited norms (both legal and otherwise) on future generations. Paradoxically, the retention of antisodomy laws signals to some foreign observers that specific African states refuse to abandon a backward-looking, "death-driven politics" (Nyong'o 2012, 41).

The Namibian state's investment in a specifically *heteronormative* futurity dates back to legal precedent set in the late nineteenth century when Namibia (then known as South West Africa) was a German colony. In a series of court cases, the German government expelled three German nationals and one British national from its African colonies for violating paragraph 175 of the German Criminal Code, which forbids sexual acts between men (Walther 2008). In these cases, the colonial legal system spoke definitively about what sex acts (penile-vaginal penetrative sex within wedlock) between which kinds of people (people of the opposite gender but same race) were acceptable to the state. These cases established legal precedent in German colonies like Namibia, where "the heterosexually constituted family occupied a significant position that formed the foundations of the political order similarly emerging with the growth of nationalism" (Walther 2008, 18). Combined with other laws and social norms of the time, this legal precedent defined the German subject as male, white, middle class, and heterosexual (Walther 2008, 23).

The legacy of heteronormative futurity informs not only politicized homophobia but also laws regulating the reproduction of Namibian women of African descent. For example, the South West African People's Organisation (SWAPO) leaders' commitment to a heteronormative future surfaced in movement edicts forbidding black Namibian women from using contraceptives in the 1980s (Lindsay 1986), a development that evokes U.S. black nationalists' opposition to birth control (Ross 2017). SWAPO developed this pronatalist policy to combat South African population-control policies that forced African women to use contraceptives or to undergo sterilization procedures, which leaders feared would lead to ethnic extinction.

Like other African national liberation movements (Epprecht 2005), SWAPO imagined a nationalist, heteronormative future for an independent Namibia premised on homophobia. Politicized homophobia can bolster nationalist movements' claims to be the only legitimate leaders of a new nation, strengthening newly secured sovereignty. As leaders note how effective homophobia is in rallying ordinary citizens, homophobia becomes a capacious, portable political strategy they can use to silence gender and sexual dissidents as well as political opponents. In an act of historical amnesia, some Namibian political leaders do not recognize homophobia or antisodomy laws as colonial inheritances. Citing Western countries' liberalization of laws governing same-sex sex as evidence of moral depravity, some Namibian political leaders emphasize their investment in heterosexual reproduction as establishing a lasting legacy. Anti-homosexuality laws and ideologies install heteronormative futurity, guaranteeing African national sovereignty.

When SWAPO freed Namibia from South African apartheid rule, it seemed possible that leaders would roll back discriminatory laws and remedy persisting racial, gender, and sexual injustices. However, just five years after liberating the country from South African apartheid rule, SWAPO leaders rolled out *politicized* homophobia. In fact, just after Zimbabwean president Robert Mugabe famously denounced lesbian and gay activists trying to secure a stall at the 1995 Zimbabwe International Book Fair as "worse than pigs and dogs" (Reddy 2002, 174), SWAPO and state leaders in Namibia began indulging in preemptive politicized homophobia, which refers to the use of homophobia to obstruct the emergence of LGBT rights advocacy (Currier 2019). Journalists stoked politicized homophobia in Namibia in October 1995 by asking a range of politicians—whose portfolios had little to do with health or the law—about their views on same-sex sexualities (Mwilima 1995). One year later, Namibian president Sam Nujoma disparaged lesbians and gay men at the SWAPO Women's Council Congress (Günzel 1996). In 1998 Jerry Ekandjo, Namibia's minister of home affairs, apparently unaware of the state's lack of enforcement of antisodomy laws, threatened to increase penalties for individuals convicted of such acts (Weidlich 1998). Then–prime minister Hage Geingob assured LGBT Namibians that Ekandjo's promise would go unfulfilled (Hamata

2000). Ekandjo subsequently encouraged police officers to "eliminate" gays and lesbians in 2000 (*Namibian* 2000). Opposition lawmakers suggested that Ekandjo was endorsing that "gay and lesbian people should be murdered" (Angula 2000). Although he stated that his call was not intended to incite violence, he maintained, "We never had moffies in mind when Swapo drafted the Namibian Constitution ten years ago" (Hamata 2000).[4] Following Ekandjo, President Nujoma asked police to "arrest, imprison, and deport homosexuals and lesbians found in Namibia," a request that went unenforced (*Namibian* 2001). SWAPO's homophobia displaced "truly emancipatory policies in Namibia," such as antipoverty initiatives, as political elites used the cover of anti-colonialism to elicit ordinary Namibians' discontent (Melber 2015, 107).

The biggest obstacle to ridding Namibia of antisodomy laws is the enduring legacy of politicized homophobia. Although older enthusiastic proponents have retired from politics, younger politicians seem eager to seize and strategically deploy the politicized homophobia they inherited from national liberation heroes. What is *new* is that members from both the ruling and opposition political parties traffic in politicized homophobia. Emulating the South African group of the same name, leaders from the Namibia Economic Freedom Fighters (NEFF) proudly announced the group's anti-homosexuality position at its launch as a political party in 2014. By staking a position on same-sex sexualities, NEFF leaders suggested that they were joining SWAPO in deploying politicized homophobia. By making "homophobia a cornerstone of their campaign" (Weylandt 2015, 128), NEFF asserted its political legitimacy through its devotion to a future free from colonial rule, one that rejected sexual diversity.

Responding to a 2014 election questionnaire soliciting political parties' positions on different issues, NEFF remained committed to an anti-gay stance, unlike other political parties that affirmed that all Namibians had the same constitutional rights, regardless of their sexual orientation (Sam 2014). Although NEFF recognized LGBT Namibians would "have the same rights as other citizens," the party claimed it would institute "programmes and mechanisms . . . to reduce homosexual practices" (Sam 2014, 61). NEFF promised that "no homosexuality shall be practiced amongst leaders" (61). NEFF leaders seemed to adhere to a principle that citizens would emulate their leaders. Hence, they would have to ensure NEFF leaders refrained from same-sex sex because "if the leaders are allowed to do that [have same-sex sex], then the rest of the nation is influenced by this practice. Therefore, we . . . don't endorse homosexuality amongst leaders" (Sam 2014, 61). In spite of NEFF's emphatic rejection of colonialism, the party revives the legacy of German laws in homophobic rhetoric that evokes the colonial court's decision to eject members of its own government from South West Africa for engaging in same-sex sex acts. Politicized homophobia remains a reliable position, enabling opposition politicians to assert their electoral viability.

Protecting the Legacy: State Resistance to Repealing Antisodomy Laws

Unlike some elites' commitment to retaining antisodomy laws, there is growing consensus inside and outside of Namibia that lawmakers should eliminate antisodomy laws. The 2011 Universal Periodic Review Working Group recommended that Namibia repeal all laws that criminalize same-sex sex, which the government rebuffed (Nakuta 2013). The Office of the Ombudsman, a Namibian state agency, observed, "The continued existence of the common law crime of sodomy is by its very nature and content discriminatory" (2013, 96). In 2016 the International Covenant on Civil and Political Rights' Human Rights Committee advised Namibian lawmakers to "abolish the common law crime of sodomy and include same-sex relationships in the Combating of Domestic Violence Act (Act No. 4 of 2003)" (*Namibian Sun* 2016b). Despite pressure from domestic and international communities, SWAPO and state leaders' investment in politicized homophobia and antisodomy laws is still palpable. SWAPO and state officials have deployed "national-readiness" arguments, which are claims that the country cannot handle discussions about same-sex sexualities or antisodomy laws (Currier 2019). For instance, in 2014, Sacky Shangala, the chairperson of the Namibian Law Reform Development Commission, claimed that "Namibia is not ready to have a debate about repealing the country's antisodomy law," a claim he used to justify his refusal to consider eliminating this law (*Namibian Sun* 2014). National-readiness arguments infantilize citizens of African nations, treating them as too immature to handle such debates. This defense rings particularly hollow, given other southern African nations' decriminalization of consensual same-sex sex between adults.

Soon after his election as president in 2015, a journalist asked Hage Geingob about his plans for sexual minority rights. In response, Geingob said,

My goodness, we are talking about poverty eradication, unemployment, food, and yet my young brother comes up with gay issues! Those are not the issues we are talking about. Those things are luxuries. I am talking about poverty eradication, lack of houses . . . Are you oppressed? Are you suppressed? Are gays oppressed here? Is there any gay who has been arrested here for being gay? Those are issues that you should report to the Police. The Police deal with such cases. Why do you create a problem where there is no problem? When I took my course in social problems, I learned that a social problem is what you make it to be. Even if there is no problem, you just complain and make it a problem. There is no problem. (Ntinda n.d.)

Geingob's refusal to contemplate sexual minority rights complicates his earlier conciliatory position on the issue. In the past, not only had he interpreted the constitution's equality clause as including sexual minority rights but he had also reassured LGBT Namibians that the state would neither prosecute nor persecute gender and sexual minorities. His later response rebuffed consideration of "gay issues," ranking socioeconomic inequalities as more pressing than sexual minority rights, characterized as "luxuries." He declined to address how politicized homophobia aggravated the socioeconomic precarity experienced by Namibian gender and sexual minorities.

Whereas some SWAPO politicians like President Geingob have dismissed sexual minority rights as a political issue, others returned to the party's inherited antiqueer vitriol to garner support from voters, combining populism and politicized homophobia. In 2016 Albert Kawana, Namibia's minister of justice, claimed that the government "has no intention to repeal the common law on sodomy, nor does it see the need to legalise gay relationships because it is a non-issue" (Shapwanale 2016b). Kawana portrayed SWAPO's position on decriminalizing same-sex sex as benign inaction; like other government officials, he seemed to fear inciting more vituperative antigay sentiments, if the ruling party initiated such legal reform. Soon after the UN recommended that Namibian lawmakers eliminate the antisodomy law, the SWAPO Party Youth League (SPYL) renewed the party's politicized homophobia. Sam Hamupolo, a SPYL spokesperson, rejected the "promotion of the behaviour of gays and lesbians" (*Namibian Sun* 2016c). Although Hamupolo recognized that the constitution protects all citizens' rights, he employed a majoritarian argument to discount sexual minority rights because "the promotion of the practices of gays and lesbians cannot be tolerated in Namibia, because that is not what the people of Namibia want" for the country in the present (*Namibian Sun* 2016c). The emphasis on present intolerance disguises practices among some Namibian ethnic groups, such as the Damara, some of whom validate gender and sexual diversity, while reinforcing heteronormative patriarchy associated with other ethnic groups, such as the Herero and Ovambo (Lorway 2007).

In addition to the ideological and political arguments above, there is a structural reason for the state's resistance to the repeal of antisodomy laws. The legal system of contemporary Namibia is based on the Namibian Constitution, which consists of three branches of government: the executive, the legislature, and the judiciary. The judicial branch creates a court system in Namibia. As such, jurisprudence is an important mechanism for change, allowing inherited laws and their legacies to be remediated in the light of current cultural norms. Homophobic, nationalist government officials may fear exposing inherited antisodomy laws to the scrutiny of contemporary customary international law and current Namibian case law. Government officials may view prosecution of antisodomy law violations as too risky, as it would open up such laws to the possibility of court-mandated change. Finally, although the government chooses not to enforce these laws, it still uses them as a legal "excuse" to incite action in specific and harmful ways.

Politicized homophobia grounded in the legacy of colonial antisodomy laws fuels state leaders' antigay denunciations, emboldening some police and military officials to punish people they perceived to be gender and/or sexually nonconforming. In 2001 Special Field Forces (SFF) members approached men in a Windhoek township who were

> wearing earrings and, in some cases, ripped them off the surprised victims' ears. . . . One of the SFF members . . . said the order had come from the President. "Where did you see men wearing earrings in our Oshiwambo culture? These things never happened before Independence. Why are they [men wearing earrings] only happening now after Independence?" (Currier 2012, 48)[5]

SFF officers interpreted men's earrings as a sign of gender and sexual nonconformity deserving of violent rebuke. In this way, the antisodomy law's persistence functions as a form of "homocriminality," a term Amar Wahab uses to capture how queer people only become legible in postcolonial states' legal frameworks as "criminals" (2012, 488). More recently, LGBT activists have been documenting violent homophobic assaults perpetrated by police and military personnel after the launch of Operation Kalahari Desert in 2019, a campaign intended to thwart crime in Namibian cities. Critics inside and outside of the government have decried the unbridled violence police and soldiers have unleashed on poor and working-class communities (*Namibian* 2019a). At an LGBT activist gathering in June 2019, several activists discussed how police were targeting gender and sexual minorities in a manner reminiscent of the SFF "earring incident" (ethnographic observation by Currier, June 4, 2019). While this homophobic behavior by police is overtly violent, government officials also use antisodomy laws to act against the Namibian population in more subtly violent ways, such as by making condoms unavailable in prisons.

The Antisodomy Law and Same-Sex Sexualities in Prison

Although the Namibian state uses antisodomy laws to justify denying incarcerated men access to condoms, an act that has long-term consequences for both the prisoners and population at large, individual government officials disagree about whether to distribute condoms to incarcerated people. Whereas Marco Hausiku, minister of prisons and correctional services, viewed giving condoms to incarcerated people as "encouraging homosexuality" in the mid-1990s, his deputy minister, Michaela Hübschle, supported decriminalizing same-sex sex to allow prison and health workers to distribute condoms openly (Mutikani 1996, 1). Officials in other government ministries have also endorsed providing condoms to incarcerated people. In 1997 Libertine Amathila, minister of health and social services, encouraged officials to distribute condoms in prisons (Nel 1997). More recently, Bernard Haufiku, minister of health, articulated support for decriminalizing same-sex sex and providing condoms to incarcerated people (*Namibian Sun* 2016a; Smith 2018). In August 2018 Haufiku insinuated that his ministry was close to striking a deal to give incarcerated people access to condoms (Smith 2018).

Some Namibian nongovernmental organizations (NGOs) are beginning to explore the unfortunate consequences of the antisodomy law, and specifically the prohibition on distributing condoms to incarcerated people. The Ombetja Yehinga Organisation (OYO), an NGO that "uses the arts to create social awareness in order to decrease the impact of the HIV/AIDS pandemic among young people" (Talavera 2007, 40), sponsors the In and Out Project, which has encouraged "offenders in correctional facilities" to get tested for HIV. OYO also collaborated with incarcerated men on the script for *Salute*, a film that "challenges the non-distribution of condoms in correctional facilities." According to the film's description, "Carlito is a young Namibian man who is sentenced to five years imprisonment because of fraud. Nothing can prepare him for his new life in custody. Naïve, he get[s] lured in the group of the General . . . a dangerous criminal who rules over his cell" (*Namibian* 2017). Financing from the Global Fund to Fight HIV/AIDS, TB, and Malaria supported the film's production. In 2018 and 2019 OYO offered free screenings of *Salute* in Namibian cities and towns, and held conversations with community members about prison sexual violence and the policy forbidding incarcerated people's access to condoms.

In a video posted to OYO's Facebook account about these community conversations about the film, many audience members voiced support for giving incarcerated people access to condoms, although a small number opposed this possibility. In the video's introduction, Adriano Visagie, who plays Carlito in *Salute*, educates viewers about the film's themes:

> In Namibia, sodomy is still a crime. This is part of the old Roman-Dutch common law we inherited at independence. This law is not often used, except in correctional facilities, where it is used as an excuse to not distribute condoms to inmates. Some people think it is morally wrong for two men to have sex, but what about HIV? Will we be able to reach zero new infections if we don't repeal this law? When touring [with] our DVD *Salute*, OYO [Ombetja Yehinga Organisation] asked people in various regions what they think about the issue of condoms in correctional facilities. Here is what they have to say. (Ombetja 2019)

An audience member from Rundu, whose identity was obscured, stated, "I don't think it's a good idea, giving them condoms, because it's just going to increase rape inside the jail. And that's not good" (OYO 2019). Other audience members offered different reasons for supporting condom provision in jails and prisons. According to a Keetmanshoop audience member who offered his thoughts in Afrikaans, "I advocate condoms in correctional facilities. I think it's a good idea because sex in prison is happening. It's a fact government does not want to acknowledge" (OYO 2019). An Oshakati audience member viewed the policy on no condoms in prisons as nonsensical: "The only option is to break this law. That is not making any sense to me. There is a problem that we need to take care of ourselves. We should just make a slight change and help other human beings out" (2019). Another Keetmanshoop audience member stated, "It's a human right for everybody to have condoms. It's not for someone to deny your right to have condoms" (2019). Many Namibian audience members expressed sympathy for incarcerated people who lacked access to condoms, viewing their vulnerability to HIV/AIDS and other sexually transmitted infections as both a human rights violation and public-health problem. With such support from ordinary Namibians, it might be possible to imagine mobilizing to repeal the antisodomy law.

Mobilizing Against Namibian Antisodomy Laws

In the past, Namibian LGBT activists considered it possible to mobilize for the antisodomy law's repeal. The notion of linking the decriminalization of same-sex sex to decolonization emerged organically in southern African LGBT activist circles. Some LGBT activists with experience in anti-apartheid and/or African national liberation movements brought their anti-colonial critique into LGBT organizing. In 1998 Steven Scholz, a member of the Rainbow Project (TRP), an LGBT activist organization, emphasized the contributions that sexual minorities made to Namibia's liberation:

> Homosexuals in this country play a very important role in the economic and social development of this country. We have gays and lesbians who even play a major role in the liberation struggle. Back then it wasn't a big issue whether you were gay or not. We all had one thing in mind and that was the liberation of this country. Why can it not be the same way now? (Tibinyane 1998, 20)

In this way, activists have framed antigay laws—in particular, antisodomy laws—as unwanted colonial inheritances and legacies. In other words, as long as antisodomy laws exist, decolonization remains unfinished. In 2005, at a regional meeting of southern African LGBT activists, Namibian activists, along with others, agreed to link the decriminalization of same-sex sex with the abolition of the death penalty as anti-colonial proposals to the African Commission on Human and Peoples' Rights (ACHPR). To be clear, Namibian lawmakers had already abolished the death penalty (Chenwi 2007), but it remained a legal punishment in some African countries. Activists believed that connecting these two issues would appeal to commissioners who favored "decolonizing legal statutes" (Currier 2012, 143). In other words, activists tried to use African nationalist tropes to persuade commissioners to recommend rescinding antisodomy laws throughout the African continent.

TRP seemed poised to mount a campaign to repeal the antisodomy law in the late 1990s and early 2000s (Currier 2012; Lorway 2014). According to the organization's constitution, TRP would "lobby for equal rights and opportunities for gays, lesbians, bisexuals and transsexuals and any other group that suffers discrimination in public life and under the law." TRP viewed the legal prohibition on sodomy as a law "inherited from the colonial regime" (Tibinyane 1998, 20). Two issues kept TRP from pursuing a law-reform campaign. First, activists feared the withering effects of SWAPO leaders' politicized homophobia, which ultimately resulted in no action around decriminalizing same-sex sex. Second, internal turmoil within TRP required leaders to address the demands of poor and working-class, black and mixed-race LGBT members who wanted the organization to take up socioeconomic inequalities. These demands displaced law reform as a strategic priority for TRP (Currier 2012). When TRP ceased operations in 2010, mobilizing for the repeal of the antisodomy law seemed to drift away as a political possibility.

Conclusion

The Botswana High Court ruling striking down that country's antisodomy law in June 2019 renewed scrutiny within neighboring Namibia of its antisodomy laws. First Lady of Namibia Monica Geingos publicly endorsed scrapping them. In a speech broadcast on the state-owned television station, she indicated that not only was the antisodomy law "perhaps the only Namibian law which discriminates against men" (*Namibian* 2019b) but also that the law's disuse is "illogical to the point that nobody has been charged and convicted with sodomy in a very long time" (Beukes 2019, 5). Missing from calls for repealing the antisodomy laws is political recognition that their existence extends colonial influence and homophobia far into the future.

The SWAPO-led government's selective decolonization leaves detrimental colonial-era laws and institutions in place. Like the antisodomy law, prisons constitute another colonial inheritance, but one that many activists and politicians have yet to question. As Florence Bernault clarifies, "Colonial conquest used the prison as an early instrument for the subjugation of Africans. . . . In Africa, the prison did not replace but rather supplemented public violence" (2003, 3). Namibian social movements have not framed prisons as a colonial-era legacy or contemporary detention practices as continuing the apartheid abuses of political prisoners, in the way that LGBT activists portrayed the antisodomy law as an unwanted colonial inheritance. Framing both the antisodomy law and prisons as unwanted colonial inheritances may constitute a cultural, discursive, and political opportunity for activists in different movements. Recognizing the power of jurisprudence to capitalize on domestic and international pressure to repeal or amend colonial-era laws may provide a definitive tool for structural change.

Ashley Currier is professor and head of the Department of Women's, Gender, and Sexuality Studies at the University of Cincinnati. Her books include *Out in Africa: LGBT Organizing in Namibia and South Africa* and *Politicizing Sex in Contemporary Africa: Homophobia in Malawi*. She can be reached at currieay@ucmail.uc.edu.

Keeley B. Gogul is an Urban Morgan Fellow at the University of Cincinnati College of Law. Her publications include "Queer Assemblage as Queer Futurity: Seeking a Utopian Solution beyond 'No Future'" in *Queer Studies in Media & Popular Culture* and a forthcoming review of *Human Rights Transformation in Practice* in *Human Rights Quarterly*. She can be reached at gogulky@ucmail.uc.edu.

Notes

1. In a fact sheet for Namibian citizens, the Legal Assistance Centre explains that Dutch settlers brought "Roman-Dutch . . . legal principles" to "South Africa in the 1600s. The common law was later influenced by principles of English law, which were introduced as South Africa came under the control of England in the 1800s and 1900s. The South African legal system was applied to Namibia while Namibia was being governed by South Africa, and so became part of the legal system that Namibia inherited at independence" (Legal Assistance Centre n.d., 1).

2. Namibian state officials could use the Combating of Immoral Practices Act 21 of 1980 to prosecute gender and sexual minorities for "immoral

practices" and engaging in certain sex acts for "immoral purposes" (Shapwanale 2016a).

3. We have been unable to explain the reason for this unofficial moratorium on the antisodomy law's enforcement. In an in-person interview, John R. Wolters, the current Ombudsman in Namibia and former state prosecutor, could not recall the source of the moratorium (interview with Currier, June 13, 2019, Windhoek, Namibia).

4. Some mixed-race gay communities in South Africa use *moffie* to refer to gay men, but Ekandjo employed it pejoratively in this instance.

5. *Oshiwambo* or *Oshivambo* refers to the Ovambo majority African ethnic group in Namibia; President Nujoma hailed from the Ovambo ethnic group.

6. The anti-rape law's expansion was a welcome or unwanted development, depending on one's viewpoint. On one hand, expanded criminalization makes male-to-male rape legally visible, independent of the antisodomy law, possibly for the first time. Eventually, this development could influence how Namibians define and understand the gendered dynamics of sexual violence as including male-to-male rape. On the other hand, prison-abolition advocates and critics of carceral feminism may regard this legal expansion unfavorably, as it means that even more people may find themselves convicted under this law and incarcerated. Instead, prison-abolition activists may promote restorative justice as an alternative to incarceration.

Works Cited

Angula, Conrad. 2000. "Ekandjo Faces Vote of No Confidence." *Namibian*, October 4, 2000. http://allafrica.com/stories/200010040047.html.

Bernault, Florence. 2003. "The Politics of Enclosure in Colonial and Postcolonial Africa." In *A History of Prison and Confinement in Africa*, edited by Florence Bernault, 1–53. Portsmouth, NH: Heinemann.

Beukes, Jemima. 2019. "Sodomy Law's Days Number—Geingos." *Namibian Sun*, June 14, 2019, 5.

Chenwi, Lilian. 2007. *Towards the Abolition of the Death Penalty in Africa: A Human Rights Perspective*. Pretoria, South Africa: Pretoria University Law Press.

Currier, Ashley. 2012. *Out in Africa: LGBT Organizing in Namibia and South Africa*. Minneapolis: University of Minnesota Press.

———. 2019. *Politicizing Sex in Contemporary Africa: Homophobia in Malawi*. New York: Cambridge University Press.

Epprecht, Marc. 2005. "Black Skin, 'Cowboy' Masculinity: A Genealogy of Homophobia in the African Nationalist Movement in Zimbabwe to 1983." *Culture, Health, and Sexuality* 7, no. 3: 253–66.

Fay, Heather, Stefan D. Baral, Gift Trapence, Felistus Motimedi, Eric Umar, Scholastika Iipinge, Friedel Dausab, Andrea Wirtz, and Chis Beyrer. 2011. "Stigma, Health Care Access, and HIV Knowledge among Men Who Have Sex with Men in Malawi, Namibia, and Botswana." *AIDS and Behavior* 15, no. 6: 1088–97.

Frank, David John, and Dana Moss. 2017. "Cross-national and Longitudinal Variations in the Criminal Regulation of Sex, 1965–2005." *Social Forces* 95, no. 3: 941–69.

Frank, Liz, and Elizabeth Khaxas. 1996. "Lesbians in Namibia." In *Amazon to Zami: Towards a Global Lesbian Feminism*, edited by Monika Reinfelder, 109–17. London: Cassell.

Günzel, Erhard. 1996. "Nujoma Blasts Gays." *Windhoek Advertiser*, December 12, 1996, 1.

Halberstam, J. Jack. 2005. *In a Queer Time and Place: Transgender Bodies, Subcultural Lives*. New York: NYU Press.

Hamata, Max. 2000. "Namibian Minister Elaborates on Anti-gay Stance." *Namibian*, November 3, 2000.

Hubbard, Dianne. 2007. "Gender and Sexuality: The Law Reform Landscape." In *Unravelling Taboos: Gender and Sexuality in Namibia*, edited by Suzanne LaFont and Dianne Hubbard, 99–128. Windhoek, Namibia: Legal Assistance Centre.

Human Rights Watch. 2008. *This Alien Legacy: The Origins of "Sodomy" Laws in British Colonialism*. New York: Human Rights Watch. Accessed December 18, 2019. https://www.hrw.org/sites/default/files/reports/lgbt1208_webwcover.pdf.

Legal Assistance Centre. n.d. "Common Law." Law in Namibia Factsheet Series No. 4 of 6. Accessed February 25, 2019. http://www.lac.org.na/projects/grap/Pdf/Law_4-Common_Law.pdf.

———. 2015. *Namibian Law on LGBT Issues*. Windhoek, Namibia: Legal Assistance Centre. Accessed August 2, 2019. http://www.lac.org.na/projects/grap/Pdf/LGBT_mono.pdf.

Lindsay, Jennie. 1986. "The Politics of Population Control in Namibia." *Review of African Political Economy* 13, no. 36: 58–62.

Lorway, Robert. 2007. "Breaking a Public Health Silence: HIV Risk and Male-male Sexual Practices in the Windhoek Urban Area." In *Unravelling Taboos: Gender and Sexuality in Namibia*, edited by Suzanne LaFont and Dianne Hubbard, 276–95. Windhoek, Namibia: Legal Assistance Centre.

———. 2014. *Namibia's Rainbow Project: Gay Rights in an African Nation*. Bloomington: Indiana University Press.

Melber, Henning. 2015. "In the Footsteps of Robert Gabriel Mugabe: Namibian

Solidarity with Mugabe's Populism—Bogus Anti-imperialism in Practice."
In *Mugabeism? History, Politics, and Power in Zimbabwe*, edited by Sabelo J.
Ndlovu-Gatsheni, 107–20. New York: Palgrave Macmillan.

Mutikani, Lucia. 1996. "No Free Condoms for Prisoners." *Windhoek Advertiser*,
June 14, 1996, 1.

Mwilima, Fred. 1995. "Hishongwa Blasts Gays: Homosexuality Is Like Cancer
or the AIDS Scourge." *New Era*, October 5–11, 1995, 2.

Nakuta, John. 2013. *2013 Baseline Report on Human Rights in Namibia*.
Windhoek, Namibia: Office of the Ombudsman. https://www.
ombudsman.org.na/wp-content/uploads/2016/09/Baseline_Strudy_
Human_Rights_2013.pdf.

Namibian. 2000. "Jerry in New Anti-gay Rant." October 2, 2000. http://allafrica.
com/stories/200010020039.html.

———. 2001. "President Nujoma Urges 'Gay Purge.'" March 20, 2001.
https://www.namibian.com.na/archive19982004/2001/March/
news/01DC0536AD.html.

———. 2017. "'Salute' Premieres Next Wednesday." October 5,
2017. https://www.namibian.com.na/170156/archive-read/
Salute-premieres-next-Wednesday.

———. 2019a. "Editorial: Citizens Fear the Police." June 14, 2019, 11.

———. 2019b. "Sodomy in Namibia and Botswana." July 4, 2019. https://www.
namibian.com.na/80410/read/Sodomy-in-Namibia-and-Botswana.

Namibian Sun. 2014. "LRDC Considers Gun Carrying Ban." June 19, 2014.
https://www.namibiansun.com/news/lrdc-considers-gun-carrying-ban/.

———. 2016a. "Condom Distribution in Prisons Advances Health
Rights." February 19, 2016. https://www.namibiansun.com/news/
condom-distribution-in-prisons-advances-health-rights/.

———. 2016b. "Govt Tiptoes around Sodomy Law." August 26, 2016. https://
www.namibiansun.com/news/govt-tiptoes-around-sodomy-law/.

———. 2016c. "SPYL Rejects Gay Rights." September 28, 2016. https://www.
namibiansun.com/news/spyl-rejects-gay-rights.

Nel, Tanya. 1997. "Face Reality—Amathila." *Windhoek Advertiser*, February 5,
1997, 3.

Ntinda, Asser. n.d. "Dr Hage Geingob Unimpressed by Gay Activist." Accessed
February 7, 2019. http://www.swapoparty.org/zoom_in_176.html.

Nyong'o, Tavia. 2012. "Queer Africa and the Fantasy of Virtual Participation."
WSQ Viral 40, nos. 1–2: 40–63.

Other Foundation. 2017. *Canaries in the Coal Mines: An Analysis of Spaces
for LGBTI Activism in Namibia*. Johannesburg, South Africa: The
Other Foundation. http://theotherfoundation.org/wp-content/
uploads/2017/06/Canaries_Namibia_epub_Draft2_CB2.pdf.

OYO (Ombetja Yehinga Organisation). 2019. "Condoms in Correctional Facilities: Yes or No?" January 29, 2019. https://www.facebook.com/OYOtrust/videos/513887345802756/.

Puri, Jyoti. 2016. *Sexual States: Governance and the Struggle over the Antisodomy Law in India*. Durham, NC: Duke University Press.

Reddy, Vasu. 2002. "Perverts and Sodomites: Homophobia as Hate Speech in Africa." *Southern African Linguistics and Applied Language Studies* 20, no. 3: 163–75.

Ross, Loretta J. 2017. "Reproductive Justice as Intersectional Feminist Activism." *Souls* 19, no. 3: 286–314.

Sam, Patrick, ed. 2014. *Spot the Difference: Namibian Elections—Make an Informed Decision*. Second edition. A report by the Namibian Institute for Democracy. https://www.nid.org.na/images/pdf/democracy/Spot_the_Difference_web.pdf.

Shapwanale, Ndapewoshali. 2016a. "The Letter of the Law." *Namibian*, July 29, 2016. https://www.namibian.com.na/153816/archive-read/The-Letter-of-the-Law-ONE-of-the-most-common.

———. 2016b. "Nam Digs In on Sodomy Law." *Namibian*, August 30, 2016. https://www.namibian.com.na/154989/archive-read/Nam-digs-in-on-sodomy-law.

Smith, Jana-Mari. 2018. "Rubbers Coming for Inmates: Haufiku 'Confident' about Discussions with Prison Authorities." *Namibian Sun*, August 15, 2018. https://www.namibiansun.com/news/rubbers-coming-for-inmates2018-08-14.

Stone, Jack, Hannah Fraser, Aaron G. Lim, Josephine G. Walker, Zoe Ward, Louis MacGregor, Adam Trickey, et al. 2018. "Incarceration History and Risk of HIV and Hepatitis C Virus Acquisition among People Who Inject Drugs: A Systematic Review and Meta-analysis." *The Lancet: Infectious Diseases* 18, no. 12: 1397–409.

Talavera, Philippe. 2007. "Past and Present Practices: Sexual Development in Namibia." In *Unravelling Taboos: Gender and Sexuality in Namibia*, edited by Suzanne LaFont and Dianne Hubbard, 39–57. Windhoek, Namibia: Legal Assistance Centre.

Tibinyane, Natasha. 1998. "Homosexuals Vow to Remain as They Are." *New Era*, February 13–15, 1998, 20.

Wahab, Amar. 2012. "Homophobia as the State of Reason: The Case of Postcolonial Trinidad and Tobago." *GLQ* 18, no. 4: 481–505.

Walther, Daniel J. 2008. "Racializing Sex: Same-sex Relations, German Colonial Authority, and *Deutschtum*." *Journal of the History of Sexuality* 17, no. 1: 11–24.

Weidlich, Brigitte. 1998. "Ekandjo Compares Homosexuality with Satanism." *Windhoek Observer*, November 14, 1998, 8.
Weylandt, Maximilian. 2015. "The 2014 National Assembly and Presidential Elections in Namibia." *Electoral Studies* 38: 126–30.

Reenvisioning Reproductive Labor

Laura Briggs's *How All Politics Became Reproductive Politics: From Welfare Reform to Foreclosure to Trump*, Oakland: University of California Press, 2017

Deirdre Cooper Owens's *Medical Bondage: Race, Gender, and the Origins of American Gynecology*, Athens: University of Georgia Press, 2017

Jeannie Ludlow

As I read Laura Briggs's *How All Politics Became Reproductive Politics* and Deirdre Cooper Owens's *Medical Bondage* in summer 2019, news stories of internment camps at the U.S.-Mexico border dominated the airwaves. It was disquieting, if unsurprising, to read histories of reproductive oppression and coercion while contemporary examples played out publicly, in ugly detail. These texts both provide historical contexts and analytical insights into the intersecting structures of racism, sexism, and classism that shape reproductive oppression historically and today.

Both Briggs's and Owens's books powerfully reframe common discourse—not superficially but substantively—and have the potential to shift readers' vision completely. They refocus our gaze on the multiple, intersecting vectors of hegemonic discourse and the lives and experiences they elide. Briggs's *How All Politics Became Reproductive Politics* traces the influence of neoliberal privatization on child-bearing and child-rearing, family and household maintenance, and care of the ill, the elderly, and other dependents—all aspects of "reproductive labor." As she explicates the political machinations behind various conservative "reforms" of reproductive policy (detailed below), Briggs challenges her readers to work toward a system of "comprehensive family rights for all kinds of people" in all types of relationships (2017, 151).

In service of this challenge, Briggs elucidates a history of movements resistant to neoliberalism's impact on reproductive labor. Her critique of "welfare reform" ties it to the exploitation of mothers of color and those living in poverty. Having laid this foundation of critique, she presents specific examples of contemporary reproductive labor that demonstrate the ongoing systemic oppression created by neoliberal individualization and

WSQ: Women's Studies Quarterly **48**: 1 & 2 (Spring/Summer 2020) © 2020 by Jeannie Ludlow.

privatization. These include the gendered, racial, and socioeconomic factors undergirding the exploitation of reproductive labor to control human movement and to punish those who do not comply through so-called immigration reform; the gendered, racial, and socioeconomic connections between access to in vitro fertilization (IVF) and assisted reproductive technologies (ARTs) and infant mortality, particularly in the black community; and the deployment of gay parenting as a normalizing discourse in the legalization of gay marriage, in contrast to the very real legal, financial, and social obstacles faced by lesbian and gay people providing care for partners and friends disabled by HIV/AIDS and other health challenges. These situations collectively demonstrate that dominant culture's (sporadic and selective) support for reproductive labor is always politically conservative. Briggs concludes with an examination of subprime mortgages as examples of conservative political exploitation of reproductive labor. Although this is not her primary focus, Briggs's careful vernacular explanation of predatory subprime lending is one of the clearest that I have read.

Briggs's writing balances breadth of information with clarity of application. The book is carefully researched for an academic audience and clearly written for a general audience, inviting and accessible. Each chapter anchors to a specific narrative that readers will either recognize or be able to relate to other current political situations. Most impressively, Briggs deftly weaves together several threads of analysis: feminist, anti-racist, economic, and political. As happens so often, these strengths also engender challenges. Weaving multiple theoretical threads, for example, can make for a complex analysis. Typically, Briggs maneuvers through these challenges with skill. Occasionally, however, her vernacular writing style dips into sarcasm or ridicule aimed at conservative ideologies. While I agreed politically with every caustic comment she made, as someone who teaches in the middle of the United States, I would think carefully before assigning those passages in class; even students who agree with Briggs might find the sarcasm off-putting, since it likely refers to ideas shared by people they know and love. In a text so obviously written for a range of audiences, these moments were unexpected. Still, reading Briggs's book while hearing news reports of border camps foregrounded the ways topicality can date a text—here, to positive effect. At times, I had the uncanny feeling that the government was working to prove Briggs right.

The stratification of reproductive labor along racial and class lines that enables the horrors explicated in Briggs's book also motivated the horrific exploitation of black enslaved women and Irish immigrant women, as demonstrated in Deirdre Cooper Owens's *Medical Bondage*. Owens's text is an impressive historiography, weaving primary research with groundbreaking theorization in a compact and multilayered text that is accessible to a variety of readers. Published a year before statues of J. Marion Sims—the "father of American gynecology"—began to be removed from public spaces, Owens's book provides much-needed reframing of the stories of the enslaved women—Anarcha, Betsy, Lucy, A.P., Phoebe, and Nanny, among others—operated on by Sims and his compatriots. By centering the experiences of these women in the history of antebellum gynecology, Owens shifts our gaze. She demonstrates that the story of the gynecological victimization of enslaved women is incomplete, at best. These women should instead be recognized simultaneously as victims of intertwined racism and sexism *and* as agents who furthered the development of modern gynecological medicine, in a complex dynamic of agency and oppression.

Owens focuses on the complexities underlying narratives of enslavement and medicine. She reminds readers that enslavers (those who owned and sold persons and those who profited from the institution of enslavement) and the doctors who assisted them (many of whom, like Sims, were enslavers themselves) had a financial interest in "a slave child's birth for varied reasons" (2017, 43). Situating this financial interest in relation to biological understandings of race, she elucidates the dualities— human/not human; strong/sick—that shaped medical professionals' perception of the women under their care. Owens makes a strong case for holding the tension of these dualities without trying to resolve them; in doing so, she argues, we can approach a more complete understanding of enslaved women's lives. Her writing skillfully illustrates this strategy. Owens demonstrates the centrality of slavery, as an institution, to the shift in health care from a model of women caring for women (midwives) to one of men's interventions on women's bodies ("medicine"). One aim of this shift was to give white men more control over the "reproductive success" of enslaved women, in order to perpetuate the institution of slavery. Owens reminds readers that, as bonded persons, enslaved women could not give consent for surgical interventions. When they were not forced into serving as surgical subjects, these same women served as nurses for other surgical subjects. Through analysis of records kept by enslavers, Owens demonstrates that these bondwomen's medical knowledge and nursing skills were vital to the very physicians who considered them less than fully human. Their knowledge and skills, Owens argues, demonstrate that these enslaved women are "the rightful 'mothers' of this branch of medicine" (2017, 14). Thus, enslaved women's bodies were both sites of domination and sites of resistance.

The book then turns to a different group of patients whose lack of agency over their own reproductive health was central to the development of American gynecology: Irish immigrant women. Owens's research into these women's experiences proves particularly instructive vis-à-vis her argument that enslaved women's reproductive success was a matter of hegemonic interest. The written records of Irish immigrant women's reproductive health care are much thinner than those of enslaved women's, underscoring the degree to which enslavers valued (financially) enslaved women's reproductive success. Owens also notes that Celts were "treated as black," perceived to be not truly white but closer to people of African descent; thus did their reproductive health contribute to the codification of whiteness in the mid-nineteenth century. Owens addresses the experiences of both groups of women, accounting for various subjectivities and situations, as she refines the concept of "medical superbodies."

As medical experts exploited black and Irish women's presumed ability to withstand intense pain, J. Marion Sims wrote of his patients' "agony" and described a surgical position that required "two white male medical assistants [to] restrai[n]" them (112). The paradoxical status of "medical superbody" interpellated complex gynecological subjects. Owens's reframing to recognize this complexity is particularly important as we continue to demand that medical care today become less racist and sexist.

Owens's historiography, like Briggs's historical analysis, provides revelatory context for contemporary systemic oppression. In addition, both texts model a more effective, counterhegemonic approach to scholarly analysis, one that centralizes the experiences of, and potential resistance by, reproductive laborers.

Jeannie Ludlow is professor of English and women's, gender, and sexuality studies at Eastern Illinois University and a former abortion patient advocate. Her essay, "Graphic Abortion: The Grotesque in Diane Noomin's 1990s Abortion Comics," was recently published in *Feminist Formations*. She can be reached at jludlow@eiu.edu.

PART III. **SCHOLARLY INHERITANCE**

REVISITING MARIANNE HIRSCH'S "FAMILY PICTURES: *MAUS*, MOURNING, AND POST-MEMORY"

Postmemory and the Imaginative Work of Those Who Come After

Caroline Kyungah Hong

In our time of perpetual crisis and the proliferation of collective trauma, Marianne Hirsch's concept of *postmemory* seems more relevant and necessary than ever. Hirsch first coined the term in the early nineties in her article "Family Pictures: *Maus*, Mourning, and Post-Memory" (1992–93). A beautiful reading of Art Spiegelman's groundbreaking graphic memoir and its use of photographs, her essay would rightly become an influential work in *Maus* criticism and comics studies at large. In it, she sketches postmemory as the purview "of the child of the survivor whose life is dominated by memories of what preceded [their] birth" (Hirsch 1992–93, 8), specifically the Holocaust. She also underscores the connections between the memory of the survivor and the postmemory of the second generation, calling attention to both "as equally constructed, equally mediated by the processes of narration and imagination" (1992–93, 9). This naming of the experiences of the second generation as postmemory was incredibly powerful and evocative even in this earliest, still somewhat fuzzy, theorization. Thankfully, Hirsch has continued to circle back to postmemory since then in order to clarify and complicate the concept.

For example, in her 2001 article, "Surviving Images: Holocaust Photographs and the Work of Postmemory," she elaborates on the significant role of repetition:

> The postmemorial generation—in displacing and recontextualizing these well-known images in their artistic work—has been able to make repetition not an instrument of fixity or paralysis or simple retraumatization (as it often is for survivors of trauma), but a *mostly* helpful vehicle of working through a traumatic past. (Hirsch 2001, 9)

WSQ: Women's Studies Quarterly 48: 1 & 2 (Spring/Summer 2020) © 2020 by Caroline Kyungah Hong.

This understanding of postmemory as potentially productive—not stuck or static, and as a condition and an approach that is haunted (a word that comes up frequently in scholarly discussions of postmemory) yet also hopeful—can be profoundly moving and motivating for those of us engaged in and with this kind of cultural work.

In Hirsch's 2012 book, *The Generation of Postmemory: Writing and Visual Culture After the Holocaust,* her fullest account of postmemory to date, she further emphasizes its "imaginative investment, projection, and creation" and, in her dual commitment to aesthetics and ethics, argues for its potential as "a form of repair and redress" (Hirsch 2012, 5, 6). She also broadens the scope of postmemory to think through "affiliative structures of memory beyond the familial" (2012, 21), and beyond the generational. In the two decades since she first used the term, it has become clear that postmemory is not limited to its applications and implications for the Holocaust, the photograph, and the graphic narrative, where Hirsch began, but is a capacious and portable concept that has impacted thinking about trauma and memory across histories, cultures, forms, and fields.

In my primary fields of Asian American and ethnic studies, postmemory has been fruitfully taken up by many scholars and critics, including one of this issue's guest coeditors, Maria Rice Bellamy, in her monograph *Bridges to Memory: Postmemory in Contemporary Ethnic American Women's Fiction* (2016). My colleague Seo-Young Chu, in *Do Metaphors Dream of Literal Sleep? A Science-Fictional Theory of Representation,* draws on Hirsch's work to theorize what she terms *postmemory han* and, like Hirsch, stresses "the power of the imagination" (S. Chu 2010, 191) to represent and work through the traumas inherited by second-generation Korean Americans. Both Sandra So Hee Chi Kim and Malissa Phung have written articles about the "affective force" of postmemory (Kim 2016, 654; Phung 2012, 5) and its diasporic dimensions, while analyzing very different texts. Long Bui has applied postmemory to an archive he calls "the refugee repertoire" to illuminate how "many in the postwar/postmemory generation aim to revise and complicate simplistic notions of the refugee or war subject" (Bui 2016, 112, 115). Viet Thanh Nguyen, in his book *Nothing Ever Dies: Vietnam and the Memory of War,* cites Hirsch's postmemory as part of his articulation of and call for what he terms "just memory" (2016, 268). Patricia Chu also writes of her indebtedness to Hirsch's insights about postmemory in her book *Where I Have Never Been: Migration, Melancholia, and Memory in Asian American Narratives of Return* (P. Chu 2019, 5). My own research has been deeply informed by Hirsch's work, ever since I cited postmemory in an essay about GB Tran's graphic memoir *Vietnamerica: A Family's Journey* (Hong 2014, 13–14).

There are many others in Asian American and ethnic studies who have also cited and been impacted by Hirsch's ideas, and there are still many more areas and sites of study where the applied discussion of postmemory could be useful and generative. Alongside the actual citation and application of postmemory itself, I also hope more of us (i.e., literary/cultural critics and academics) can take up the open and generous approach to criticism and critique that Hirsch has modeled with this concept—theory that is living and changes and deepens over time, scholarship that is rich and rigorous but also always "intensely personal" (Hirsch 2012, 15), and academic work that doesn't deny or downplay its feminist (and antiracist and decolonial) commitments. After all, writers and artists are not the only ones engaged in postmemory work.

As a second-generation Korean American, my own postmemory (or postmemory han, à la Seo-Young Chu) is vexed, characterized by "contradictory needs, desires, refusals and aversions," and defined by both "proximity" and "distance" (Hirsch n.d.). I was raised in a family that trafficked in secrets and lies. I knew little of my parents' and grandparents' experiences in Korea, and I was never privy to our family history or stories about Japanese colonization or the Korean War. As a teenager, I imagined what their lives might've been like, cobbled together from a few clues here and there—a handful of black-and-white photographs, my paternal grandfather's fluent Japanese, my mother's distrust of everyone—plus what I saw on *M*A*S*H* and what little I learned on Saturdays in Korean school. And now I often think about what I'll eventually share with my young daughter about the various traumas I've survived and wonder how she, too, will experience postmemory.

In the meantime, I find it less fraught to consider postmemory beyond the familial and generational, to focus on other collective formations and structures, particularly through my work as an Asian Americanist. Asian American studies as a field was established about fifty years ago, and its primary concerns, questions, and methods have been shaped largely by postmemorial generations of students, teachers, writers, artists, and scholars. When I read, watch, study, and write about Asian American literature and culture, and especially when I step into the classroom and teach my students—who come after me, who comes after them—about the extraordinary texts and movements that are born out of the traumas of immigration, exclusion, incarceration, war, and other state-sanctioned violence, I, too, am engaging in the creative work of postmemory, forging real and imagined links across the contradictions of Asian America's pasts and futures.

Caroline Kyungah Hong is an associate professor of English at Queens College, CUNY. She serves as cochair of the Circle for Asian American Literary Studies and a board member of the Association for Asian American Studies and the *Asian American Literary Review*. She can be reached at caroline.hong@qc.cuny.edu.

Works Cited

Bellamy, Maria Rice. 2016. *Bridges to Memory: Postmemory in Contemporary Ethnic American Women's Fiction*. Charlottesville: University of Virginia Press.

Bui, Long. 2016. "The Refugee Repertoire: Performing and Staging the Postmemories of Violence." *MELUS* 41, no. 3: 112–32.

Chu, Patricia P. 2019. *Where I Have Never Been: Migration, Melancholia, and Memory in Asian American Narratives of Return*. Philadelphia: Temple University Press.

Chu, Seo-Young. 2010. *Do Metaphors Dream of Literal Sleep? A Science-Fictional Theory of Representation*. Cambridge, MA: Harvard University Press.

Hirsch, Marianne. 1992–93. "Family Pictures: *Maus*, Mourning, and Post-Memory." *Discourse* 15, no. 2: 3–29.

———. 2001. "Surviving Images: Holocaust Photographs and the Work of Postmemory." *Yale Journal of Criticism* 14, no. 1: 5–37.

———. 2012. *The Generation of Postmemory: Writing and Visual Culture After the Holocaust*. New York: Columbia University Press.

———. n.d. "An Interview with Marianne Hirsch." *Columbia University Press*. https://cup.columbia.edu/author-interviews/hirsch-generation-postmemory.

Hong, Caroline Kyungah. 2014. "Disorienting the Vietnam War: GB Tran's *Vietnamerica* as Transnational and Transhistorical Graphic Memoir." *Asian American Literature: Discourses and Pedagogies* 5: 11–22.

Kim, Sandra So Hee Chi. 2016. "Suji Kwock Kim's 'Generation' and the Ethics of Diasporic Postmemory." *positions: asia critique* 24, no. 3: 653–67.

Nguyen, Viet Thanh. 2016. *Nothing Ever Dies: Vietnam and the Memory of War*. Cambridge, MA: Harvard University Press.

Phung, Malissa. 2012. "The Diasporic Inheritance of Postmemory and Immigrant Shame in the Novels of Larissa Lai." *Postcolonial Text* 7, no. 3: 1–19.

Postmemory and the "Fragments of a History We Cannot Take In"

Tahneer Oksman

"The embrace of history and fiction is what I was concerned with, or rather the effort to disentangle the grip of history while remaining in its palm, so to speak. Especially this particular piece of history and this particular novel" (Morrison 2019, 307). So writes Toni Morrison in "The Source of Self-Regard," an essay included in a recently published collection of her works carrying the same name. Based on a speech she gave in 1992 at the Portland Arts & Lecture series, Morrison initially said these words about her novel *Beloved*, just four years after it won the Pulitzer Prize for Fiction.[1] I could not help but think about Morrison's *Beloved*, and indeed, her career-long concern with imagination and history in relation to African American literature and culture, as I revisited Marianne Hirsch's groundbreaking essay, "Family Pictures: *Maus*, Mourning, and Post-Memory," in the wake of Morrison's recent death.

Hirsch's essay, which introduced her now widely employed term, *postmemory*, around the same time that Morrison delivered her speech, was composed, like *Beloved* was, at a moment when the atrocities of the early and mid-twentieth century had begun to recede into the background in light of fresh communal emergencies, like proxy wars related to the Cold War and the subsequent fall of the Soviet Union, and more locally, the AIDS epidemic and the U.S. economic crisis of the early 1980s. As Holocaust scholar Michael Rothberg points out, by then, too, "Intellectuals interested in indigenous, minority, and colonial histories challenged the uniqueness of the Holocaust and fostered research into other histories of extreme violence, ethnic cleansing, and genocide" (2009, 8). Two years following the Rwandan genocide, 1996, marked the publication of Alan

WSQ: Women's Studies Quarterly 48: 1 & 2 (Spring/Summer 2020) © 2020 by Tahneer Oksman.

S. Rosenbaum's widely cited edited volume, *Is the Holocaust Unique?: Perspectives on Comparative Genocide*. Many scholars, artists, and writers were starting to think about negotiations between communal and individual experiences, past and present, and about how to maintain the relevance of history in light of urgent contemporary unfoldings. And finally, the children of survivors—the second and third generations—were asking themselves about the impact that the previous generations' trauma had had on their own lives; they were starting to consider themselves "possessed by a history they had never lived" (Epstein [1979] 1988, 14).[2]

As Hirsch attests in the introduction to her 2012 book, *The Generation of Postmemory: Writing and Visual Culture After the Holocaust*—a work in which she partly recounts the factors that led to her earlier scholarly pursuits—it was Morrison's *Beloved* that helped her see that "latency need not mean forgetting or oblivion" (2012, 11).[3] For Hirsch, as for Morrison, a careful fostering of imagination, or of transparent mediation from within the "palm" of history, is what might help us maintain powerful and evocative associations between then and now, between here and there. It is what might help us feel more proximate to a distant past we think we already know. And, as Hirsch reminds us, the "connective," not the comparative, is what drives this mission, a determination rooted in feminist methodologies (2012, 21). As she writes, postmemory is "not identical to memory: it is 'post'; but, at the same time . . . it approximates memory in its affective force and its psychic effects" (2012, 31). It is a structure—affiliative or familial—that ethically binds even as it attests to, and stems from, as she writes in her pioneering essay, "fragments of a history we cannot take in" (Hirsch 1992–93, 27).

Photography is at the heart of Hirsch's theorization of this network. "Family Pictures" opens with descriptions of the author's encounters with various photographs from different points in her own personal story, images brought about in starkly divergent contexts, containing disparate representations—of those who survived and those who did not. But the images all gesture to the same impenetrable past. "Photography is precisely the medium connecting memory and post-memory," she writes, describing the "contradictory and ultimately unassimilable dimension of photography—its hovering between life and death" as a useful prop for grasping at the horrors of events that feel, and that in many ways *are*, ungraspable (1992–93, 9). Hirsch uses the first volume of Art Spiegelman's *Maus*—a book she taught in several introductory courses at Dartmouth as early as 1987, before the second volume saw publication—as a kind of linchpin for her conceptualization of postmemory (2012, 9). It would receive its own Pulitzer Prize four years after *Beloved* (*Maus* won in a "Special Citations" category). For Hirsch, Spiegelman's use of photography in *Maus*, not to say the graphic memoir's distinguished and in some ways originary manipulations of various modes, mediums, and registers, including comics, singularly brought to the surface the "levels of mediation that underlie *all* visual representational forms" (1992–93, 11; italics in original). In essence, Hirsch found a work in *Maus* that properly embraces history without embalming it, that never relinquishes, even momentarily, an awareness of how our understandings of personal and collective pasts are always formed through and framed by a variety of intersecting forces.

About halfway through "The Source of Self-Regard," Morrison transitions from what she describes as a move from African American "*history*" to "*culture*" (2019, 315; italics in original). She talks about her latest novel at the time, *Jazz*, a book published in 1992 that focuses mainly on Harlem in the 1920s. Bringing together her thoughts on these two novels, she argues that, with both texts, she was trying to explore what she describes as "self-regard," or the way a person sees herself under different circumstances. With "jazz," she explains, as a work, a form, and an idiom, of "creative agency," of "individual reclamation of the self," she senses "the way in which imagination fosters real possibilities" (2019, 319, 320). I wonder, revisiting Hirsch's essay as we hasten toward the middle of this new century, what comes *after* postmemory, with the phasing out of those directly involved in, or living at the time of, the Holocaust, with the passing, in time, too, of the next generation? Does memory, or postmemory, simply transition into history, into a distant, untouchable legacy? After 9/11, and in a time when the digital image, the digital archive, has transformed our relationship to photography as something no longer as easily identifiable for its indexicality, its traceability in relation to the real world, will the photograph, in theory and practice, remain as useful or impactful? Are there hopeful, productive, and ethical ways to move beyond memory in order to more fully inhabit the present, with all of its "real possibilities"? These questions, already being asked by many, are undoubtedly waiting to be addressed by scholars, artists, and writers galvanized by the legacies of those, like Hirsch, who hazard to make their mark.

Tahneer Oksman is an associate professor of academic writing at Marymount Manhattan College. She is the author of *"How Come Boys Get to Keep Their Noses?": Women and Jewish American Identity in Contemporary Graphic Memoirs* and the coeditor of the anthology *The Comics of Julie Doucet and Gabrielle Bell: A Place Inside Yourself*. She is currently working on a book about comics, loss, and grief, and can be reached at toksman@mmm.edu.

Notes

1. The original speech, revised and updated in the print essay, can be found online. See Morrison 1992.
2. Helen Epstein's *Children of the Holocaust* is widely cited as one of the first books to explore this question.
3. Hirsch also fleshed out and refined her concept of postmemory in earlier works, including her 1997 book, *Family Frames*, and in numerous other articles and collections.

Works Cited

Epstein, Helen. (1979) 1988. *Children of the Holocaust: Conversations with Sons and Daughters of Survivors.* New York: Penguin.

Hirsch, Marianne. 1992–93. "Family Pictures: *Maus*, Mourning, and Post-Memory." *Discourse* 15, no. 2: 3–29.

———. 1997. *Family Frames: Photography, Narrative, and Postmemory.* Cambridge, MA: Harvard University Press.

———. 2012. *The Generation of Postmemory: Writing and Visual Culture After the Holocaust.* New York: Columbia University Press.

Morrison, Toni. 1992. Lecture. Portland Arts & Lectures series. The Archive Project. Podcast audio. March 19, 1992. https://literary-arts.org/archive/toni-morrison/.

———. 2019. "The Source of Self-Regard." In *The Source of Self-Regard: Selected Essays, Speeches, and Meditations,* 304–21. New York: Knopf.

Rosenbaum, Alan S., ed. 1996. *Is the Holocaust Unique?: Perspectives on Comparative Genocide.* Boulder, CO: Westview Press.

Rothberg, Michael. 2009. *Multidirectional Memory: Remembering the Holocaust in the Age of Decolonization.* Stanford, CA: Stanford University Press.

Reparative Remembering

Sonali Thakkar

In the opening pages of "Family Pictures: *Maus*, Mourning, and Post-Memory," Marianne Hirsch (1992–93) describes a photograph of a woman who sits on a bench in front of a pretty house, surrounded by trees in bloom, a newspaper in hand. It is a photograph of her husband's aunt Frieda, dispatched to relatives in England and Bolivia in 1945 as an announcement that she, Frieda, had survived the Riga ghetto and concentration camp. I want to begin with a few observations about Hirsch's reading of this photograph, since it economically conveys the key elements of her approach. It also opens up what I will argue is the most generative aspect of her theorization of postmemory—namely, the identification and description of a practice of reparative remembering that speaks to ongoing debates in literary and cultural theory about the politics of futurity and negativity.

Nothing in Frieda's photograph refers directly to the Holocaust; it includes no sign of the camps, yet Hirsch argues that it is a Holocaust photograph. In turning our attention to such family photos, Hirsch asks how the history and memory of the Holocaust is transmitted and mediated by the familial and the intimate. Hirsch's formulation of this question initially seems to depend on a familiar and problematic contrast, even opposition, between history and memory: the newspaper in Frieda's hand, Hirsch observes, is a "curious prop—perhaps representing the public history which is the official alternative to the private memory she, as a witness, brings to her addressees" (1992–93, 5). But Hirsch's juxtaposition of history and memory is not organized around dichotomies of objectivity and authenticity, or archive and testimony.[1] Rather, she maps history/memory onto the public/private distinction that, in the tradition of feminist scholarship,

WSQ: Women's Studies Quarterly **48**: 1 & 2 (Spring/Summer 2020) © 2020 by Sonali Thakkar. All rights reserved.

she posits in order to undo. In a 2018 forum on "Holocaust and the History of Gender and Sexuality," the historian Atina Grossman observes that "it may well have been feminists' facility with teasing out and contextualizing the 'personal' in the 'political'—or historical—that generated the distinctive insights of our scholarship on the Holocaust" (Farges et al. 2018, 82). Hirsch's reflection on what it would have meant for Frieda's relatives, "sitting around their kitchen table in La Paz," to receive this picture is a meditation on history as it is lived in the relations between partners, between parents and children, and among extended family networks (1992–93, 4).

Hirsch's emphasis on how familial relations mediate memory offers a theory of traumatic transmission that is constitutively structured by a feminist perspective and that therefore differs substantially from other influential accounts of trauma and testimony from the same period. For example, Hirsch draws on Shoshana Felman and Dori Laub's nearly contemporaneous *Testimony: Crises of Witnessing in Literature, Psychoanalysis, and History*. Unlike Felman and Laub, however, whose work focuses on the dyads of analyst and patient, and critic and text, Hirsch focuses on familial form and pays more attention to the intergenerational inheritance of trauma. She also attends to the way testimony might circulate in ordinary encounters, amid the banality of the everyday (I think here of *Maus*, and of Vladek narrating his story to Artie as he pedals furiously on his exercise bike). In Hirsch's account, the existence of the second generation complicates the meaning of the past, which does not lose its gravitational pull but is no "black hole" either—a term Laub borrows from Nadine Fresco's work on the children of survivors (Felman and Laub 1992, 64). Instead, the past is transformed by the present and future as they come into being. In my reading, the contribution of Hirsch's article is to show how the extension and reproduction of the familial redistributes trauma and its negativity without necessarily weakening or ameliorating them.

We see these dynamics at work in Hirsch's reading of Frieda's photograph: "Frieda's picture," Hirsch writes, "says only 'I am alive,' or perhaps, 'I have survived'" (1992–93, 5). There is an extraordinary drama to this missive, which announces a survival that defies all odds. But it is not just Frieda who carries on. The scattered family that reconstitutes itself around this photo must then "get up from their kitchen tables . . . [and] integrate her image and the knowledge it brought into their lives" (Hirsch 1992–93, 4–5). This image of the ordinary forced to make space for the extraordinary, the juxtaposition of kitchen table and concentration camp, and most of all the question of "integration" all indicate how Hirsch's work is preoccupied with continuity and even futurity. What comes after the drama of survival, not only for the survivor but also for those who make up the intimate and ordinary worlds the survivor must reenter?

Hirsch's answer is the child, the paradigmatic figure of postmemory in her early formulation of the concept. It is not the survivor but the child of the survivor in whom the past is refracted. But if the child presents an answer, it also poses a problem. Hirsch's treatment of the second generation is not redemptive (that is, she does not sentimentalize the child). Nonetheless, the child continues to hold open the future, while the lost or dead child, such as Art Spiegelman's brother Richieu, signifies the future foreclosed: "A child who died unnaturally, before he had the chance to live" (Hirsch 1992–93, 23). Moreover, in her later work, Hirsch expands the concept of postmemory to describe a broader social structure, in which the intergenerational inheritance of trauma organizes politics, demanding an engagement with the past if it is not to overwhelm the future. As such, her vision of the future, and of a politics that might secure it, appears dependent on what Lee Edelman (2004) has called "reproductive futurism." But in fact, postmemory complicates the child's association with futurity. The concept's power stems from its illumination of the affective experience of entering a world that remains organized by the violence of an event that transpired before one's arrival. From the perspective of the inheritors of postmemory, the landscape that unfolds before them is not one of political optimism and possibility but rather of relative limitation and disempowerment. As a former student of Hirsch's, I found myself reflecting on postmemory's influence on my own work while writing this piece. I located it in this association of the child with historical belatedness and genealogical constraint—qualities that I find in the figure of the racialized and colonized child, who must contend with an inheritance that confounds natality's promise to make the world anew.

Yet Hirsch's perspective on the past's circumscription of the present and future is poignant without being melancholic, because this circumscription is not absolute. The structure of postmemory allows and even demands agency and creativity of the second generation, not least with respect to practices of commemoration and representation. Hirsch identifies these qualities in Spiegelman's *Maus*, but we see them at work, too, in her own relationship to Frieda's photograph. Recounting the photograph's arrival in the homes of Frieda's family, she signals her own creative investment, writing that she can "picture" and "imagine" the scene of its reception (Hirsch 1992–93, 4). At the same time, her reading of the photograph recognizes the limitations of her knowledge and the speculative dimensions of her reflections. Postmemory, I want to suggest, is reparative, in Eve Kosofsky Sedgwick's sense of the term, which Sedgwick derives from Melanie Klein's formulation of the depressive position. In Sedgwick's account, the depressive position relieves one from the drama of powerlessness and omnipotence by refocusing attention on the "middle ranges of agency—the notion that you can be relatively empowered or disempowered without annihilating someone else or being annihilated" (2011, 20). Sedgwick's summary of the depressive position—"It's not all about you"—in fact encapsulates the structure of postmemory (2011, 20). Hirsch helps us to see that the relationality at work in the transmission of memory and testimony is not histrionic, nor is agency zero sum. What she offers us is a model of reparative remembering.

Sonali Thakkar is an assistant professor of English at the University of Chicago, where she is also affiliated with the Center for the Study of Gender and Sexuality. She is completing a book titled *The Reeducation of Race: Jewishness and Plasticity in Postcolonial Politics*. She can be reached at sonalit@uchicago.edu.

Notes

1. On the opposition of history and memory, see, for instance, Nora 1989. For a forceful critique, see Klein 2000.

Works Cited

Edelman, Lee. 2004. *No Future: Queer Theory and the Death Drive*. Durham, NC: Duke University Press.

Farges, Patrick, Doris Bergen, Anna Hàjkovà, Elissa Mailänder, and Atina Grossman. 2018. "Forum: Holocaust and the History of Gender and Sexuality." *German History* 36, no. 1: 78–100.

Felman, Shoshana, and Dori Laub. 1992. *Testimony: Crises of Witnessing in Literature, Psychoanalysis, and History*. New York: Routledge.

Hirsch, Marianne. 1992–93. "Family Pictures: *Maus*, Mourning, and Post-Memory." *Discourse* 15, no. 2: 3–29.

Klein, Kerwin Lee. 2000. "On the Emergence of Memory in Historical Discourse." *Representations* 69: 127–50.

Nora, Pierre. 1989. "Between Memory and History: Les Lieux de Mémoire." *Representations* 26: 7–24.

Sedgwick, Eve Kosofsky. 2011. *The Weather in Proust*, edited by Jonathan Goldberg. Durham, NC: Duke University Press.

Works in Progress: Sketches, Prolegomena, Afterthoughts

Marianne Hirsch

Between the publication of *Maus I* (1986) and *Maus II* (1991), Art Spiegelman changed his cover self-portrait. In *Maus I*, Spiegelman depicts himself as a cartoon mouse with a human body and long tail, sitting with his back to the reader at his drafting table, smoking and drawing; and in *Maus II*, Spiegelman has morphed into a man holding a mouse mask in his hands. Now Spiegelman's pens are beside him in a cup and the cover of *Maus I* hangs on the wall of his studio. In my 1992 essay, "Family Pictures: *Maus*, Mourning, and Post-Memory," I interpret this shift as a symptom of the increasingly self-conscious contradictions shaping the work's distinctive animal fable and the multiple mediations separating the artist from his memoir. On the surprising and also very welcome occasion of revisiting this 1992 essay in 2020, I see Spiegelman's shifting self-presentation differently. It now appears to me to be an integral aspect of the work of postmemory itself.

In her comment on my essay, included in this issue of *WSQ*, Caroline Kyungah Hong generously, and helpfully for me, characterizes postmemory as "capacious," "portable," and "open . . . to criticism and critique," as "theory that is living and changes and deepens over time" (2020, 131). Indeed, for me, this early essay on *Maus* was an introductory sketch, followed by refinements, renegotiations, and elaborations over the course of nearly three decades. If it was, and still is, a work in progress, however, it is due not so much to my rush to publish an unfinished argument, but to the ways in which memory and the past are, in Sonali Thakkar's terms in her response in this volume, "transformed by the present and future as they come into being" (2020, 138). The provisional quality of my early essay is no doubt also a reaction to the inspiring work on the memory of

WSQ: Women's Studies Quarterly **48**: 1 & 2 (Spring/Summer 2020) © 2020 by Marianne Hirsch.

painful pasts done by scholars, artists, and activists across the globe, and by the many conversations in this burgeoning field that I've been fortunate to join. In what follows, I offer just a few of the things I've rethought and am still rethinking.

First, the "post." It originally appears hyphenated, as *post-memory*, in 1992, which was inspired by Andrea Liss's (1991) discussion of photographs as "post-memories" in her essay "Trespassing through Shadows." But by 1997, when my revised *Maus* essay appeared as the first chapter of my book *Family Frames: Photography, Narrative, and Postmemory*, I had dropped the hyphen. In my rationale for the term there and in several subsequent publications, I argued that the relationship between postmemory and memory does not merely consist in a temporal lag, but also indicates the oscillation between proximity and distance, continuity and rupture. One of my colleagues has suggested that the many current "posts"—postmodernism, postsecularism, posttraumatic, and more—could be seen as "post-it" notes and afterthoughts. What happens if the post-it falls off? Is the initial concept still the same? What remains of *memory* after it is incorporated into *postmemory*? How do I remember once I realize that my own memories are not only transmissible and available to others who were not there, but possibly determinative in their lives as well? I now wonder if it was *this* anxiety that made me drop the hyphen, creating a hybrid term that better signaled the belatedness, supplementarity, and citationality of postmemory? Or would the hyphen have pointed to these contradictions more effectively? In any case, both versions exist, and both are regularly cited and used in relation to different painful histories.

Second, the Holocaust. Beginning with *Maus* in the early 1990s, and approaching it through my own family history, I have located my inquiry squarely in relation to the generations of Holocaust memory—the anxiety about the aging and death of survivors, the heavy responsibility facing their descendants to tell their stories accurately and affectively, without appropriating them. *Maus* illustrates the precarious gatekeeper position of the "generation after," while finding ways to give shape to this history precisely by way of an unknowing desire to know and to feel. And yet, of course, what I call a "structure" of intergenerational transmission is not in any way limited to the Holocaust, but rather describes the experiences of, and the aesthetic forms used by, what Eva Hoffman calls the "postgenerations" of many other traumatic histories. Looking closely at some of these—in ways that the works cited by Caroline Kyungah Hong (2020) in this issue do—certainly reveals the uniqueness of each of these histories, and the serious limitations of the Holocaust as a general template for traumatic memory and its transmission. As the field of memory studies took hold across the globe, and especially in the Global South, the work on multiple diverse histories has made me see the memory of the Holocaust differently. As Tahneer Oksman (2020) shows in her essay in this issue when she productively invokes Toni Morrison alongside Art Spiegelman, or as Sonali Thakkar suggests in her reference to "the figure of the racialized and colonized child" (2020, 139), approaches to memory are more generative if they reveal historical, political, structural, and/or aesthetic connections between diverse histories, rather than using one as a starting and reference point, as has happened with the Holocaust.

Third, the family. *Maus* powerfully transmits a specific family story of trauma and survival, transmission and blockage. At the same time, it makes clear that even the most intimate familial acts of transmission are already mediated by publicly available images and narratives that form a collective imaginary shared within a contemporary cohort. To grant the domestic intimacy of, as Thakkar puts it in this issue, "history as it is lived" within the family of survivors (2020, 138), as well as the more general availability of collective memories, I have distinguished between *familial* and *affiliative* postmemory. The memory scholars Aleida Assmann (2010) and Jan Assmann (1997) have distinguished between *communicative memory*, which is intimate and embodied, and which is practiced across roughly three generations between grandparents, parents, and grandchildren, and what they call *cultural memory*, which, disembodied, is institutionalized in archives, history curricula, memorials, and museums. But do these institutions not also attempt to animate, or to reanimate, the history they are documenting by invoking the affects of postmemory through the use of familial tropes? At the same time, I have wondered whether affiliative postmemory could not also extend beyond our ancestors to our less proximate contemporaries. In other words, might our relationship to victims and survivors of violence and persecution in our own generation demand similar kinds of responses and responsibilities as those of previous ones? And what would those responses be? *Maus* performs Artie's oscillation between identification and disidentification with his parents' suffering, threatening at times to slide into an excessive appropriation. But our contemporaries ask not so much for identification, or even empathy, but for something more akin to solidarity, accompaniment, cowitnessing (Kacandes 2001), and coresistance (Kricorian 2019). Indeed, as Thakkar—by way of Eve Kosofsky Sedgwick—reminds us, the practice of postmemory models an engagement that stresses: "It's not all about you" (2020, 140).

Finally, gender. As a father/son story, *Maus* typifies the predominance of men and the exclusion of women as narrators of catastrophic histories. Anja Spiegelman's story is told by her husband, who burned her diaries, and who highlights his own roles of caretaker and hero. As Vladek tells it in *Maus I*, "She went through the same what me: terrible!" (1986, 158). My essay suggests that the mother's absence is fundamental to the very structure of *Maus*. Yet the book also gives us hints of another story, one that contradicts Anja's fragility and suicidal depression, and one I neglected on first reading. In a few scenes, Anja appears as an activist in the resistance, delivering and hiding packages, and she shows bravery and determination in other scenes as well. In *MetaMaus*, Spiegelman includes interviews with women who knew Anja in the camp and who fill out this submerged picture of agency and courage.

"What comes after postmemory?" Tahneer Oksman provocatively asks, citing Toni Morrison's reflections on moving from "history" to "culture" (2020, 135). For Oksman, this means moving from a preoccupation with the past, such as we see in *Maus* and in my work, to a way of "more fully inhabit[ing] the present, with all its 'real possibilities'" (2020, 135). As scholars, artists, and activists who are presently working on memory urge, the task of postmemory is precisely to locate us in the present and, in whatever ways possible, to point us to a more hopeful, progressive future. And that, surely, continues to be work in progress.

Marianne Hirsch is William Peterfield Trent Professor of English and Comparative Literature at Columbia University and professor in the Institute for Research on Women, Gender, and Sexuality. She has worked extensively on the second-generation memory of the Holocaust and has written several books on family narratives in literature and photography. She can be reached at mh2349@columbia.edu.

Works Cited

Assmann, Aleida. 2010. "Reframing Memory: Between Individual and Collective Forms of Constructing the Past." In *Performing the Past: Memory, History and Identity in Modern Europe,* edited by Karen Tilmans, Frank van Vree, and Jay Winter, 35–50. Amsterdam: Amsterdam University Press.

Assmann, Jan. 1997. *Das kulturelle Gedächtnis: Schrift, Erinnerung und politische Identität in frühen Hochkulturen*. Munich: Beck.

Hirsch, Marianne. 1992–93. "Family Pictures: *Maus*, Mourning, and Post-Memory." *Discourse* 15, no. 3: 3–29.

———. 1997. *Family Frames: Photography, Narrative, and Postmemory*. Cambridge, MA: Harvard University Press.

Hoffman, Eva. 2004. *After Such Knowledge: Memory, History, and the Legacy of the Holocaust*. New York: Public Affairs.

Hong, Caroline Kyungah. 2020. "Postmemory and the Imaginative Work of Those Who Come After." *WSQ Inheritance* 48, nos. 1/2: 129–32.

Kacandes, Irene. 2001. *Talk Fiction: Literature and the Talk Explosion*. Lincoln: University of Nebraska Press.

Kricorian, Nancy. 2019. "Pilgrimage As/Or Resistance." In *Women Mobilizing Memory*, edited by Ayşe Gül Altınay, María José Contreras, Marianne Hirsch, Jean Howard, Banu Karaca, and Alisa Solomon, 105–9. New York: Columbia University Press.

Liss, Andrea. 1991. "Trespassing through Shadows: History, Mourning, and Photography in Representations of Holocaust Memory." *Framework* 4, no. 1: 29–41.

Oksman, Tahneer. 2020. "Postmemory and the 'Fragments of a History We Cannot Take In.'" *WSQ Inheritance* 48, nos. 1/2: 133–36.

Spiegelman, Art. 1986. *Maus: A Survivor's Tale*. New York: Pantheon.

———. 1991. *Maus II: A Survivor's Tale: And Here My Troubles Began*. New York: Pantheon.

———. 2011. *MetaMaus: A Look Inside a Modern Classic, Maus*. New York: Random House.

Thakkar, Sonali. 2020. "Reparative Remembering." *WSQ Inheritance* 48, nos. 1/2: 137–40.

PART IV. **RECLAIMING FEMINIST, QUEER, AND INTERSECTIONAL INHERITANCES**

Recovering the "Most Neglected Feminist Leader of the Twentieth Century": Crystal Eastman, Historical Memory, and the Bequest of an Intersectional Inheritance

Amy Aronson

Abstract: At the time of her death in 1928, Crystal Eastman was one of the most conspicuous political women in the United States. A cofounder of the National Woman's Party, the Woman's Peace Party, and the American Civil Liberties Union (ACLU), Eastman also drafted the nation's first serious workers' compensation law and has been credited as a coauthor of the Equal Rights Amendment. Yet nearly a century later, her legacy is oddly ambiguous. Over time, she has become a strangely elided figure—commemorated, paradoxically, as one of the most neglected feminist leaders in American history. This article explores Eastman's political identity, connecting it to the question of her complex legacy in historical memory today. I argue it was her intersectional imperative—her drive to bridge multiple social justice movements all under one emancipatory rubric—that destabilized her historical standing and intelligibility. By reexamining her public life and career in light of new sources and frameworks, I aim to redefine the transgressive nature of her politics for a new generation of women's studies scholars. **Keywords:** Crystal Eastman; intersectionality; historical memory; feminism; National Woman's Party; legacy

In her last piece of published writing, Crystal Eastman took stock of her own life for the first time. An early twentieth-century labor lawyer, antiwar activist, civil liberties champion, and feminist trailblazer, she was invited to contribute an essay to a 1927 series in the *Nation* called "These Modern Women." In it, seventeen twentieth-century feminists were asked to reveal the most influential sources of their political identities to the world (Showalter 1989). The project was the brainchild of *Nation* editor Freda Kirchwey, Eastman's longtime friend and colleague from the suffrage and women's peace movements, who would soon write Eastman's obituary.

WSQ: Women's Studies Quarterly 48: 1 & 2 (Spring/Summer 2020) © 2020 by Amy Aronson. All rights reserved.

At the time, Eastman was one of the most conspicuous political women in the country. A cofounder of the National Woman's Party, the Woman's Peace Party—today, the Women's International League for Peace and Freedom (WILPF)—and the American Civil Liberties Union (ACLU), she also drafted the nation's first serious workers' compensation law and has been credited as a coauthor of the Equal Rights Amendment (ERA). Through these endeavors and more, Eastman exercised institutional as well as policy leadership within many of the defining social movements of the twentieth century: labor, feminism, free speech, peace. Yet a century later, her legacy is oddly ambiguous. Indeed, numerous scholarly accounts have rendered Eastman marginal within the institutional narratives of the very movement organizations she helped to found and to lead. Some histories omit her almost entirely.[1] Over time, she has become a strangely elided figure—commemorated, paradoxically, as one of the most neglected feminist leaders in American history (Cook 1998, 405).

Newly discovered details about Eastman's only piece of autobiographical writing offer clues to this perplexing legacy. Scholars have long known that Kirchwey revised the conclusion to Eastman's *Nation* article prior to its publication, but that original ending was presumed lost. It turns out, however, that the untouched manuscript still exists; it had been buried among the last bits of literary estate held in mixed files and folders by Eastman's descendants. All that had been evident about the substance of Kirchwey's revision was Eastman's outraged response to it (Cook 1978, 46). Now it is clear that her strong reaction occurred not merely because the changes were made without her consent (Kirchwey 1927).

Ironically, Kirchwey's editorial effort reflected her desire to make Eastman's story more accessible to public memory. As published, Eastman's life conveyed a time-honored message of generational inheritance within the women's movement. Readers were treated to an inspiring but uncomplicated narrative of succession from Annis Ford Eastman, the pathbreaking feminist foremother, to her daughter Crystal, the savvy, modern-era feminist leader. Kirchwey drew upon cultural narratives about mothers and daughters that had been circulating in women's organizations, as well as in magazines and other popular media, for decades (Walters 1994). Throughout the nineteenth century, many feminist groups wielded the idea of maternity, and of mother-love, to warrant women's rebellion against the patriarchal order of the father. Feisty foremothers were seen to push open doors for participation in public life for the next generation of women to step through. Yet by the twentieth century, many young feminists in Crystal's cohort had begun to rebel against this organizing idea of their movement elders. The modern generation wanted to be seen as self-supporting women, to break away from the mentality and methods of their mothers' movement and create a "sisterhood" of their own. By the 1910s, disidentification with mothers became a defining political act for feminist daughters (Henry 2004; Faludi 2010).

For Eastman, however, none of these available narratives fully pertained. She adored her feminist mother. She never felt the need to disidentify to become herself. Indeed, she titled her last essay "Mother-Worship" (Eastman 1927). Yet Eastman was a radical and renegade in her politics all her life—anything but a dutiful daughter in the way that role was understood both by the women's movement and the wider culture at the time. Rather, Eastman saw herself as an original admixture of suffrage successor, rebellious modern, and her own brand of dutiful daughter all at once. She was an original compound. Indeed, *that* was the woman the mother she worshipped taught her she was born and raised to be. Eastman objected to Kirchwey's simplification of her story to conform with any pat narrative or party line. She angrily crossed out the published ending on every copy of the article she gave to friends, family, and colleagues. Alongside the altered final paragraph in the copy she saved in her scrapbook, she disowned it, noting for posterity, "None of this is mine."[2] This article explores Eastman's own conception of her political identity, connecting it to the question of her complex legacy in historical memory today. By reexamining her public life in light of new sources and frameworks, I aim to redefine the transgressive nature of Eastman's politics for a new generation, recovering her timely bequest to next-wave scholars of women's studies as we contemplate the centennial of suffrage.

Locating Eastman: Sources, Connections, Intersections

Eastman cut a striking figure in her lifetime—striking, yes, but difficult to pin down. She was "one of the leading spellbinders," according to a 1914 article in the *Washington Herald*, and she was defined by her "monstrous faith in humanity," a rather oxymoronic phrase, by the progressive *Pearson's* magazine in 1917. Friends and coworkers often noted her "magnificent presence," as the Harlem Renaissance novelist and poet Claude McKay described it, her boundless embodiment of "all that was fundamentally fine, noble and genuine in American democracy" (1937, 83). And, as her ACLU colleague Roger Baldwin remembered, Eastman was "outspoken (often tactless), determined . . . and courageous," plainly visible, and difficult to ignore (1975, 54).

Nevertheless, something about her political identity has left her vulnerable to fragmentation and misunderstanding over time. One factor is archival: the only collection of her letters is mainly concentrated on her adolescent and college days, tapering off to almost nothing by the time of her first full-time job. Information about her most pivotal adult years must therefore be gleaned secondhand, from the archives of the organizations with which she was involved or affiliated, or the papers of her colleagues, allies, and political adversaries. While this dispersion of material attests to the range of Eastman's work, it also diffuses her political voice, eroding recognition of the salience of her contributions.

This scattered archival record, however, evokes an even more indicative explanation for the peculiar obscurity that has marked Eastman's story. Since the late 1970s, when the historian Blanche Wiesen Cook anthologized important selections of her writing, Eastman has surfaced in scholarship many times. However, she typically appears in sporadic utterances and momentary glimpses, as a cameo in narratives in which she actually played a more meaningful part. Such intermittent visibility has rendered Eastman both familiar and elusive. As a walk-on, she can seem almost out of context in the very movement organizations to which she devoted her life. At times, she seems to arise as a problematic figure, errant within the arenas where her influence was significant.

Cook has explained Eastman's position as a nearly direct result of her radicalism and militancy. She rightly described an exceptionally bold woman, and suggested Eastman's leftist revolt against the political and economic power structure all but ensured her obscurity. As Cook succinctly puts it: "History tends to bury what it seeks to reject" (1978, 2). Yet documents once submerged in disparate archives and collections now bring to light additional dimensions of Eastman's politics. New evidence suggests her most radical position, in fact, may have been her resistance to established political boundaries or consensus schools of thought of all kinds. Indeed, across her political life, Eastman's impulse was to question or challenge doctrinal requirements almost as an organizing principle in itself. She tended to see such requirements as antidemocratic and stifling to individual vision, contrary to the successful pursuit of social justice through direct democracy and grassroots social change.

Eastman never considered joining the Socialist Party, or, later, the Communist Party, even though she first identified as a socialist while still a college student, publicly blessed the Russian Revolution in 1917, and befriended prime movers of the Communist Party in Britain when she lived there in the 1920s.[3] After her brother, the radical writer and editor Max Eastman, briefly joined the Socialist Party in the winter of 1912, she twice applauded his critique of party reasoning, commending the political and organizational value of candor and independent thinking in the face of whatever the party line. "That straight talk to the Socialists," she told him, "does us all good" (Eastman 1912, 1913).

Eastman determined early on that one social problem alone cannot be fixed without fixing the others. In 1907, the same year she completed her education and embarked on her public life, she envisioned herself as "one of these circus-chariot-ladies" with one hand "driving a tandem of the arts and the law [and] the other hand holding aloft two streaming banners,—love and liberty" (*Vassar Bulletin* 1907). Traversing the "disciplinary" boundaries of arts and the law as well as the public and private arenas—love and liberty—Eastman identified her political identity as a multimovement activist with a foot in many quarters. Throughout her political career, she strived to confederate social justice struggles, coalescing her heartfelt investments in their intersecting ideals and constituencies. She talked about gender with the socialists and the antimilitarists, about class, imperialism, internationalism and even maternalism with the feminists. Steering under the banners of multiple movements at once, she pushed to forge ties among shared experiences of inequality, all in an effort to link organizational agendas and collective actions under one vast emancipatory rubric.

In her persistent confrontations with the complex relations of oppression and privilege in society as well as among and within activist groups, Eastman was politically distinctive—and also ahead of her time. She intuitively understood that there are interconnections among systems of oppression which must be attended to rigorously and simultaneously. Although she did not always foreground race and racism per se in her social critique and protest—she sometimes folded racial inequality into her socialist concern with the class struggle and anti-imperialism or her feminist and pacifist concerns with anti-violence and anti-militarism— her legacy invites comparison with the contemporary theorization of intersectionality.[4]

In the three decades since the critical race theorist Kimberlé Crenshaw

(1991) named the interactivity of multiple oppressions in identity, intersectionality has experienced a marked "expansion of its definitional scope" (Gopaldas 2013, 90). Indeed, Crenshaw and other scholars now chart the movement of the concept from identity alone to extenuating fields of struggle, describing its progress across disciplines, issues, and geographic boundaries as a "lively and provocative travelogue" (Carbado, Crenshaw, Mays, and Tomlinson 2013, 303). Contemporary research examines intersectionality not only as critical method (MacKinnon 2013; Carastathis 2014; Ramsay 2014), but as social movement strategy (Chun, Lipsitz, and Shin 2013), model for coalition building (Cole 2008), mechanism for cross-movement policies (Verloo 2013), and means of negotiating heterogeneity in an era of "niche activism" (Levitsky 2007, 271). Just as this recent scholarly work theorizes the ability of intersectionality to facilitate solidarity, enabling individuals and groups to conceptualize how social justice struggles are linked, Eastman, too, perceived the interlocking structures that maintain inequality and strived to create a coalition identity and public actions to combat them in concert.

Contemporary women's studies scholars now reflect that socialist feminists in the 1970s were reaching for intersectional connections among the social movements around them—connections like those Eastman pursued beginning in the 1910s (Gordon 2016). In a much earlier era, she tried to engage cross-movement policy ideas and mobilize actions designed to harmonize the aims of multiple groups. Yet then as now, history, exigency, and interpersonal alliances kept asking her to choose: one single-issue campaign; one struggle to create a better world; one identity—laborite, suffragist, pacifist, or revolutionary, militant or mother.

Eastman did not see herself that way—and the mother she worshipped instilled as an article of faith that the sacrifice of her own vision was tantamount to a deadly sin. Expansive, straddling, disquieting to dominant perspectives and institutional rank, Eastman was perpetually transgressive in ways that have been less apparent in the past. Her intersectional identifications could make her an iconoclast or gadfly within every organization she knew. Its competing demands within a world of practical politics and organizational dynamics positioned her more precariously than many of her colleagues. Indeed, Eastman's arguments at times left her stranded, as if she had tried to build a bridge from the middle of the water outward, rather than solidly anchored from one side to the other. Yet this perspective constituted her truest political identity and so became the defining paradigm of her public life.

Transgressing Consensus: Intersectionality and Historical Memory

Historical memory is replete with the interests and social relations that condition what a culture chooses to remember about the past. As a result, it is almost always easier to win remembrance when one's ideas or actions conform to canonical values and/or hegemonic powers. Both recognition and renown more often accrue to those who do not challenge the mainstream of their historical moment, or who can at least be seen as part of an emerging political, social, or cultural consensus in some relation to it (McLaughlin 1998, 217).

Eastman's public life bucked such trends in a number of revealing respects. In the big picture, she saw the climate of the times shift dramatically over her relatively short career. Her first real job—her work on industrial accidents and workers' compensation—belonged to the progressive mood of the moment: it was part of an emergent wave of reform efforts generally, and specifically of similar worker rights legislation sweeping the country at the time. Her next full-time position was as campaign manager for the Wisconsin suffrage drive in 1911 and 1912. While the campaign keenly experimented with newer methods of publicity and political mobilization, Eastman's work was legitimized by the long-standing National American Woman Suffrage Association (NAWSA), and the Wisconsin effort deployed rhetoric modeled on other contemporaneous campaigns for the vote. Even in her increasing suffrage militancy—Eastman was the very first person contacted by Alice Paul and Lucy Burns to help launch the constitutional suffrage drive through what would become the National Woman's Party—her more defiant utterances, in rattling the seats of power, served to enhance her visibility and prominence. She enjoyed acclaim in the militant wing of the movement and notoriety in Washington and in the press, useful factors that might have clarified and even strengthened her hold on historical standing over time.

From 1908 to 1912, Eastman's work was sufficiently consistent with a national climate of progressivism to drive rising public recognition of her. However, in the buildup to American intervention in World War I between 1914 and 1917, as the political climate shifted in more conservative and nationalistic directions, she maintained her cross-movement vision of human equality, international democracy, and world peace. Just as she began to challenge the larger political disposition of the country, her insistent positions became policy departures from the organizations with which she had once been fully compatible. Although her goals across movements did not change, her voice seemed more insurgent in a dynamic relationship with a cultural climate growing less and less tolerant of both organizational protest and citizen dissent. In this context, she experienced a reputational rise and fall.

Eastman's relative "fall from grace" alone might have left her more vulnerable to eclipse in historical memory. In almost every arena of American life, success stories are more readily remembered, incorporated, and retold. Indeed, Kirchwey's revisions specifically intended to secure Eastman's reputation that way, advancing a narrative of successful feminist succession in the midst of the surprisingly difficult era for women's organizing after the vote was won.[5] Nevertheless, cultural rebels can reap lasting reputational benefits that carry them to historical renown (McLaughlin 1998). Properly situated and supported, countercultural figures can become both recognizable and memorable in history. Eastman's increasingly oppositional attitude, then, might have served to secure her place in historical memory, just as it did other rebels in her orbit.

Yet that didn't happen for her. For several reasons, Eastman lacked the contextual clarity that might have allowed a historical reputation as *rebel* take hold and endure. For one thing, no matter where one may be located on the political spectrum, historical reputation is promoted through affiliation with recognized alliances, institutions, and mentors. These connections are known to impart definition, signal stature, and help to maintain the ideological intelligibility more readily embraced by historical narrative and collective memory.

However, Eastman did not benefit from this "halo effect" as much as might be expected given her resume. Indeed, her reputation may have been sullied somewhat by the nature of her connection to some of her more high-profile alliances at the start of her career. As a young graduate student just one year out of college and emerging into a new world of women's professional work in the Progressive Era, she met two prominent, older male mentors with whom she would become romantically linked: the Columbia professor and Marxist economist Vladimir Simkhovitch, and the urban reformer and progressive journalist Paul Kellogg. As a first-year law student, she fell in love with Simkhovitch, who was married to a prominent Barnard professor and the head of the Greenwich House settlement, where Eastman worked nights to pay her way through school. While the year-long affair ended without any apparent effect on the Simkhovitch marriage, a taint of sexual notoriety, which accumulated around Eastman through her career, may have begun there, undermining her personal standing, and the professional credibility and support that typically accrues from it, just as her public life took shape.[6]

Most of all, however, Eastman's historical reputation suffered from her radical resistance to resting definitively within any single network of alliances, any single movement or organization at all—as a reformer, a rebel, or anything else. After all, she was not the only radical woman in her time or her political milieu. Her enthusiasm for socialism and even revolution was shared by a number of her organizational colleagues—feminists, laborites, as well as antiwar activists—many of whom are better remembered today. In fact, numbers of radical women in her orbit, such as Emma Goldman and Margaret Sanger, are now recognized specifically for their radical politics, as rebel touchstones of their positions and their times. The same is true for many of Eastman's more direct organizational allies. Her antiwar colleague Emily Greene Balch, for example, was a radical internationalist who took many of the same stands Eastman did, losing her position on the faculty of Wellesley College as a result. Balch, like Eastman, was stamped as a dangerous agitator in her time, yet by 1946 Balch was awarded the Nobel Peace Prize.

One difference between the two women was that Balch also served as the first International Secretary of the Women's International League for Peace and Freedom. Indeed, after her dismissal from Wellesley in 1918, she established WILPF's headquarters in Geneva, Switzerland, between 1919 and 1922, and she remained closely connected to the organization for the rest of her life. In 1934 Balch again served as head of the League, working tirelessly there for a year and a half without pay (Gwinn 2010). There are numerous differences between the two women's lives, but one pertinent point of departure is that Eastman, unlike Balch, consistently resisted identifying herself with any single organization or cause. She claims a legitimate place in the leadership of multiple leftist organizations, but never in her life allocated her energy to one at a time.

A critical consequence of such cross-movement allegiance is illustrated by Eastman's experience in the post-suffrage women's movement itself. At the 1921 convention of the National Woman's Party, the first meeting of the organization after the vote was won, Eastman met a challenging moment by putting forward an intersectional program designed to advance from single-issue suffragism to an extensive, more race- and class-conscious, transnationally minded future feminism. Her proposals were influenced by ideas that were circulating in the international women's movement at that time, several of which she had already incorporated into her own Woman's Freedom Congress, held in New York City in 1919. That meeting had delineated intersectional dimensions within the women's struggle with panels concerning class ("Labor Legislation for Women"), and race ("The Future of the Colored Woman"), as well as sessions pertaining to sexuality and reproduction ("Birth Control and the Illegitimate Child"), and the financial reorganization of domestic and family life ("The Cooperative Movement and the High Cost of Living") ("Program of the Woman's," reel 33). At the NWP convention itself, Eastman further advocated feminist resolutions about disarmament—"to give expression to the overwhelming pacifist sentiment at the Convention"—and also a "resolution of protest against the disenfranchisement of Negro women" since she found NWP members "almost unanimous in [their] indignation on that subject" (Eastman 1921, 10).

By contrast, Alice Paul, the NWP leader commemorated today as a nearly peerless suffrage champion and, oftentimes, as the sole author of the ERA, rejected such intersectional connections as "distractions" (Cott 1984, 51). She pressed for another clear and targeted women's campaign. When a vote was quickly called for, Eastman's minority resolutions lost, decisively, two-to-one. The papers headlined the success story, heralding, "Miss Paul wins triumph" (*New York Tribune* 1921). Years later, Paul herself remembered Eastman's intersectional ideas as foreign and far afield. While Paul certainly had her own political personality and interests, it remains notable that she recalled her longtime colleague, who died, effectively, in the NWP's employ, as a leftist, not a feminist. Despite the currency of similar ideas within the women's movement in Europe and elsewhere, she dismissed Eastman's program as "embracing everything Russia was doing [and] taking in all kinds of things that we didn't expect to take in at all." (Cott 1984, 48) In Paul's memory, the intersectional Eastman became an outsider—nominal and not part of the *we*—despite a history with the movement across the American, British, and international arenas that was, in its totality, as ample as Paul's own. Nevertheless, Paul's political displacement assigned, and subsequent recollection consigned, Eastman to marginal, indeed negligible, status. "We didn't give a second thought to it," she remarked (Cott 1984, 48).

Here as elsewhere, Eastman's intersectional aims problematized her stances and her standing. Such uncertain positioning, both in ideological frameworks and social networks, diminished her institutional status time and again, obfuscating the ownership and belonging from which historical legacies are built. In resisting the reputational anchor of single-issue or dominant-organization association, Eastman raised some of the "definitional dilemmas" now connected with intersectionality (Collins 2015). By their very nature, her cross-movement identifications blurred her political identity, muddling her placement in historical memory.

The particular mix of those involvements further disrupted her access to recognition and remembrance. In general, members of subcultures contend with complex reputations that can destabilize their public image. Among other things, they carry divided reputations; simultaneously, they are viewed very differently by different groups (Fine 2001, 11). This problem was not only present but compounded in Eastman's case. For she moved not merely in a subculture, but a counterculture—an oppositional subculture, likely to provoke even more divergent understandings between insiders and outsiders, and so to need even greater solidarity from within. And beyond that, she was an *intersectional* countercultural activist, identifying herself simultaneously with several protest struggles at once. This complex posture did not merely divide her reputation, it fractured it, confounding the ability to understand where she stood both inside and outside each movement domain.

However compatible this position was with her political identity, in practice Eastman's intersectionality redoubled definitional dilemmas by almost everywhere challenging sympathetic and hostile boundaries alike. A clearer relationship to any of those boundaries might have secured her historical reputation as a political rebel. But instead, her intersectional posture persistently troubled consensus, opening quandaries—over priorities, strategies, tactics—even among her allies. Indeed, her arguments seemed to challenge the very process of self-definition, already more precarious and hard-won for these groups, from within. In the end, the very clarity of Eastman's intersectional identity vexed her position even within the array of social change organizations she saw as her collective political home. As she bridged movement contexts and agendas, surging by turns as a dynamic champion and challenging voice, she complicated the political affiliations and interpersonal alliances from which historical recognition is built. The tandem she was driving at the dawn of her career ultimately came apart beneath her feet. She fell through the essential planks of historical memory.

Claiming Our Inheritance: Eastman's Legacy and the Intersectional Future

Broadly speaking, historical memory shows a tendency to fashion either the great or the evil, constructing remembrance around those seen to do one big thing wrong (who then can do little that is right), or those who do one big thing right (and so can do no wrong) (Gugushvili, Kabachnik, and Kirvalidze 2017). This predilection leaves far too little room for the range of political identities that are more culturally complicated. Eastman's intersectional aspirations persistently unsettled premises, pressing even her allies to confront the unexamined biases in their thinking and policies. The tragic irony was the way her inclusive vision often seemed to divide people, to divide loyalties. Yet her story, in its achievements and its altercations, grants us fresh provisions as scholars of women's studies and women's lives. It further endows our inheritance of complex women, challenging us to consider and reconsider the ways leaders may blaze a trail by providing road maps to follow and by pointing out hazards, missteps, shortfalls, and wrong turns along the way. It also bequeaths another urgent call for broad-minded engagement with the complexities of our different identifications, with the voices of all those whose political investments raise fervent questions from within.

Nearly a century after Eastman's death, progress has eroded on many of the issues she cared about: gender equality and human rights, nationalism and globalization, political censorship and media control, worker benefits and family balance, and the monumental questions of war, sovereignty, force, and freedom. At the same time, the fierce, in-your-face attitude of her advocacy has surged in feminist inquiry and progressive change organizing a century after the vote was won (Kazin 2012). Given these timely dimensions, Eastman's efforts and experiences endow a critical bequest to twenty-first-century feminist politics and scholarship. She left a searching legacy born of her challenges to every aspect of inequality and to every solipsistic explanation and response. She saw each strand of social inequality as irreducibly entangled with every other into a knot that demanded intersectional interventions. She stressed both public and private, fusing spheres that had been long understood as separate. And she refused to abandon any one of these strands to any other, an undying commitment to her vision of social justice that left her involved in every campaign and marginalized in each.

At the centennial of suffrage, we are all feminist successors. To both the promise and the perils of Eastman's political intersectionality, today we are her heirs. The question for tomorrow is: What mandate will we make of it?

Amy Aronson is an associate professor at Fordham University. She is the author, editor, or coeditor of five books. Her new book, *Crystal Eastman: A Revolutionary Life*, was published by Oxford University Press in January 2020. She can be reached at amaronson@fordham.edu.

Notes

1. For example, Kathryn Kish Sklar and Beverly Wilson Palmer (2009) erroneously state that Eastman was not present at the 1919 International Congress of Women After the War, where WILPF was officially formed. Indeed, they claim she was not even *missed*, writing, "Many WILPF members were not displeased when Eastman was refused a passport in 1919 and could not attend the Zurich conference" (259). Eastman is similarly omitted from Carrie A. Foster's (1995) history of WILPF. Several books on free speech in America—see Stone 2005 and Finan 2007—hardly note Eastman's pivotal role in the founding of the ACLU or that Roger Baldwin, often credited as ACLU's sole founder, was hired to assist her during a maternity leave.
2. Eastman's original scrapbook provided courtesy of her grandchildren.
3. Eastman befriended Arthur MacManus, a leading British Communist whose ashes were placed within the Kremlin Wall Acropolis. However, according to the FBI, she took no active part in the movement in England (Hurley 1923).
4. Eastman certainly addressed racism. She worked with African-American groups in the suffrage campaigns, denounced the Chinese Exclusion Act of 1882 after it rendered Chinese immigration permanently illegal in 1902 (a ban that lasted until 1943), and included a panel on Black women in her Woman's Freedom Congress in 1919. An outspoken anti-imperialist, Eastman also pressed Congress in 1916 for a Pan-American Union to promote cooperation between the United States and Latin America.
5. Paradoxically, the suffrage victory vitiated the sense of purpose, and, for some, the feelings of female superiority that had long fired women's commitment and public participation. Many leaders retired, and the movement itself began splintering along lines of class, race, age, and region after the vote was won. Culturally, younger women in the 1920s began turning toward personal fulfillment as a measure of their empowerment, while the rising mass media and culture of consumerism were redefining the very notion of American citizenship and the theaters for its public expression. See Showalter 1989 and Glickman 2001.

6. Indeed, Mary Simkhovitch spoke glowingly of Eastman in her memoir, saying, "Crystal Eastman, brilliant suffragist and especially known for her masterly work on the Pittsburgh Survey, and her work on industrial accidents, was one of us" (1938, 13).

Works Cited

Baldwin, Roger. 1975. "Recollections of a Life in Civil Liberties, Part 1." *Civil Liberties Review* 2, no. 2: 31–72.

Carastathis, Anna. 2014. "The Concept of Intersectionality in Feminist Theory." *Philosophy Compass* 9, no. 5: 304–14.

Carbado, Devon W., Kimberlé Williams Crenshaw, Vickie M. Mays, and Barbara Tomlinson. 2013. "Intersectionality: Mapping the Movements of a Theory." *Du Bois Review of Social Science Research on Race* 10, no. 2: 303–12.

Chun, Jennifer Jihye, George Lipsitz, and Young Shin. 2013. "Intersectionality as Social Movement Strategy: Asian Immigrant Women Advocates." *Signs* 38, no. 4: 917–40.

Cole, Elizabeth R. 2008. "Coalitions as a Model for Intersectionality: From Practice to Theory." *Sex Roles* 59, nos. 5/6: 443–53.

Collins, Patricia Hill. 2015. "Intersectionality's Definitional Dilemmas." *Annual Review of Sociology* 41: 1–20.

Cook, Blanche Wiesen. 1978. *Crystal Eastman on Women and Revolution.* New York: Oxford University Press.

———. 1998. "Crystal Eastman." In *Portraits of American Women: From Settlement to the Present,* edited by G. J. Barker-Benfield and Catherine Clinton, 403–28. New York: Oxford University Press.

Cott, Nancy F. 1984. "Feminist Politics in the 1920s: The National Woman's Party." *Journal of American History* 71: 43–68.

Crenshaw, Kimberlé. 1991. "Mapping the Margins: Intersectionality, Identity Politics, and Violence Against Women of Color." *Stanford Law Review* 43, no. 6: 1241–99.

Eastman, Crystal. 1912. "Letter to Max Eastman." June 20, 1912. Box 6, folder 191. Crystal Eastman Papers. Schlesinger Library, Harvard University.

———. 1913. "Letter to Max Eastman." January 15, 1913. Box 6, folder 192. Crystal Eastman Papers. Schlesinger Library, Harvard University.

———. 1921. "Alice Paul's Convention." *Liberator,* April 1921, 9-10.

———. 1927. "Mother-Worship." *The Nation,* March 16, 1927, 283-84.

Faludi, Susan. 2010. "American Electra: Feminism's Ritual Matricide." *Harper's,* October 2010.

Finan, Christopher M. 2007. *From the Palmer Raids to the Patriot Act: A History of the Fight for Free Speech in America.* Boston: Beacon Press.

Fine, Gary Alan. 2001. *Difficult Reputations: Collective Memories of the Evil, Inept, and Controversial*. Chicago: University of Chicago Press.

Foster, Carrie A. 1995. *The Women and the Warriors: The Women's International League for Peace and Freedom, 1914–1946*. Syracuse, NY: Syracuse University Press.

Glickman, Lawrence B. 2001. "The Strike in the Temple of Consumption: Consumer Activism and Twentieth-Century American Culture." *Journal of American History* 88: 99–128.

Gopaldas, Ahir. 2013. "Intersectionality 101." *Journal of Public Policy & Marketing* 32, no. 1: 90–94.

Gordon, Linda. 2016. "'Intersectionality,' Socialist Feminism and Contemporary Activism: Musings by a Second-Wave Socialist-Feminist." *Gender & History* 28, no. 2: 340–57.

Gugushvili, Alexi, Peter Kabachnik, and Ana Kirvalidze. 2017. "Collective Memory and Reputational Politics of National Heroes and Villains." *Nationalities Papers* 45, no. 3: 464–84.

Gwinn, Kristen E. 2010. *Emily Greene Balch: The Long Road to Internationalism*. Chicago: University of Illinois Press.

Henry, Astrid. 2004. *Not My Mother's Sister: Generational Conflict and Third Wave Feminism*. Bloomington: Indiana University Press.

Hurley, W. L. 1923. "Letter to William J. Burns." January 11, 1923. Record group 65. FBI Records, U.S. National Archives.

Kazin, Michael. 2012. *American Dreamers: How the Left Changed a Nation*. New York: Vintage Books.

Kirchwey, Freda. 1927. "Letter to Oswald Garrison Villard." July 26, 1927. Box 40, folder 2073. Oswald Garrison Villard Papers. Houghton Library, Harvard University.

Levitsky, Sandra R. 2007. "Niche Activism: Negotiating Organizational Heterogeneity in Contemporary American Social Movements." *Mobilization: An International Quarterly* 12, no. 3: 271–86.

MacKinnon, Catharine A. 2013. "Intersectionality as Method." *Signs* 38, no. 4: 1019–30.

McKay, Claude. 1937. *A Long Way from Home*. New Brunswick, NJ: Rutgers University Press.

McLaughlin, Neil. 1998. "How to Become a Forgotten Intellectual: Intellectual Movements and the Rise and Fall of Erich Fromm." *Sociological Forum* 13, no. 2: 215–68.

New York Tribune. 1921. "Woman's Party Will Work for Feminism Only." February 19, 1921, 6.

Pearson's. 1917. "In the Limelight." November 1917, 216-17.

"Program of the Woman's Freedom Congress," March 1, 1919. Mary Ware Dennett Papers, Schlesinger Library, Harvard University, reel 33.

Ramsay, Nancy J. 2014. "Intersectionality: A Model for Addressing the Complexity of Oppression and Privilege." *Pastoral Psychology* 63, no. 4: 453–69.

Showalter, Elaine. 1989. *These Modern Women: Autobiographical Essays from the Twenties.* New York: Feminist Press.

Simkhovitch, Mary Kingsbury. 1938. *Neighborhood: My Story of Greenwich House.* New York: W. W. Norton & Company.

Sklar, Kathryn Kish, and Beverly Wilson Palmer. 2009. *The Selected Letters of Florence Kelley 1869–1931.* Champaign: University of Illinois Press.

Stone, Geoffrey. 2005. *Perilous Times: Free Speech in Wartime from the Sedition Act of 1798 to the War on Terrorism.* New York: W. W. Norton & Company.

Vassar Class of 1903 Fourth Annual Bulletin. May 1907. Vassar College Archives, Vassar College.

Verloo, Mieke. 2013. "Intersectional and Cross-Movement Politics and Policies: Reflections on Current Practices and Debate." *Signs* 38, no. 4: 893–915.

Walters, Suzanna Danuta. 1994. *Lives Together/Worlds Apart: Mothers and Daughters in Popular Culture.* Berkeley: University of California Press.

Washington Herald. 1914. "Mrs. Benedict Due Today." March 10, 1914, 5.

"Doing Josephine":
The Radical Legacy of Josephine Baker's Banana Dance

K. Allison Hammer

Abstract: For over a century, Black women performers have challenged racism, sexism, and heteronormativity. However, the ephemeral traces of historical performances are always in danger of being erased or misinterpreted. In the 1920s and 1930s, Josephine Baker both shocked and delighted audiences at Parisian dance halls with her scandalous banana belt. For many critics, the belt symbolizes either her agency or her submission to primitivist caricature and racial/sexual objectification. Instead, through what I call *female phallicism*, I theorize the belt as a multiple dildo harness that intervened in complex ways in colonial racial and sexual discourses. The banana belt offers contemporary critics a multidimensional, dialogic space for dismantling racial and sexual hierarchies. **Keywords:** queer theory; transgender theory; Josephine Baker; African American performance; 1920s Paris; femme; dildo

The American darky is the performing fool of the world today.
—Claude McKay, Banjo

The misogynistic, racist, and homophobic cultural retractions of the Trump era have compelled me to study with increased intensity the archives of queer and feminist rebellion. Through this process, I rediscovered Josephine Baker's *la danse des bananes* and the potential feminist and queer inheritances hiding in the folds of her multiple rubber protrusions. Granted, for the majority of critics, the garment confirms Baker's positionality as an ingenue—"a feather mannequin" (Francis 2013, 128). Baker's early dance performances only substantiate for some Claude McKay's dire

WSQ: Women's Studies Quarterly 48: 1 & 2 (Spring/Summer 2020) © 2020 by K. Allison Hammer.

assessment that "the American darky is the performing fool of the world today" ([1957] 1970, 14). And for Erin D. Chapman, Baker's agency is merely "a trick of the light," a "collaborative heist accomplished by performer and photographer" (2012, 106). On the surface, she becomes the exemplar of colonial dominance over the Black female body. Topless, in primitive drag, Baker appears to be just this.

Certainly, it must be acknowledged that as a celebrity performer and activist, Baker at times displayed an exuberant willingness to reconcile France's rhetorical humanism with its active colonialism abroad (Francis 2013, 130). All of Baker's stage and screen appearances in France were based on French colonialism in Southeast Asia and North Africa—French negrophilia and primitivism—with plot lines resembling nineteenth-century, French romantic, Orientalist fiction (Brown 2008, 252–54). However, Baker was not necessarily demonstrating complete submission in these dances.

As I followed my own playful musings on their silly, phallic quality, I began to see the radical potential of Baker's bananas. I imagined the belt not as an absolute sign of Baker's oppression or complicity within colonialist regimes, but rather as a historical example of what I call *female phallicism*.[1] Baker embodied the phallic through a femme aesthetic, which creates friction within racist, sexist, and heteronormative ideologies. In this reading, the belt becomes a multiple dildo harness that covertly destabilizes white male hegemony and the phallogocentric economy, as theorized by Derrida. Baker therefore performed in *La danse sauvage* and *la danse des bananes* the queer plasticity and transferability of the phallus. Because of its femme orientation, the belt offers a new host of sex and gender potentialities, which extends Judith Butler's, Jack Halberstam's, and Paul B. Preciado's theorizations of the dildo as a sexual and political tool.

With her phallic embezzlement, Baker refuted early twentieth-century scientific racism that provided a rationale for the dehumanization of Black women and men. Using Black comic techniques of parody and dissent stemming from slavery, she used the improvisatory choreography of the variety stage to relay through movement the modernist New Woman's virility, which would exclude Black women. In the moment of the performance, Baker opened a complex dialogic space, which is as much Baker's legacy as the fantastic garment itself.

Bananas and Other "Body-Like Things"

What happens when we approach the phallus as funny, performative, and widely available to a range of gender identities? Through female phallicism, I consider how femme or feminine-identified cis and transgender individuals develop nonnormative relationships to the phallic, in this case through what Judith Butler euphemistically called "body-like things" (1993, 84). Butler's "The Lesbian Phallus" continues to destabilize the penis/phallus equation through her enduring critique of Freud and Lacan, both of whom she argues naturalized this fusion by disavowal and negation. As Butler claims, both the notion of the bodily ego in Freud and the projective idealization of the body in Lacan suggest that corporeal morphologies result in part from an externalized identification, which means that there is no basis for the fusion of the symbolic phallus and the biological penis (Butler 1993, 90).[2] For Butler, the idealized, phantasmatic figure of the phallus is subject to contradictions, and this is where the lesbian phallus intervenes as a consequence of the "transvaluative denial of its substitutability, dependency, diminutive size, limited control, [and] partiality" (81). Female phallicism is one possible phallic rebellion, which demonstrates the indissolubility of psyche and body *as tension* (66).

Female phallicism highlights with acuity the willfulness that is required to keep sexual morphologies distinct. The Western psychoanalytic notion of castration grounds the heteronormative, colonial epistemology of the body. Outside of two sexes and two distinct kinds of bodies exists only a no-man's-land of pathology and disability (Preciado 2018, 5). However, I argue that the body of a woman with a phallus connotes simultaneously the threat of castration, which Butler observes is a way of "being the phallus," as it is thought that women "are" the phallus, and the male fear of castration anxiety, which stems from "having the phallus" and fearing its loss (1993, 84). The phallus on the body of a femme/feminine-identified performer, as opposed to what appears for Butler to be a masculine-identified lesbian, accentuates this collapse of "being" and "having," and creates even greater friction within morphologies that supposedly secure sexual difference. One cannot both possess the phallus and represent its absence at the same time without compromising the supposed integrity of masculine and feminine morphologies that Lacan insists sustain language, the Law of the Father, the act of naming—our very place in society and culture.

Female phallicism also shifts the theoretical focus from the phallic viability of the transmasculine toward that of the femme/feminine, altering and extending the radical proliferation of "synthetic" forms of desire and pleasure offered by Halberstam and Preciado. Halberstam theorizes how the dildo can be viewed not as a phallic signifier but as a sexual object that questions the originality of the penis and helps confer masculinity on subjects not assigned male at birth, which allows us to see how masculinity is authenticated (Preciado 2018, 64). Using drag kings as the prime example, Halberstam insists that dicks *are* dildos—the "real thing" *is* the simulacrum, to cite Baudrillard's term. Working both against and alongside Butler's framework, Preciado widens Halberstam's claim through what he calls the *countersexual revolution*. In an important callback to Butler's view of the psyche and body *as* tension, Preciado asserts that the dildo reconfigures the erotogenic boundaries of the fucking/fucked body, as it questions the idea that the limits of the flesh coincide with the limits of the body (2018, 73).[3] Further, the dildo, like other technologies of sex relegated to the side of the "unnatural," lurks at the outer limits of racist, male-dominated capitalist system(s) (Preciado 2018, 135).

Female phallicism revises both Halberstam's and Preciado's claims for the dildo by offering a future direction for theorizing trans women's and nonbinary individuals' connection to the phallus and to phallic pleasures and performances, accomplished through the synthetic *or* through various phallic relationships to the penis. This direction can be useful for seeing how the relationship between the penis and phallus as "privileged signifier" is decoupled through transgender embodiment. I approach the ways the dildo as a femme/feminine phallic signifier and sexual object engages in a cataclysmic destabilization of the Cartesian body/mind division as well as the phenomenology of subject/object relations. Baker uses not just one but sixteen dildos to intervene on discourses of sexual difference, colonialism, and the fucker/fucked dichotomy.

In Baker's performance, the multiple phalluses become a source of what I call *body continuity* discovered within the gestural language of the dance. Body continuity, as understood through Baker's performances, resists the phallogocentric logic of Lacan's "mirror stage" in which a subject only achieves "wholeness" through a relation to a penis. Instead, Baker attains body continuity through her disruptive, funny, and highly erotic multiple dildo harness. Body continuity accounts for the often private ways that Black women have accessed female phallicism within the licentious public sphere of the variety stage, which is not subject to the same epistemological and ontological laws and regulations of more formal Western dance theater (Brown 2008, 15).[4] Such a seizing of the phallus as a source of body continuity simultaneously unsettles the terms of colonial desire. Baker achieved through movement a sense of wholeness, of her own humanity, which was denied to Black women through race science and colonial control. Her performance can be read as challenging Lacan's notion that wholeness is achieved in relation to a phallus/penis, and instead proposes that this idealization of wholeness can be achieved through female phallicism. Body continuity is the a priori ground for female phallicism in the moment of the performance. Further suggesting the substitutability and malleability of the phallus, body continuity achieved through performance offers a feeling of wholeness and integrity, of ownership over one's life and a sense of purpose in the world. As Butler insists, "Bodily contours and morphology are not merely implicated in an irreducible tension between the psychic and the material but *are* that tension" (1993, 66). Body continuity in the performance is an attempt to temporarily reconcile that tension, in this case through a phallic claim. In what Jayna Brown (2008) calls the "hall of mirrors," Baker's performance can be perceived as critiquing the phallogocentric mirror stage, in which the infant discovers an idealized image of a self, but through the phallus (or lack of the phallus) as privileged signifier. The contested space of the dance hall requires "multiple directional strategies of perception," in which the dancer is subject to the gaze but also gazes back and questions it with her body (Brown 2008, 17). In possession of the multiple dildo harness, Baker's eye-crossing and angular bodily poses render Lacan's theory comically reductive. As Preciado insists, by virtue of its detachability, its universal penetrating ability (of the anus, vagina, mouth), and thus its refusal to become a stable signifier of heteronormative sex, the dildo symbolizes diasporic "dispossession and nomadism" (2018, 7). Claiming the dildo in particular undoes colonial binaries and thus allowed Baker to claim the privilege of mobility for Black people.

Through female phallicism, Baker found another way to engage in "doing Josephine," a phrase Baker coined to assert her power as a Black woman and as a performer/celebrity. She conveys through this phrase how Black women in the first half of the twentieth century used vernacular dance to resist oppressive social regimes (Brown 2008, 1). Further, the bananas' fecundity surpasses the colonizer's own member. Anne Cheng insists on Baker's complexity when she argues that even if Baker is in some way playing into the colonizer's vision of Black femininity, she is doing so with a "ring of embarrassingly fruitful phalluses" (2011, 46). This is not surprising, given the fact that Baker embraced a range of gender aesthetics in the course of her career, including androgyny and male drag.[5] Through close examination of her early performances, the phalluses in *la danse des bananes* swung according to a hybrid choreography, foregrounded by *La Revue Nègre* and her discovery of a body continuity.

"Doing Josephine" in the Capital of the Black Atlantic

Baker's erotic and humorous redeployment of phallic power occurred within the complex cultural textures of early twentieth-century colonialism and modernism. As Bennetta Jules-Rosette observes, Baker entered Paris at the height of the colonial period, after the city had been "transformed by war, industrialization, migration, overcrowding, and urban redesign" (2007, 151–52). Paris was a city caught in its own contradictions. While Paris often appeared more tolerant than U.S. cities, colonial violence taking place in the Antilles and Africa created a long shadow that proved difficult to conceal (Braddock and Eburne 2013, 4). Assimilationist colonial policy made Paris a "safe haven," a fact that France capitalized on to improve its own image and resolve the contradiction between liberating principles and colonization (Francis 2013, 142).

Paris was also a place of wish fulfillment, of an imagined Black modernity that wasn't available in the "real" (Braddock and Eburne 2013, 5). Baker's bananas were not mere entertainment, or mere surface, but rather, through an *active* female phallicism, penetrated the surface to a deeper reality. This view contradicts the majority of scholars, for whom Baker predominately recalls only the visual politics of Saartije Baartman (Cheng 2011, 3). Renamed Venus Hottentot in the early 1800s by British and French natural scientists, Baartman was originally studied to make a comparison between apes and Black people (Cheng 2011, 3). Binding Baker to the history of the late nineteenth-century "human zoos" that took place in Paris, Francis asserts that by turning the colonial scene into a sexual fantasy, Baker "bypassed" rather than confronted the brutal reality of colonial Africa (2013, 130). Baker scholars, including Terri Francis, Tracy Sharpley-Whiting, Erin D. Chapman, and others, often conceive of Baker as a sexual and racial fetish trapped within the crisis of Black female existence, which demanded the internalization of destructive myths (Francis 2013, 125). Those who are critical of Baker's complicity within French colonial policies and her seeming willingness to become an example of successful assimilation often take as a given Baker's race and gender and the meaning of those categories for early twentieth-century European audiences. However, her iconic banana dance offers simultaneously the European idealization of primitive innocence and the denigration of primitive sexuality, which accounts as well for the polarization in contemporary reception in which Baker often appears either as a naive victim or a parody of European racism or sexism (Cheng 2011, 41). But neither view presents the complex politics of representation in her dances.

The unrefined, erotic space of the variety stage embraced many of the styles and aesthetics of strip tease and burlesque, which follows a different trajectory than scientific racism (Cheng 2011, 36). Appearing at the turn of the twentieth century in European dance halls, theaters, and cinema, strip tease and burlesque both asserted and threatened the "boundary between bodies and things" (36). While scientific racism insisted on clinical distance, strip tease or burlesque elicited circuits of desire that drew the audience to the performer (38). The bananas seem to signal Baker's primitive objectification, yet they also make a profound statement about her ability to penetrate her audiences rather than the other way around. Her "embarrassingly fruitful" reversal of the fucker/fucked dichotomy becomes clear in the ways the audience reacted to her performance in an extreme manner.

Baker nearly incited a riot when she appeared seminude in a pas de deux called *La danse sauvage* in *La Revue Nègre* at the Théâtre des Champs-Elysées, at 9:30 p.m. on October 2, 1925. Jules-Rosette describes her as a "Dionysian spectacle": "Clad only in beads and a belt of feathers, with glaring spotlights focused on her, Baker began to gyrate. No one knew what to expect" (2007, 47). The appearance of control over the crowd isn't surprising given that Black performers knew how to anticipate and manipulate the needs of white audiences, though their dancing was not limited to these needs or expectations (Brown 2008, 6). Baker's own pronouncements should not be taken as the authentic final word on the dance, but her memory of the dance suggests her sense of body continuity developed here as an interior response, precipitating *la danse des bananes*:

> Driven by dark forces I didn't recognize, I improvised, crazed by the music, the overheated theater filled to the bursting point, the scorching eye of the spotlights. Even my teeth and eyes burned with fever. Each time I leaped I seemed to touch the sky and when I regained earth it seemed to be mine alone. I felt . . . intoxicated. (Jules-Rosette 2007, 47–48)[6]

Baker registers the heat in the performance space as the earth became "[hers] alone." Rather than allow what the press called her "image of the frenetic savage dancer" to determine her existence, she used it as a challenge (47–48). The dark forces could describe the conflicting, ambiguous moment of display, which she resists by turning her gaze inward. In this moment of autoerotic body continuity, the space becomes "[hers] alone," in light of not *despite* the white audience's needs and expectations. As Brown articulates, vernacular dance is public and collective and yet also catalyzes "intensely private, articulations of bodily interiority" (2008, 15). Female phallicism in *La Revue Nègre* (invoked through the ironic phallic suggestion of a single pink flamingo feather) gave Baker an "interiority" wherein the dance motion existed "in and of and for" herself (Brown 2008, 6).

In *La Revue Nègre*, Baker opened a dialogic zone of multisignification during which she negotiated with the audience for power. Janet Flanner, writing for the *New Yorker* under the pen name Genêt, recalled how Baker's dance partner, the muscular Black male "savage" Joe Alex, carried her upside down as she performed the splits. Genêt described an "instant of complete silence," followed by a "scream of salutation" that erupted through the theater (Flanner [1972] 1988, xx). In the concentrated moment of the performance, Baker finds her pleasure through erotic withholding. It was only after this "instant of complete silence," that the audience was allowed to "let down" and find their "scream" (xx). Some audience members rushed the stage, while others fled in anger and disgust. In reviews of the performance, critics simultaneously applauded and denigrated her supposed close association to the "savage" (Brown 2008, 226).

La danse des bananes communicated with even more intensity Josephine Baker's multisignifying "tumulte noir." The dance was the headlining act in the 1926 *Folies Bergère* production *La Folie Du Jour*, under the direction of Paul Derval. The cast featured three Black men as "natives," who transported the explorer's belongings and took care of the white explorer's canoe, bringing it safely to dock. The explorer relaxed while Baker, as Fatou, danced within an imagined African scene complete with a tropical river, a tree with branches gracing the stage, potted plants, and a tent (Francis 2013, 134–35). As Gillett notes, European newspapers announced that Baker had introduced the Charleston to Paris, but now the dance had to be renamed the banana dance (2013, 117). Here, Baker located her resistance to the colonizer through the banana garment and her own improvisations, which demonstrates the power of the dance hall as an often contradictory, dialogic space. Her dance moves offered the blend of polyrhythmic and polycentric movements found in the capital of the Black Atlantic but with many of her own improvisations (Francis 2013, 135–36). She incorporated the characteristic shimmy—then flung herself to the floor, rising slowly to face the colonizer with her arm reached out overhead, holding the pose for an extra beat (2013, 136). While this move could be seen as acquiescence to the colonizer's sexual desires, according to performance critic Brenda Dixon-Gottschild, Baker became in *la danse des bananes* a "female personality that is in possession of the male" (*Joséphine* 2006). Baker found the verb for her sexual agency, the "doing word" that Hortense Spillers claims Black women perpetually "await" in terms of their sexuality (2003, 157). However, the object of the *doing* was not a vagina or breast, but a bunch of semi-erect rubber phalluses. The semi-erect quality offered a masculine arousal in *trans*ition, an in-between state that allowed for further destabilization of the penis/phallus equation. As Preciado argues, the erect penis claims a self-authenticating presence that is threatened when the excluded elements—the flaccid penis, the clitoris, the vagina, the anus, or the dildo—reappear (2018, 66). Baker's flaccid dildos, which became aroused through her own movement, signaled this threat.

In both dances, Baker actively conjured stereotypes that seemed to signal her objectification, but Baker's female phallicism illuminated the sexual and racial contradictions present in the fetish. Baker's multiple dildo harness doesn't so much become what Butler describes as an "alternative fetish" resulting from the "transferable, substitutable, and plastic" nature of the phallus, but rather Baker allows us to question the actual meaning of the term *fetish* (Butler 1993, 89). As Cheng explains, the racial fetish "defiles instead of clarifies" dichotomies, because of the ways fetishization unleashes cycles of identification and disidentification (2011, 48). Baker's female phallicism brought to the stage these sexual and racial contradictions, which foreground "the crisis of meaning in the fetish *and* in the cross-cultural exchange between European whiteness and the 'other'"

(Cheng 2011, 47). While it is untenable to suggest that she had total control over this conjuring, she enacted body continuity through female phallicism, and thus redeployed the racial and sexual fetish, creating a very different kind of epistemological crisis than the one most critics describe.

Conforming to the modernist obsession with the aesthetics of the surface, *la danse des bananes* presented a series of masks that also reveal hidden desires (Cheng 2011, 45). According to Cheng, the dance produced the scene of "the Black female lack masking the Black dick making the hunger of the white imperial phallus" (2011, 45). Here Cheng points to Baker's confounding side-by-side performance of the castrated female subject and the male subject "in possession" of the Black dick. However, I argue that in both dances, she provoked "the hunger of the white imperial phallus," not necessarily only for the female sex object but for the "Black dick" evoked through both Joe Alex's and Baker's phallic protrusions. Instead of perceiving this scene as one in which the "desiring European audience" reacted to the "phallic maternal body" in an "uncomfortable affinity to Black masculinity, the ape to which the bananas allude," I argue that the desiring European audience confronted instead the possibility of a female phallus—a "monstrous" hybridity that is neither Black, phallic, and maternal, *nor* Black, phallic, and masculine (Cheng 2011, 45). Female phallicism theorizes the crisis in categorization that occurred when a femme/feminine subject possessed the Black phallus, and the white imperial phallus hungered for a Black *female* dick, precipitating a profoundly queer "disturbance."

Baker's *multiple* phallic powers suggest she doesn't "mimic" the phallic power of the white colonizer or the Black male "savage" Joe Alex, but exceeds them both—exponentially. In ultrafemme jewelry, makeup, shoe style, etc., Baker represents castration but also wears the phallus. Given the separation between penis and phallus, and the reality that the phallus is never fully attainable by anyone, all men, even straight men, simultaneously experience penis envy *and* castration anxiety. Baker made this separation between penis and phallus evident in her performance. Further, the homoerotic, profoundly queer connotation of Baker as penetrator (of both men and women in the audience) suggests how the dildo in a performance context destabilizes heteronormativity. Importantly, the wearer's sexual identity cannot be established, especially when the dildo is attached to femme/feminine-presenting body and aesthetic (Preciado 2018, 73). Baker drew on homoerotic desires of both men and women, blurring the boundaries that delimit the homosexual taboo, which might help to further explain the frenzied response to her performances.

In *la danse des bananes*, synthetic multiples dethrone the anatomical and suggest the resignification of the phallus that Butler promises in the "Lesbian Phallus," while at the same time performing a destabilization of racial categories. Through multiple dildos, Baker undermines the colonizer's ability to take command within the "culture, rationality, progress" impulse of the scientific-medical discourses (Preciado 2018, 121). As Preciado suggests, as movable object "fixed on to flesh," which can be untied, separated, and reattached, the dildo allows us to "decolonize and rehabilitate the fetish as the cultural technology that enables fabrication of any sexual body" (2018, 63, 7). If sexuality itself is "fabricated," regardless of the synthetic or biological nature of the sex, then authentic masculine power, claimed through anatomy and the otherness of the fetish, loses its force and meaning. The dildo thus threatens the male phallic guarantee of control.

With its comedic playfulness, associations with bigness (as in "top banana"), and reference to plantations in the French Antilles, the banana itself became an ideal metaphor for colonial hierarchies in Baker's performances. Much of Baker's skillful dethroning of the white colonizer occurred through covert and nuanced comic subversion. Jean-Claude Baker, her unofficially adopted son and one of her most dedicated biographers, highlights these elements of the dance.[7] He also connects the dance to the inheritance of resistance found in Black folk styles of the South. Jean-Claude Baker (with Chris Chase) writes:

> It's a Charleston, a belly dance, Mama Dink's chicken, bumps, grinds, all in one number, with bananas flying. (Taylor Gordon, a Black American singer who caught the show, remembered that "the vivacious Josephine Baker was flopping her bananas like cowtails in fly time.") (Baker and Chase 1993, 135)

Taylor Gordon's description of Baker "flopping her bananas like cowtails in fly time" conveys how, through comedic female phallicism, Baker achieved body continuity, evident in her sense of ownership of these bananas. The bananas weren't just moving on their own or moving as an unintended effect of the dancer's motion; rather, as Dixon-Gottschild notes, these were "like phalluses stimulated by female agency" (*Joséphine* 2006).

Baker's detractors forget how central the comedic sensibility has been to Black resistance. When Whiting cites Baker's "childlike comedic posture" as part of her complicity in the "[Black] Venus narrative," she underestimates her comedy as a possible expression of suppressed rage (Francis 2013, 135; Watkins 1999, 25). As Mel Watkins, Bambi Haggins, and many others have argued, when the comedy occurs in the guise of the child (or the naive, as Baker often did), the actor actually expresses power over the "adult"—in this case, the colonizer—as a form of subterfuge in order to gain a sense of superiority (Haggins 2007; Watkins 1999, 25). The reading of Baker's comedy as complicity also ignores Black Americans' survival tactics from the time of their arrival in the New World—"to foster a dual mode of behavior and expression—one for whites and another for themselves" (Watkins 1999, 32). What Haggins calls *laughing mad* is a "liberatory act," which continues throughout the history of Black comedy (2007, 1).

In the banana dance, Baker's female phallicism ran through the comedic. As Brown reminds us, variety stages of the early twentieth century featured mainly comedies: "Black farce and satire, often smuggled in behind the wide white mouth, shine light on the fissures in hegemonic claims, revealing the ways hierarchies breed their own instabilities" (2008, 5). Brown emphasizes *play*, and how "playing in the field of racialized fantasies" was for the Black variety performer "her stock and trade" (2008, 6). Baker received inspiration from the culture of private joking among Black people that was not accessible to whites. Coding her rage, and *out*rage— using female phallicism—she held close the private world of Black humor and utilized mimicry to contest the vision of Black women as naive and simpleminded sexual prey (Watkins 1999, 35). In *la danse des bananes*, the dildo operated through a combination of parody and dissent, in harmony with the types of parody and mimicry that racialized Others have used to critique and covertly dismantle dominant ideologies (Preciado 2018, 105). Through the parodic powers of the dildo harnessed on the variety stage, Baker attained a sense of body continuity denied to her as a Black woman.

The banana belt evolved over time, under Baker's direction and guidance. Later versions contained pointed spikes that looked less realistic but more provocative. Jean-Claude Baker asserts in the caption for a photograph of Baker in the spiked *Ziegfeld Follies* version of the belt (fig. 1), published in Vogue in 1934: "Many will claim to have invented it [the banana

Fig. 1. Josephine Baker dancing at the Folies-Bergère, Paris. Photography by Walery (1863–1935).

belt], but only Josephine would dare to strategically fashion herself a sub-stitute phallus" (Baker and Chase 1993, 155).

Spikes adorned her pelvic region, accentuating her female virility with cheeky upward points. She also raised the comic effect through these now treacherously sharp, phallic protrusions, as even the idea of dancing the Charleston in such gear sounds as ridiculous as it does potentially sexy. Baker held both hands like pistols shooting off in the distance—an obvi-ous phallic reference, as guns are often considered metaphors and stand-ins for the penis. In a photograph series of Baker performing the conga in New York City circa 1930, the bananas appear as minimalist spikes, more confrontational and lethal, demonstrating also the gravity of her phallic play (Billy Rose Theatre Divisin n.d.).

Conclusion

Baker arrived on the modernist scene at a critical moment in Paris's his-tory, at the time a fertile ground for Black artistic and political ferment. Her early dances exemplify both the powerful artistic growth centering in Paris and the subversive element covertly contained within some of these arts. Through not one but sixteen rubber banana dildos, she com-ically confronted her audiences with the exploitative reality of colonial power and the racist and sexist ideologies that structure Western society (Braddock and Eburne 2013, 2). However, due in part to feminist criti-cism, the process of Black cultural classification, and the role of the Black arts movement in criticizing artists for their performance of racialized self-hate, Baker is stuck in what Brown calls a narrative of race betrayal (Brown 2008, 282). For these critics, the early twentieth-century variety stage rep-resents "an era to get over, the dark ages before we discovered ourselves" (2008, 282). However, Baker is not frozen in her historical moment, but with the slapping of the semi-erect bananas, leaps from the temporal frame into the anti-racist, gender-radical "not yet."

The queer, feminist, and transgender inheritance of Baker's bananas suggests that Butler's call to arms has already been answered at key his-torical junctures like this one, in ways that are not always perceptible on the surface. Butler's question remains relevant today: "Yet are we to accept the priority of the phallus without questioning the narcissistic investment by which an organ, a body part, has been elevated/erected to the struc-turing and centering principle of the world?" (1993, 79). Through female phallicism rather than transmasculinity, Baker brings the dildo forward as a radical inheritance, fulfilling the later queer and transgender movements' extension and radicalization of the "Anti-Oedipus" proposal, the notion that the entire discourse of "castration" belongs to a heteronormative, colonial epistemology of the body (Preciado 2018, 5).

For contemporary scholars, the banana belt is our inheritance—a reminder to be attentive to potential acts of phallic rebellion. By "flopping her bananas like cowtails in fly time," Baker discovered, again and again, a body continuity denied to her in the larger social and political arenas, presciently following Jack Halberstam's directive to "pick up the dildo and write your own way out of history" (2018, xvi). This fantastic garment offers an inheritance that must not be stuffed in a box or a drawer but rather be kept in the forefront of our critical consciousness. Not only did Baker invent one of the most *queer* multiple dildo harnesses in the history of Black women's performance, but she also gained a sense of her own humanity in the moment of the dance, a right not bestowed upon all bodies, both in her time and today.

K. Allison Hammer is a senior lecturer in women's and gender studies at Vanderbilt University. Their research engages in critical analysis of gender and sexuality in literature, film, and performance. Their work has appeared in *Studies in Gender and Sexuality*, *Feminist Formations*, and *Transgender Studies Quarterly*. They can be reached at k.allison.hammer@vanderbilt.edu.

Notes

1. Importantly, *female phallicism* is distinct from the term *phallic woman*, which is often used as a slur against women who possess masculine strength and bravado.
2. According to Butler's reading of Lacan, in "Mirror Stage," Lacan rewrites Freud's theory of narcissism through concepts of projection and misrecognition, which allows Lacan to establish the body as an idealization of totality and control. Phallogocentrism is born in the moment that the organ, engaged by the narcissistic relation, becomes the model or principle by which any other object or Other is known, at which point the organ is installed as a "privileged signifier." While the mirror stage is epistemological, and thus describes how we know what we know, Lacan's *signification of the phallus* describes how the epistemological is embedded in the symbolic domain of signification, which establishes the conditions for knowability, and thus signifiability.

3. However, I argue against Preciado's nonporous delineation between penis, as "organic embodiment" of the hegemonic tradition, and the dildo as cyborgian intervention. I fear such a distinction could have negative consequences for trans women who either do not have access to, choose not to have bottom surgery, or have simply not considered that path for themselves. I argue instead for different theorizations of the penis that don't automatically assume its hegemony. I also disagree with Preciado's idea of the dildo as new "origin," wherein the penis becomes a copy of the dildo (2018, 22). The idea of an origin conflicts with his otherwise horizontal schematic of sex and gender possibilities.

4. Vernacular dance has been undertheorized, as cultural studies approaches based on semiotics often miss the importance of "bodies in motion" (Brown 2008, 13). Studies that *do* consider dance focus on ballet and modern dance rather than vernacular; Black dance and "primitive" dance only offer "inspirational illustrations of folk technique" (2008, 14).

5. Adding to the queer and trans dimension of Baker's performance style, Baker envisioned herself as a kind of Napoleon figure; she even purchased a set of antique portable steps, which she placed at the foot of her bed, like those Napoleon used (Jules-Rosette 2007, 92).

6. We need to be careful not to assign "authenticity" to Baker's words on her own performances, and yet as Terri Francis asserts, it is impossible to separate Baker's persona from her personhood, since "her life, body, and words, once made public, circulated as consumable signs in an orbit beyond her ultimate control but that was nonetheless generated by her" (2013, 128).

7. Testifying to the near erasure of the belt as radical inheritance, the only surviving footage of the banana dance was lost for sixty years, and recovered stuffed in a box in Rochester, New York. This is the footage that Jean-Claude cites, which is of the version performed in the United States, evident in the fact that she is not topless but wears a bra (Baker and Chase 1993, 135).

Works Cited

Baker, Jean-Claude, and Chris Chase. 1993. *Josephine: The Hungry Heart.* New York: Random House.

Billy Rose Theatre Division, The New York Public Library. n.d. "Josephine Baker." New York Public Library Digital Collections. Accessed May 13, 2019. http://digitalcollections.nypl.org/items/23f94090-2ae3-0131-934c-58d385a7b928.

Braddock, Jeremy, and Jonathan P. Eburne. 2013. "Introduction." In *Paris, Capital of the Black Atlantic: Literature, Modernity, and Diaspora,* edited by

Jeremy Braddock and Jonathan P. Eburne, 1–14. Baltimore: Johns Hopkins University Press.

Brown, Jayna. 2008. *Babylon Girls: Black Performers and the Shaping of the Modern.* Durham, NC: Duke University Press.

Butler, Judith. 1993. *Bodies That Matter: On the Discursive Limits of "Sex."* New York: Routledge.

Chapman, Erin D. 2012. *Prove It On Me: New Negroes, Sex, and Popular Culture in the 1920s.* Oxford: Oxford University Press.

Cheng, Anne Anlin. 2011. *Second Skin: Josephine Baker and the Modern Surface.* Oxford: Oxford University Press.

Flanner, Janet. (1972) 1988. *Paris Was Yesterday: 1925–1939.* Edited by Irving Druttman. New York: Harcourt, Brace, Jovanovich.

Francis, Terri. 2013. "Embodied Fictions, Melancholy Migrations: Josephine Baker's Cinematic Celebrity." In *Paris, Capital of the Black Atlantic: Literature, Modernity, and Diaspora*, edited by Jeremy Braddock and Jonathan P. Eburne, 124–146. Baltimore: Johns Hopkins University Press.

Gillett, Rachel Anne. 2013. "Jazz Women, Gender Politics, and the Francophone Atlantic." *Atlantic Studies* 10, no. 11: 109–30.

Haggins, Bambi. 2007. *Laughing Mad: The Black Comic Persona in Post-Soul America.* Brunswick, NJ: Rutgers University Press.

Halberstam, Jack. 2018. "Foreword." In *Countersexual Manifesto*, by Paul B. Preciado, ix–xvi. New York: Columbia University Press.

Joséphine: First Black Superstar. 2006. Directed by Suzanne Phillips. BBC Wales: Forget About It Film and TV. DVD.

Jules-Rosette, Bennetta. 2007. *Josephine Baker in Art and Life: The Icon and the Image.* Urbana: University of Illinois Press.

McKay, Claude. (1957) 1970. *Banjo: A Story without a Plot.* New York: Harcourt, Brace, Jovanovich.

Preciado, Paul B. 2018. *Countersexual Manifesto.* New York: Columbia University Press.

Spillers, Hortense J. 2003. "Interstices: A Small Drama of Words." In *Black, White, and in Color: Essays on American Literature and Culture*, 152–75. Chicago: University of Chicago Press.

Watkins, Mel. 1994. *On the Real Side: Laughing, Lying, and Signifying—The Underground Tradition of African-American Humor That Transformed American Culture, From Slavery to Richard Pryor.* New York: Simon and Schuster.

"We Always Somebody Else": Inherited Roles and Innovative Strategies in Black Women's Stand-Up Comedy

Jalylah Burrell

Abstract: This article traces Marsha Warfield's stand-up comedy career as the practice rose to prominence and revolutionized comedic performance in the 1970s. Warfield's uses of humor offer complex representations of Black womanhood, and this essay links her work to companion projects by Black feminist activists and writers in the 1970s and 1980s. It also discusses the strategies Warfield developed to take the stage as herself, which resisted the inherited roles and routines that circumscribe Black women's humorous expressivity. **Keywords:** Black feminism; stand-up comedy; Marsha Warfield; humor; jokes; comedic performance

The theatrical legacy that minstrelsy has left continues to require that the woman on stage—especially the black woman—carry the fantasies of the social order.

> —Annemarie Bean, "Black Minstrelsy and
> Double Inversion, Circa 1890"

Marsha Warfield emerged on the stand-up comedy scene in the wake of a sea change in society. The 1970s represented a catalytic moment in both Black feminisms and stand-up comedy, but Black women comedians' critical contributions to both have been underexamined. The activism of the Combahee River Collective, an influential convening of Black feminist activists, and the artistry of a Black women writers' renaissance emphasized the simultaneity of oppression—a constant of Black feminist thinking—to provide visibility to as well as complex renderings of Black women's experiences as sources that have generated enduring critical and

WSQ: Women's Studies Quarterly 48: 1 & 2 (Spring/Summer 2020) © 2020 by Jalylah Burrell. All rights reserved.

creative insights and opportunities. At the same time, a shift was taking place in stand-up comedy: cutting-edge comedians George Carlin, Robert Klein, and Richard Pryor abandoned a mannered and sanitized style of stand-up comedy for a style more resonant with the uncomfortable and unvarnished truths drawn from the performer's individual experience (Bennet 1974, 91). While these men sold out stadiums, however, women comedians, still combating the social construction of humor as a masculine practice, remained largely excluded from comedy-club main stages and cable network specials, and were hindered from exercising the expanded expressive possibilities of stand-up comedy (Zoglin 2008, 183).

One of the few women who made significant incursions into the mainstream stand-up comedy scene in the 1970s was Marsha Warfield, whose early career exhibited a "new and powerful feminism" similar to what Mary Helen Washington observed in the work of Black women writers of the era (1981, 2). Washington attributes the telling of "the Black woman's unspoken truths" to Toni Morrison, Ntozake Shange, Toni Cade Bambara, and a number of their contemporaries (1981, 11). Just as these Black women writers were rendering Black womanhood visible—a priority of Black feminist ideology—Black women comedians with similar truth-telling impulses were struggling to make stand-up comedy do the same (King 1988, 72). While Black feminism affirms Black women's "right to interpret our reality and define our objectives," many Black women comedians in the 1970s and early 1980s found it difficult to exercise that right in stand-up comedy (King 1988, 72). Take Danitra Vance and Whoopi Goldberg as examples. Goldberg has been reticent to place her work under the umbrella of stand-up comedy. In her documentary on Jackie "Moms" Mabley, she claims, "I'm not actually a stand-up stand-up, I'm sort of like a lean-up 'cause, you know, I started, like, with the characters, and so all of my characters told stories. That was the way I felt I could communicate" (*Whoopi Goldberg Presents* 2013). Danitra Vance, the first Black woman repertory player on NBC's *Saturday Night Live*, similarly dismissed stand-up comedy as a viable form of performance. In the comedy-club circuit, Vance recognized a "tradition" of performers yielding to audience expectations to secure laughs (Vance 1994, 383). Unwilling to let audiences remain "who they were when they came in," she made the decision to "say to hell with the audience," in part by pivoting to performance art and theater (Vance 1994, 384). Goldberg and Vance both observed that what was possible for Carlin, Klein, and Pryor, was not possible for them. To achieve success on stage performing material that reflected the truth of their experiences, Black women were compelled to draw on a range of strategies, notably pivoting to character-based solo comedic performance, a move Warfield was unwilling to make.

Warfield began performing stand-up in Chicago in 1974, a recently divorced twenty-year-old telephone-company employee who had taken inspiration from a newspaper article about a local stand-up comedy showcase. Within three years, Warfield was in Los Angeles performing at the storied Comedy Store, racking up appearances on network talk and variety shows, and improvising alongside Robin Williams and Sandra Bernhard as a cast member of Richard Pryor's short-lived NBC variety show. Her star would only continue to rise: She toured the national comedy-club circuit as a headliner, worked notable benefits and roasts, opened for soul superstars on national tours, and secured the role of Roz on the NBC sitcom *Night Court* in 1986 (*Ebony* 1988, 98). At the tail end of her six-season tenure on *Night Court*, she hosted her own daytime talk show on NBC, *The Marsha Warfield Show*. A recurring role on the NBC sitcom *Empty Nest* followed. In a 1990 *Los Angeles Times* profile, Warfield gushed, "I am in the dream-come-true part of my life now. Who wouldn't want to be me?" (King 1990, 2). By Warfield's own admission, what was distinctive about that *dream-come-true* was not fame and fortune, but that she had wrested those rewards by taking the stand-up stage as herself: "Just to stand up in front of an audience and say, 'I am a human being, I am a man, I am woman, and this is what I think.' For a Black performer, it seems to me that this transition happened in my lifetime" (pers. comm., March 4, 2015). For Black women performers, this transition has been impeded by the snarled legacies of the American comedic tradition. For Marsha Warfield, this transition was facilitated by surfacing this history in her act.

In this article, I discuss a metaphor for Black women's comedic performance—"We always somebody else"—drawn from a play by the Black woman humorist Alice Childress, about another Black woman humorist, Jackie "Moms" Mabley. I use the metaphor to illustrate the challenges of eliciting laughter from an audience whose referents for the performer are girded in a gaze that Toni Morrison assails in *The Bluest Eye*. In the novel's afterword, Morrison frames her writing in relationship to an "immutable inferiority originating in an outside gaze" ([1970] 2004, 210). Like Morrison's novel, Marsha Warfield's stand-up comedy "pecked away at a gaze that condemned her," but unlike her contemporary Morrison, Warfield and her peers' bodies of work have been largely ignored in scholarship and popular histories. In this article, I discuss the comedic strategies Warfield employed to animate the complexities of her personhood and thinking to achieve what Daphne Brooks calls "representational autonomy" in her discussion of comedic performer Aida Overton Walker (Brooks 2006, 283). Although Marsha Warfield's unique career positions her as an outlier in the history of Black women comedians, it is an exceptionalism made possible by the pressure other Black women like Walker exerted on comedic performing practices in the early to mid-twentieth century. Black women artists had long taken to tent shows, hole-in-the-wall clubs, and chorus lines to, as Brooks puts it, "imagine how performance culture might serve as a site of revision and self-making for black women and their overdetermined bodies in the cultural imaginary" (2006, 286). Resolved to fully exercise the expressive freedoms of stand-up comedy in the 1970s, Warfield developed an act attentive to the moves earlier Black women performers innovated to assert flashes of autonomy, notably those of Jackie "Moms" Mabley.

A north star of Black women's comedic performance, Marsha Warfield revered Jackie "Moms" Mabley despite dismay for the conditions of her success. "I wanted to do anything I could for her," Warfield said in a 1979 *Jet* magazine article presenting prospective heirs to Mabley's throne (1979, 61). Warfield added: "I had thought about getting a job as her chauffeur or secretary, anything, so I could somehow maybe, get some information or soak up some knowledge she had" (*Jet* 1979, 61). That dream never came true. Mabley, an early practitioner of many of the performance practices that would come to be known as stand-up comedy, passed away in 1975 just as Warfield was getting her sea legs in the Chicago stand-up scene. In the following decade, Warfield's proposed ploy of chauffeuring Mabley for access to her genius appeared as a plot point in Alice Childress's 1987 play *Moms: A Praise Play for a Black Comedienne*. Luther, a character briefly in Mabley's employ as pianist and chauffeur, is revealed to be something of an oral historian, having interviewed Slappy White and sixteen other Black comedians "to discover the heart, as well as the art, of comedy" (Childress 1987, 12). The gig served as a pretense for access. After his hiring, the chauffeur balks at being christened Luther, an appellation Mabley bestowed on all of her pianists: "I'm sorry. My name's not Luther. . . . How'd you like someone to change your name?" Childress uses Luther's anger at this individual affront to call forth Black women's misnaming in American culture.

In her parsing and puncturing of this ill-gotten "rhetorical wealth," Hortense Spillers rattles off some of Black women's false monikers to "demonstrate the powers of distortion that the dominant community seizes as its unlawful prerogative" (1987, 69). Similarly, Childress uses Mabley's response to Luther to spotlight comedy as a channel for powers of distortion.

> [*To audience*] Like it or not, mine's been changed. A boy-child's born and he knows who the hell HE is . . . for the rest-a his no-good life . . . [*Laughs*] Say he get married seven times . . . he's forever MISTER Jones. But me, a poor woman, gotta change my name all the time. First you name for your father, then you marry that MISTER Jones. He might walk out on you. Then comes divorce. Next time you Mrs. Smith, Mrs. Green, Mrs. Johnson, or Mrs. Whosis. You never know who the hell you are cause, dammit . . . we always somebody else. (Childress 1987, 7)

As the play elaborates, Mabley underwent one of those name changes. Long before she bore the moniker "Funniest Woman in the World" or racked up millions of album sales, the comedian was born Loretta Mary Aiken and lifted her stage name from Jack Mabley, a former beau (Jacobson 1974, 46). Her grandmotherly persona was also an invention: "Moms" was a character she developed and inhabited from the age of twenty (Jacobson 1974, 46). Childress endows her imagined Mabley with lines that approximate the real-life comedian's hazy personal history: Mabley was reportedly forced to marry an older man as an adolescent, left home to seek work as a minstrel before she was fourteen, was sexually assaulted in her teenage years and, as a lesbian, compelled to painstakingly negotiate her self-presentation on and off the stage amid the realities of homophobia, racism, and sexism (*Whoopi Goldberg Presents* 2013). Childress's play uses Mabley's biography to make a claim about the trials of performance and personhood for Black women. By contrasting the experience of a presumably Black "boy-child," whose identity is imbued with a measure of authority, from that of a "poor woman," Childress foregrounds the simultaneity of race, class, and gender oppressions as a determining factor in the roles available to Black women. Childress's theatrical rendering of Mabley's practice advances Black feminist thought by addressing how Black women comedians have operated within a repertoire of roles and routines derived from contemptuous conceptions of Black personhood distinct from those of Black men and foundational to the American comedic tradition.

As Childress's play theorizes, the ridicule and misrepresentation of Black womanhood is an engine of the American comedic tradition. Black women's comedic performance and spectatorship is characterized by a contention with this force. Warfield's desire to sputter this engine, to "speak a truer word" about herself (Spillers 1987, 65), relied upon her observing how these roles bounded Mabley's act. Misogynoir, a term coined in 2008 by Moya Bailey to specify "the violence of representational imagery depicting black women," adjoins Childress's efforts to provide a black feminist survey of the American comedic landscape (2013, 341). When prompted to explain its genesis, Bailey provided examples from comedy: the satirical publication *The Onion* calling nine-year-old Best Actress nominee Quvenzhané Wallis an epithet the night of the 2013 Academy Awards ceremony, and Bailey's subsequent observation that "Black women were disproportionately targeted in the jokes students tell themselves" (Bailey and Trudy 2018, 762). Misogynoir speaks to how the great distances between the somebody elses' invented by "a world that looks on in amused contempt and pity" and the self, are a distinct conundrum for Black women comedians (Du Bois 1903, 3). Misogynoir also specifies ridicule and misrepresentation of Black womanhood as an inheritance of nineteenth-century America's most popular entertainment form, blackface minstrelsy.

Blackface minstrelsy propagated a host of *somebody elses* for Mabley and other Black women comedians to attempt to exploit or elude. While it began as a vehicle for white male performers to mount demeaning imaginings of Blackness by darkening their complexions, exaggerating their features, and mangling their speech, after the Civil War the body of performers diversified but remained dominated by men. As her biographer Elsie A. Williams documents, Mabley performed in blackface in popular revues in the 1920s, but its impact on Mabley's oeuvre and Black women's comedic practice is not limited to Black women's occasional participation in it (1991, 159). The most influential progenitor of the American comedic tradition, blackface minstrelsy curated humor as a means to elevate the powerful and demean the vulnerable. As Mel Watkins explains: "Without doubt, minstrelsy did establish a set of derogatory stereotypes in American humor. These not only became standard elements in popular stage humor (and later radio, film, and television humor) but also common referents in the everyday humor of nearly all Americans—blacks included" (1994, 129). For Black women, these stereotypes include Sapphire, Mammy, Jezebel, and Topsy, and they respectively mobilize projections of sassiness, servility, lasciviousness, and ferality onto Black girlhood and womanhood. These stereotypes are a burdensome legacy and are still not the extent of the violence blackface minstrelsy enacted on Black womanhood. Eric Lott's reading of images of Black womanhood in minstrelsy is instructive when he writes, "It seems . . . the extraordinary energy of antebellum misogyny, perhaps even that contempt for white women intermittently repressed through men's 'protection' of them from savage black manhood, was displaced or surcharged onto the 'grotesque' black woman" (1992, 33). This energy fuels not only the thematic preoccupation with misrepresentations of Black womanhood in the casual and professional expressions of humor that misogynoir names, but also audiences' staunch aversion to the comedic agency of Black women performers.

The American comedic tradition's proliferation owes much to the limited power of those who it lampoons. Should they jeer from the audience, they are drowned in the din of a guffawing crowd. Should they employ a comedic logic that runs contrary to America's collective constructed funny bone from the stage, they are likely to bomb. To wane the force of its disdain for Black women, Mabley taught her audiences how to read against the grain. A hallmark of Mabley's act was the rewriting of nursery rhymes. Mabley would preface the recurring bit by characterizing nursery rhymes as lies intended to perpetuate the power relations of the "good old days," a frequent target of her humor:

> You teach 'em that Mother Hubbard went to the cupboard to get her dog a bone. I say that Mother Hubbard had her gin in that cupboard. You tell 'em Jack and Jill went up the hill after some water. I tell 'em that water don't run uphill. You tell 'em that the wolf ate up Red Riding Hood's grandmother. I tell 'em that if he did, then he must have used tenderizer on her as tough as grandmother was. That wolf had a hard time. (Mabley and Markham 1964)

Mabley's first revision reveals the nursery rhyme as an instrument of indoctrination to feminine propriety. Her second revision calls into question the natural order that nursery rhymes instill. Her third revision worries dominant narratives of history; the grandmother, who could possibly be a stand-in for Mabley, succumbs to the wolf's attack, but not without a fight. That Mother Hubbard is a comic nursery rhyme is not incidental. Mabley's revisions suggest a critique of the American comedic tradition and

American society. Toni Morrison similarly vitiates the children's primer in *The Bluest Eye* to critique an American literary tradition. "See Jane. She has a red dress. She wants to play. Who will play with Jane?," becomes a series of letters. Both Mabley and Morrison reconfigure resources that introduce order and narrative to inaugurate imagination and legibility as a means to not only reorient audience members or readers but also point to new possibilities for future Black women artists confronting "the limits of black female representation" (Allen 2005, 103).

Marsha Warfield entered the field of stand-up comedy with her own definition of humor, a vision for how humor could serve as a vehicle for her thoughts, and an awareness of the tough terrain of Black women's comedic performance. Excerpts from Marsha Warfield's early act, featured prominently in Debra J. Robinson's 1983 documentary *I Be Done Been Was Is*, provide insight into her refusal to let the landscape detour her vision. The film includes discussions of Warfield's stand-up strategy—particularly her use of monologues designed to reveal both the inner workings of her mind and how the American comedic tradition fixes Black women as stock characters and subjects of scorn. The film contrasts Warfield's direct approach to Alice Arthur's—another Black woman comedian featured in the documentary—who is shown inhabiting characters as a regular part of her performance practice. Arthur used characters when taking the stage because performing as herself often seemed too daunting: "I get to say a lot of things that I would never say as Alice Arthur" (*I Be Done* 1983). Reflecting on her favorite bits from the documentary, Robinson cited Arthur's impression of Diana Ross (pers. comm., March 19, 2015). The documentary witnesses a pitch-perfect rendition of the Motown star, from the compulsive pulling of just-tossed hair from her oval face, to the permanent shrug of her shoulders. In this impression, Robinson recognized a revolutionary act: "It's not a man in drag. How many women do you see imitating other women?" (pers. comm., March 19, 2015). Robinson was referring to a long history of female impersonation by Black and white male performers that found an early audience in minstrelsy and became a staple of Black male comedians' acts. White minstrel imitations of Black women conceived them as libidinous; Black male minstrels, compensating for their emasculated depiction by white minstrels, emphasized masculinity in their renderings of Black womanhood (Bean 2001, 181). LeRhonda S. Manigault-Bryant calls this performance strategy "promoting masculine power while hiding it" in her discussion of Tyler Perry's Madea character

(2014, 176). In both cases, the humor is generated from obfuscating and assaulting Black women's personhood—not, as in Arthur's case, through an expert and exaggerated evocation of the idiosyncrasies of a Black woman superstar.

Where Arthur's act, for Robinson, served as a breath of fresh air from tired comedic tropes, Marsha Warfield would offer a slightly different perspective on the employment of characters. Characters allowed Arthur to assume the stage uninhibited, but for Warfield they lacked the necessary dimension to animate the complexity of her thinking. Moreover, they did not reflect the vision she had for her performance:

> I don't try to do characters . . . I think they are limiting. I try to do people. If I'm talking about a particular person, I want to show you that person. If I'm talking about a particular thing I want you to see that. If I say "a big house," then you might imagine a big house. But if I show you a big house. "I mean, man, this house was big!" You know, the staircases and the whole thing. Then you can see it. And that's all I'm trying to do is show you what I'm thinking about and not a particular person. I don't want to be somebody else. I like me. (*I Be Done* 1983)

Warfield's approach affirmed her own value, challenging the contempt for Black women that characterizes the American comedic tradition. It also transformed observational comedy from the categorical to the introspective. She dispensed with the, "Did you ever notice?" template, and replaced it with I-statements and observations. While many stand-up comedians' acts have historically depended on converting their audiences to their way of seeing or affirming their audience's points of views, Warfield wanted to explicitly reveal how she was thinking about what she was seeing.

Warfield reveals her nuanced thinking on the girl groups of the early 1960s on the final track of her 1981 album, *I'm a Virgin*. On "Penis Envy Pt. II," Warfield acknowledges the artistry of these Black women and sources its limits in both the diminished power that they held in the music industry and the compulsion to mitigate stereotypes of Black womanhood through a politics of respectability.

> The only thing that kept me from being a singer was that the black women that sang in the sixties were tongue-tied and I wasn't fortunate enough to have a speech impediment. Kept me out of that business. Remember

those singers? How gentle is the rain that falls softly on the meadow? Tonight, you're mine completely. Hey Mr. Postman, look at me. Is there a
letter? Oh yeah! (Warfield 1981)

Warfield begins by cloaking herself in the bloated conceit of a starry-eyed
never-been, coolly naming just one hurdle—"the only thing"—impeding
her path to the rare feat of jukebox glory when logic suggests that many,
many more obstacles exist. By adopting this guise, Warfield is able to include a note of true admiration for the girl groups whose gagging she is
about to lampoon. With her impressions of the Supremes' "A Lover's Con-
certo," the Shirelles' "Will You Love Me Tomorrow," and the Marvelettes'
"Please Mr. Postman," Warfield exaggerates the turgidity of the vocals to
magnify the opacity of the lyrics, and their sublimation of young women's
desire through cliché, earnestness, and manufactured girlishness. In her
setup to the impressions, Warfield plays with the idiomatic and diagnostic
meanings of being tongue-tied to situate her own tongue in history. Warfield's choice of words dulls her caricature of the tongue-tied performances
by insinuating their source as outside the will of the girl groups and a condition of their entry into the world and business of Black popular music.
History has muzzled Black women performers, and failing to acknowledge
that within the architecture of her joke would have been reckless. When
she notes that she "wasn't fortunate enough" to be tongue-tied, she is ges-
turing at the moment, almost two decades since those songs were recorded; she is locating the explicit content of her act within the spectrum of
Black women's performance, and affirming the aesthetic value of the recordings. The bit could have taken shape as just a dismissive impression,
but Warfield opted to show "a big house. . . . You know, the staircases and
the whole thing" (*I Be Done* 1983). Warfield's depiction of herself as an
ill-equipped girl group–aspirant attributes discipline and skillfulness to
earlier Black women performers' negotiations of their subordinated status and cultural misrepresentations. It also announces her deviation from
performance paths that require the suppression of any part of her identity.

From the beginning of Marsha Warfield's stand-up comedy career, she
sought to practice "smart, funny, assertive, independent stand-up" (Marsha Warfield, pers. comm., March 4, 2015). While she enjoyed Mabley's
comedy, she did not employ models while developing her act. After a
smashing debut in the "virgin spot"—reserved for stand-up newbies—at a
Chicago comedy showcase in the early 1970s (Kohen 2012, 33), Warfield

spent a few months developing material despite having no idea "how to structure an act, how to stand-up" (Marsha Warfield, pers. comm., March 4, 2015). Warfield understood humor as a complex way of thinking, not as mere participation in the American comedic tradition. She explained, "Some people think math. Additive. I think everything in humor" (Marsha Warfield, pers. comm., March 4, 2015). Consonant with intersectionality, the most common term for Black feminisms' analytic emphasis on the multiplicity of identities and multiplicative impact of oppressions, Warfield's conception of humor girded her use of stand-up as a vehicle for a Black woman's truth-telling (Crenshaw 1989, 149; King 1988, 47).

In 1976 Warfield moved out to Los Angeles to advance her career, but she maintained her idiosyncratic approach, booking television, film, and club gigs without an agent and adopting a stage persona that challenged audience expectations. Her success in the fourth annual San Francisco Comedy Competition and regular gigs at the Comedy Store in Los Angeles witness the efficacy of this approach. Not long before the comedy competition, Warfield bought a car and then taught herself to drive. Recalling her inversion of these steps, Warfield laughed at her gall (pers. comm., March 4, 2015). Newly licensed, Warfield drove to the Bay Area to appear at adjudicated showcases and was crowned winner over four other finalists, including future *Saturday Night Live* cast members Dana Carvey and A. Whitney Brown. At the time of this writing, Warfield remains the only woman to have won (San Francisco Comedy Competition, n.d.). She was also one of few women to perform in the main performance space of the Comedy Store. Her first sets there earned her kudos from eventual heavy hitters David Letterman and Jay Leno (Kohen 2012, 133). Fellow stand-up comedian Merrill Markoe, who would go on to be founding head writer of the *Late Show with David Letterman*, remembered Warfield as one of the Comedy Store's "brave performers." In Warfield's delivery, Markoe observed an "unintimidated timing," that wrested the success of a set from the exclusive control of the audience (Kohen 2012, 134). Markoe admired Warfield's assuredness, assertiveness, and patience: "She would deliver a punch line, and then just stand silently and stare at the audience, deadpan. She would wait for them to laugh. Usually they did, but if for some reason they didn't, she never looked shook" (Kohen 2012, 134).

Warfield's career owes to hard work and good fortune, but it is also a product of her buying the car and then learning how to drive. Markoe's assessment of Warfield's strength in negotiating audiences hostile to a stand-up on the basis of the comedian's identity recalls Warfield's recollection of her start in stand-up that she didn't know "how to structure an act, how to stand-up" (Marsha Warfield, pers. comm., March 4, 2015). To traditionally structure an act and career as a Black woman—or as Alice Childress's (1987) character rendering of Jackie "Moms" Mabley put it, as a perpetual "somebody else"—would not have been effective. Black women comedians have limited access to the industry platforms and powers that endorse talent and enable careers. They are also hard-pressed to land the specific targets of their jokes when audiences are primed to see them as the steadfast targets. Warfield confronted audience discomfort with her presence on stage as an agent of truth—and not the familiar subject of distortion—by manipulating that discomfort, not attempting to assuage it through self-deprecation or resorting to stereotype. By assuming an unshakable stage persona and stretching the spacing between her set's jokes, Warfield displaced some of the inadequacies associated with Black women stand-up comedians onto audiences unsure of their ability to "get" the joke.

By not traditionally structuring her act, Warfield did not have to cede control of her self-presentation to mollify audiences, working through stereotypes as Mabley was compelled to do or working through character as many of her contemporaries opted to do. Warfield expressed a desire to "be as close on stage to who I am as possible," and distinguished this imperative from the defensive strategies Black women performers have adopted to shield themselves from virulent disdain and violent misinterpretations:

> Jackie Mabley had to become "Moms" to perform. I never wanted to put that barrier between myself and the audience. When they say, "Ladies and Gentleman, Marsha Warfield," that's all I really wanted anybody to ever say . . . How they see me is going to differ from table to table, to person to person, to night to night, and that's okay, because I can't control how people see me, but I *can* control how I can conduct myself. (Marsha Warfield, pers. comm., March 4, 2015)

On the first track of Warfield's comedy album *I'm a Virgin,* she scales the barrier between Black women and audiences that Mabley helped manage through character and costuming. The album opens with an emcee's introduction: "It is my pleasure to present to you tonight, the incomparable wit of Ms. Marsha Warfield." Warfield receives the applause and reintroduces herself, "Let me introduce myself to some of you who don't know who I am. My name is Marsha Warfield and I'm a virgin" (Warfield 1981). The audience returns her greeting with fits of laughter. She lets them dissipate before continuing: "I don't know why some people don't believe me when I say that, but I wouldn't lie to you" (Warfield 1981). The audience is less sure of how to respond, uncertain if it is a comment on their earlier use of laughter as a signal of disbelief to her claim of sexual inexperience, and they remain quiet until an audience member yells something indiscernible. The audience eats up her retort, "You know, it's usually some asshole to my right who doesn't believe me," which allows the audience to project any anxieties they still hold for their earlier transgression onto the "asshole" (Warfield 1981). Warfield takes a moment to clarify: "Like I said I, I wouldn't lie to you. I really am Marsha Warfield." The audience's relief is palpable in their laughter. They were correct to disbelieve her. Warfield shifts the terrain again when she says, in reference to her supposed virginity, "I gave it up though. Not a lot of money in that." Warfield is able to introduce herself and the album's frank discussions of sexual pleasure by confusing audience expectations. Through creating uncertainty about the joke's intended targets early in her act, she can more effectively land targets as the act progresses.

Warfield's stand-up conduct plays with deviant representations of Black women and the strategic postures they beget to surface a cultural disbelief that a Black woman could be a virgin. She then feigns prurience to surface a cultural investment that she dispensed with virginity to make money, thus aligning herself with the Jezebel stereotype. DoVeanna S. Fulton, a critic of a subsequent crop of Black women comedians expresses "worry" about the circulation and reception Black women comedians' acts "by viewers who lack historical and cultural knowledge" (2004, 92). In a discussion of Black women's work on the 2001 Showtime special *Queens of Comedy*, Fulton ponders the boosted "chances of misinterpreting contemporary Black women's humor" given their wide circulation and their use of expletives and what she describes as "hard-core" styles (2004, 92). Warfield's audience was likely no more knowledgeable about the complexities of Black womanhood than the audience at the *Queens of Comedy* taping, but Warfield uses their knowledge of stereotypes to destabilize expectations and provoke laughter. She exposes the house that minstrelsy built as a landmark her comedy need not reside in but move through and around.

Warfield's introduction also pretends to position herself as a novice, recalling her performance in the reserved "virgin spot" for her debut stand-up set. The double signification implies Warfield is green behind the ears, yet her tone exudes calm confidence and her patient pacing allows audience laughter, uncertainty, and anxiety to swell and subside—qualities her Comedy Store colleague Merrill Markoe so admired. She exhibits neither self-deprecation nor sass, dispositions the American comedic tradition enforces on Black women performers. "My name is Marsha Warfield and I'm a virgin," is, after all, not *really* her introduction—it is an introduction of other selves that have stood in for her. In a discussion of Kim Wayans's sketch comedy in the 1990s, Carol Allen describes this maneuver as "exposing [a] false front" in order "to slip through and assert her own subjectivity" (Allen 2005, 105). Warfield's introduction finally occurs when she wraps up the bit by saying, "I like sex a lot. I really do. Especially since I found out women are supposed to have orgasms too. How many of you knew that? Two women? Who know each other" (Warfield 1981). Warfield, who would not publicly identify as lesbian until later in life, introduces herself on stage as someone who celebrates women's sexual pleasure, and observes both its elusiveness in heterosexual encounters and regular achievement in sex between women. Because Warfield's initial bogus introductions suggest to her audience that their perception of truth and order are askew, her actual introduction is divested of some of its pejorative meanings and taboo associations, leaving her audience uncertain as to whether what they witnessed was evidence of deviance or a product of their delusive world view. This series of introductions completes a multifarious approach to stand-up comedy that allowed Warfield to perform as herself while deflating some of the disdain and discharging some of the roles blackface minstrelsy cleaved to the Black woman comedian.

Phyllis Diller once described stand-up comedy as "ultra-final funny" (Kohen 2012, 14). The self-deprecating comedian elevated stand-up—and by extension, herself—from comedic actors, singers, and dancers. "It's just brain to brain" was how Diller described it (Kohen 2012, 14). Both the practice and study of comedy by women is troubled by this extraction of stand-up comedy from an ecosystem of comedic performance. For Black women in particular, performance practices like blues, musical theater, and dance are where the bulk of Black women's known history of comedic performance lies. Despite the avant-garde imprimatur that stand-up comedy has steadily accumulated in distinction from other forms of comedic performance, it is not more pure or intellectual, but the form can accord a performer a measure of freedom that generally eludes Black women performers, and that Marsha Warfield was intent on exercising. She has cited the women's movement, antiwar protests, and Black power as motivating her to pursue a career in stand-up (Marsha Warfield, pers. comm., March 4, 2015). She entered the field to "knock down sacred cows," not to climb an artificial hierarchy of performance (pers. comm., March 4, 2015). While her ingenious strategies allowed her to tell her truth in the manner she desired, the scope of their interventions also reveals the fundamental limits of stand-up comedy for Black women in the 1970s and after.

Acknowledgments

I would like to thank the special issue editors Maria Rice Bellamy and Karen Weingarten, and the anonymous reviewers for their comments and helpful suggestions.

Jalylah Burrell is a postdoctoral fellow at the Center for the Study of Women, Gender, and Sexuality at Rice University. She can be reached at jalylah@gmail.com.

Works Cited

Allen, Carol. 2005. "'Shaking That Thing' and All Its Wonders: African American Female Comedy." *Studies in American Humor* 12: 97–120.

Bailey, Moya. 2013. "New Terms of Resistance: A Response to Zenzele Isoke." *Souls* 15, no. 4: 341–43.

Bailey, Moya, and Trudy. 2018. "On Misogynoir: Citation, Erasure, and Plagiarism." *Feminist Media Studies* 18, no. 4: 762–68.

Bean, Annemarie. 2001. "Black Minstrelsy and Double Inversion." In *African American Performance and Theater History: A Critical Reader*, edited by Harry J. Elam and David Krasner, 171–91. New York: Oxford University Press.

Bennet, Joan. 1974. "Standup Comedy: Roles Replacing Oneliners." *New York Times*, June 30, 1974. https://www.nytimes.com/1974/06/30/archives/standup-comedyroles-replacing-oneliners.html.

Brooks, Daphne A. 2006. *Bodies in Dissent: Spectacular Performances of Race and Freedom, 1850–1910*. Durham, NC: Duke University Press.

Childress, Alice. 1987. *Moms: A Praise Play for a Black Comedienne*. Alexandria, VA: Alexander Street Press.

Crenshaw, Kimberlé. 1989. "Demarginalizing the Intersection of Race and Sex:

A Black Feminist Critique of Antidiscrimination Doctrine, Feminist Theory, and Antiracist Politics." *University of Chicago Legal Forum* 1: 139–67.

Du Bois, W. E. B. 1903. *The Souls of Black Folk*. Cambridge, MA: A. C. McClurg and Co.

Ebony. 1988. "Introducing: Actress/Comedian Marsha Warfield." May 1988, 92–94, 98.

Fulton, DoVeanna S. 2004. "Comic Views and Metaphysical Dilemmas: Shattering Cultural Images through Self-Definition and Representation by Black Comediennes." *Journal of American Folklore* 117, no. 463: 81–96.

I Be Done Been Was Is. 1983. Directed by Debra J. Robinson. Shorewood, WI: D. Robinson. Videocassette (VHS).

Jacobson, Mark. 1974. "Amazing Moms." *New York Magazine*, October 14, 1974, 46–49.

Jet. 1979. "Who Will Succeed Moms Mabley as Top X-Rated Comedienne?" November 15, 1979.

King, Deborah K. 1988. "Multiple Jeopardy, Multiple Consciousness: The Context of a Black Feminist Ideology." *Signs* 14: 42–72.

King, Susan. 1990. "Warfield Lives a Dream." *Los Angeles Times*, April 14, 1990. https://www.latimes.com/archives/la-xpm-1990-04-14-ca-871-story.html.

Kohen, Yael. 2012. *We Killed: The Rise of Women in American Comedy*. New York: Farrar, Straus and Giroux.

Lott, Eric. 1992. "Love and Theft: The Racial Unconscious of Blackface Minstrelsy." *Representations* 39: 23–50.

Mabley, Moms, and Pigmeat Markham. 1964. *The Best of Moms and Pigmeat*. Chess Records.

Manigault-Bryant, LeRhonda S. 2014. "Pause, Auntie Momma! Reading Religion in Tyler Perry's Fat Drag." In *Womanist and Black Feminist Responses to Tyler Perry's Productions*, edited by LeRhonda S. Manigault-Bryant, Tamura A. Lomax, and Carol B. Duncan, 165–86. New York: Palgrave Macmillan.

Morrison, Toni. (1970) 1994. *The Bluest Eye*. New York: Penguin Books.

San Francisco Comedy Competition. n.d. "Past Winners and Finalists of the San Francisco Comedy Competition." Accessed October 26, 2019. http://sanfranciscocomedycompetition.com/about-the-competition/past-winners.

Spillers, Hortense J. 1987. "Mama's Baby, Papa's Maybe: An American Grammar Book." *Diacritics* 17: 65–81.

Vance, Danitra. 1994. "Live and In Color!" In *Moon Marked and Touched by Sun: Plays by African-American Women*, edited by Sydné Mahone, 381–404. New York: Theatre Communications Group.

Warfield, Marsha. 1981. *I'm a Virgin*. Laff Records.

Washington, Mary Helen. 1981. "New Lives and New Letters: Black Women Writers at the End of the Seventies." *College English* 43: 1–11.

Watkins, Mel. 1994. *On the Real Side: Laughing, Lying, and Signifying—The Underground Tradition of African-American Humor That Transformed American Culture from Slavery to Richard Pryor*. New York: Simon & Schuster.

Whoopi Goldberg Presents: Moms Mabley. 2013. Directed by Whoopi Goldberg. New York: HBO Studios.

Williams, Elsie A. 1991. "Moms Mabley and the Afro-American Comic Performance." In *Women's Comic Visions*, edited by June Sochen, 158–78. Detroit: Wayne State University Press.

Zoglin, Richard. 2008. *Comedy at the Edge: How Stand-up in the 1970s Changed America*. New York: Bloomsbury.

PART V. **REPRESENTING MARGINALIZATION AND CONTEMPORARY DIS/INHERITANCE**

Birthrights and Black Lives: Narrating and Disrupting Perverse Inheritances

Stacie Selmon McCormick

Abstract: This article examines how Lezley McSpadden's *Tell the Truth & Shame the Devil: The Life, Legacy, and Love of My Son Michael Brown* and Danielle Allen's *Cuz: The Life and Times of Michael A.* draw upon the medium of life-writing to disrupt discourses that have historically pathologized black motherhood. Both books widen the lens to show the collateral damage of state-sanctioned violence as well as histories of racial and gender oppression. In doing so, these texts reveal how black mothers often bear perverse inheritances (such as the denigration of black motherhood that was founded in slavery and has been perpetuated across time) that they must simultaneously combat while endeavoring to protect their children. **Keywords:** black motherhood; Black Lives Matter; life-writing, incarceration

This is not a story to pass on.
—Toni Morrison, Beloved

In the closing section of Toni Morrison's *Beloved*, the narrator assesses the cumulative impact of slavery and its hauntings—the toll it takes on Sethe, a formerly enslaved mother; the generational trauma with which her children must contend—and determines: "It was not a story to pass on" (1988, 275). A version of this line repeats more declaratively to announce: "This is not a story to pass on." This phrasing contains many possible readings: This is not a story to *retell*, or this is not a story to *miss*, or perhaps most consequentially: this is not a story to pass down to future generations because it is too painful. If we consider the underlying implications

WSQ: Women's Studies Quarterly 48: 1 & 2 (Spring/Summer 2020) © 2020 by Stacie Selmon McCormick.

of the generational trauma that Morrison interrogates in *Beloved*, then we have to consider that for black people, those living in slavery's long shadow, the passing on of troubling narratives to future generations is not entirely within one's control. These are the familiar discourses that so many black people live out in the afterlife of slavery (Hartman 2007). These conditions—"skewed life chances, limited access to health and education, premature death, incarceration, and impoverishment (Hartman 2007, 6)—continue to be passed down as a kind of perverse narrative inheritance with which black people must contend. The Black Lives Matter era of the twenty-first century has raised new awareness of the devastating impact of the passing down of slavery's afterlives onto black subjects and communities. The counternarratives that spring up from this moment designed to circumvent state-sanctioned oppression—"I can't breathe" and "Hands up, don't shoot"—evince an effort on the part of black people to shift the discourse and to articulate their vulnerability and pain. Extended versions of such efforts can be found in the rise of accounts by black mothers attempting to offer another vantage point from which to comprehend this long-standing bodily and psychic violence.

Because they sit at the nexus of patriarchal and racist constructions of motherhood, black mothers often bear the burden of inherited narratives about black motherhood. Concomitantly, black mothers are working to counter the perpetuation of such narratives and their impact through their own acts of life-writing. This article analyzes Lezley McSpadden's *Tell the Truth & Shame the Devil: The Life, Legacy, and Love of My Son Michael Brown* and Danielle Allen's *Cuz: The Life and Times of Michael A.* for their efforts to challenge the tropes that inscribe black motherhood in precarious terms and reinforces them through their children (Morgan 2018, 860).[1] Coauthored with Lyah Beth Leflore, Lezley McSpadden's *Tell the Truth & Shame the Devil* tells the story of her son Michael Brown, who was killed by a police officer in Ferguson, Missouri, in 2014. In the book, McSpadden recounts Michael's life and the aftermath of his death using her own story as a framework through which to understand her son. The book became the first to be published by one of the Mothers of the Movement—a group of mothers who have all lost children to violence and gone on to advocate for racial justice. Danielle Allen's *Cuz* presents the story of Allen's cousin, Michael A., a vibrant young black man who grew up in Los Angeles and got caught up in the "tough on crime" policies of the 1990s that sent many young people away to prison for life sentences. Michael A. was tried as an adult at age fifteen for attempted carjacking. In combination with the three-strikes law, Michael's carjacking conviction sentenced him to an eleven-year prison term, until he was finally released on parole. Approximately three years following his release, Michael was shot and killed by a former girlfriend and prison mate named Bree, indicating that one never fully escapes from the carceral system. Even though Danielle Allen is the principle narrator of *Cuz*, Michael A.'s mother Karen figures prominently, and her story bears remarkable similarities to Lezley McSpadden's.[2] Together, both works reveal how black mothers are implicated in and resist the social forces that imperil their children's livelihoods.

In this article, I argue that Lezley McSpadden and Danielle Allen both draw upon the medium of life-writing to speak back to and disrupt discourses that have historically pathologized black motherhood. In their efforts, they widen the lens to show the collateral damage of state-sanctioned violence and histories of racial and gender oppression to show how black mothers often bear perverse inheritances (such as the denigration of black motherhood that is founded in slavery and perpetuated across time) that they must simultaneously combat while endeavoring to protect their children. I will analyze how both McSpadden and Allen center black mothers amid larger social narratives that render them veritably invisible, thereby unsettling readings of state-sanctioned violence against black subjects as a primarily male struggle. Their works reframe this terror as a multileveled issue that threatens black communities holistically. Additionally, I will explore how each mother's legitimacy is threatened by the state, which calls attention to the ongoing ways black maternal authority is challenged and how black mothers continue to feel the effects of the pathologies that often frame black motherhood. Finally, I look to how they use narrative to intervene in and present a counterdiscourse that advances new conceptions of black motherhood in the contemporary moment.

Rejecting Perverse Inheritances and Reclaiming Maternal Authority

Black mothers have historically had to contend with the effects of how racism and patriarchy structure black motherhood (see Roberts 1993). As a result, myths about black motherhood continue to circulate in American culture—myths that are expressed in documents like the 1965 Moynihan Report, a report that that largely names black mothers as responsible for the "tangle of pathology" that contributes to the so-called fractured state of black families. Allegations of maternal absenteeism and inherent alienation continue to frame black motherhood.[3] Black single mothers often experience this denigration even more intensely because, as Dorothy Roberts explains, "Society penalizes Black single mothers not only because they depart from the norm of marriage as a prerequisite to pregnancy, but also because they represent rebellious Black culture" (1993, 26).[4] Assailing black mothers and black motherhood deepened in the Reagan era with the prominence of the trope of the welfare queen. As more black mothers enrolled in social support programs like welfare, the program became racialized and sexualized with accusations of black women gaming the system or somehow being "unworthy" of such support (Nadasen 2007, 53). The onslaught of public disparagement of black mothers constitutes a practice of what Andrea Freeman calls the "unmothering" of black women, whereby the cumulative effect of racial stereotypes rooted in slavery "divorce black women from common conceptions of good mothering" (2018, 1569). These are the narratives black mothers inherit.

The precedents for the narratives embedded in the Moynihan Report and beyond, however, can be traced to the slave era. Indeed, as Hortense Spillers interrogates in her transformational work, "Mama's Baby, Papa's Maybe: An American Grammar Book," the intangible aspects of property transference for black women became an "American grammar" that continues to marginalize black women and mothers in American discourse and society writ large. Spillers explains how U.S. slavery restructured laws of primogeniture (the law of the father) so that enslaved children followed the condition of their mothers (Spillers 2003, 203–4). Such restructuring ensured the continuation of a system long after slavery that reified the status of both black mother and black child as abject (Morgan 2018, 871). Importantly, however, Spillers calls for a refusal of this reification and encourages an advancement of a new American grammar that makes visible and disrupts the perpetuation of these negative narratives.

Indeed, black women have pushed against efforts to define black motherhood in overwhelmingly negative terms most forcefully in their life-writing. Figures such as Harriet Jacobs, Mamie Till-Mobley, and Myrlie Evers-Williams have all used the genre of life-writing to assert their legitimacy as mothers (as opposed to merely vessels of production) amid the state-sanctioned racial terror visited upon their families. In their respective works, they elevate the voices of black mothers to disrupt the discourses that render them and their loved ones insignificant. Their acts of writing speak to Lucy E. Bailey's assertion that "narrative inheritances can be hegemonic, bestowed, and unwelcome, as well as potential sites of resistance to counter others' expectations and narrate anew" (Bailey 2018, 98–99). This *narrating anew* describes precisely what black mothers across time have aimed to do in response to the ways black motherhood has been impugned.

Both *Tell The Truth & Shame the Devil* and *Cuz* engage in the practice of *narrating anew* in response to the devastating archive of violence that veritably erases the black mothers and children situated at the nexus of such violence.[5] Both works advance the body of work established in black women's life-writing because they respond to the post–civil rights and post–Reagan era discourse about black mothering, and directly confront the grammars that render them as absent-presences in their children's lives, where they are called up primarily as scapegoats for the ways American social structures have often failed black children. These works sit at the intersections of personal narrative and political discourse—or what Angela Ards terms the "ethics of self-fashioning" that can be traced in black women's life-writing to more thoroughly present the experience of black women within the eras of mass incarceration and Black Lives Matter (Ards 2016, 4). As such, these works raise new concerns about black motherhood that account for contemporary conditions while also resisting inherited narratives. They construct new American grammars that enable the visibility of black motherhood and black familial bonds, those narratives that are less visible than the ones of black abjection that predominate cultural discourse.

"I'm Mike Mike's Mother, and I've Always Existed"

Of the tragic volume of deaths that are foundational to the Black Lives Matter era, Michael Brown's death, which occurred on August 9, 2014, in Ferguson, Missouri, is perhaps the most broadly engaged and theorized. It could be that his death came on the heels of the acquittal of George Zimmerman, Trayvon Martin's killer, or that, in the aftermath of his death, scores of activists and protesters took to the streets to fight against state-sanctioned police violence. Regardless, Ferguson became ground zero in the fight for black lives, and for many, Michael Brown's death was a clarion call for an end to the devaluing of black life in the United States and beyond and the desire for new possibilities and futures. Yet, in prominent written accounts of this tragedy, Lezley McSpadden functioned in some ways as an absent-presence. Fred Moten and Stephano Harney's essay, simply titled "Michael Brown," stands as a notable instance of the way Michael Brown's mother often did not enter the frame in a meaningful way in early discourses on Michael Brown's killing, and of the way the story we have of his life is limited because of this absence. They write:

> In the interest of imagining what exists, there is an image of Michael Brown we must refuse in favor of another image we don't have. One is a lie, the other unavailable. If we refuse to show the image of a lonely body, of the outline of the space that body simultaneously took and left, we do so in order to imagine jurisgenerative black social life walking down the middle of the street—for a minute, but only for a minute, unpoliced, another city gathers, dancing. We know it's there, and here, and real; we know what we can't have happens all the time. (Harney and Moten 2015, 81)

While Harney and Moten are correct to call attention to the image of Michael Brown that we don't have because the state had so thoroughly framed Michael Brown's life and the Ferguson community in criminality and abjectness, they also assume that there are no available subjects to offer that image (or that it can never be available to us). In fact, McSpadden in *Tell the Truth & Shame the Devil* rejects the narrative inheritance that renders her as an absent-presence in her son's life. She also intervenes in the singular way of knowing her son (that Harney and Moten lament) in order to offer us a window into the "jurisgenerative black social life" of her son. Or, as Alessandra Raengo would likely put it, McSpadden offers us an image of her son that advances black sociality, which is an affirmation of the "primacy, vibrancy, and generative capacity of black social life" (2017, 121). Raengo notes that the critical posture of black sociality vividly materializes the networks of solidarity, grief, and grievance that undergird Black Lives Matter advocacy (2017, 130). Working in opposition to social death, McSpadden's narrative raises the beloved community that surrounded Michael Brown while at the same time resists the narratives that inscribe her and her son in pathological terms.

Importantly, McSpadden foregrounds the narrative about her son by presenting her own, thereby offering context into the social conditions structuring his life. Although he was a welcomed arrival and adored by his family, the birth of Michael Brown started Lezley McSpadden down a path of dead ends, leaving her unable to attain support for her own advancement. She lacked adequate childcare and struggled to find educational resources for her children. Because she bravely begins her son's story with her own, we not only gain insight into the systemic troubles Michael Brown faced, but also into the challenges young black mothers like McSpadden experience regularly. While she does not advocate for remedies to address the circumstances for her own upbringing, she elevates them as a reminder that the dynamics of Michael Brown's story are much larger than many perceive.

At the outset of her book, McSpadden directly confronts a prominent rendering of black single mothers—the myth of the "welfare queen"—thereby signaling her intentions to narrate her life anew and outside of the discourse of the state. She writes,

> I never finished high school. It was once one of the most uncomfortable and embarrassing facts about my life. . . . I've worked for years barely making minimum wage, sometimes at two jobs, to put clothes on my children's backs and shoes on their feet, even Mike Mike's [Michael Brown's nickname] size 13 feet. I've even received public assistance, because a mother will put her pride to the side and accept help from others to make ends meet and care for her children. (2016, 5–6)

Here McSpadden unpacks prevailing tropes of mothers who bear similarity to her and refuses to take on a posture of shame about her life's circumstances. More than just calling up the narrative inheritances with which black mothers must contend, McSpadden incorporates her own coming-of-age story for readers to engage with alongside Michael Brown's. In positioning these stories in necessary relation to each other, McSpadden reveals all the ways black girls and women are similarly imperiled by the violence of racism and patriarchy.

Indeed, McSpadden's individual story is a testament to the intersectional oppression that black women and girls experience. MsSpadden details the violence she experiences as a toddler at the hands of her father when she naively reveals to her mother that he was involved with another woman (McSpadden 2016, 16–17). We also learn of the abuse she and her mother experienced from a man McSpadden was instructed to call Mister. The violence became so severe that she moved out of her mother's home and into her grandmother's. This move initiated a long struggle with domestic instability for McSpadden during which she moved frequently in search of a supportive home. This precarity also extended into her teenage years, leading up to the birth of her son Michael. Eventually, McSpadden had to drop out of school due to a lack of structural support (including the lack of support she received from Michael Brown's father at times) to simultaneously continue her education and raise her child. Patricia Hill Collins illuminates, "Stepping out of the realm of Black discourse reveals that far too many Black men who praise their own mothers feel less accountable to the mothers of their daughters and sons" (Collins 2000, 174). Ultimately, Lezley McSpadden was left alone to parent her children, similar to the experience of her own mother, who also struggled under the weight of domestic violence and inconsistent support from her children's fathers. McSpadden's experience reminds us of the need to build lifelines to address issues affecting black working mothers, particularly single mothers who have little structural support, issues such as "childcare, the chronically poor education offered to Black children in underfunded, inner-city public schools, the disproportionate numbers of young Black men who have arrest records or are incarcerated, and the large numbers of African-American children currently in government-run foster care" (Collins 2000, 177). McSpadden had to confront most of these issues as she navigated raising her child. So her narrative not only does the work of giving a more complex picture of her individual circumstances, but it allows us to see beyond McSpadden as an individual and contextualize her story within a larger framework of structural inequality that imperils black girls and women.

The struggles McSpadden encountered negatively impacted her ability to be physically present for her children, particularly because she had to take on a disproportionate amount of employment to counter the structural disadvantages she faced. In fact, she writes about being at work when she learns of her son's death, and notes that her work often took her away from her children, including causing her to miss Michael's graduation ceremony (McSpadden 2016, 166). These absences, to a biased onlooker, would appear to be confirmation of the social stigma of black maternal absenteeism, but McSpadden reframes them to show that, even though economic conditions bounded her to work, she was often supporting her children from a distance.

The demands of work not only kept McSpadden from being able to be a visible presence in her children's lives at key moments but also left her vulnerable to state intervention in the way she cared for her children. This was most devastatingly exhibited in the aftermath of Michael Brown's killing. In her book, McSpadden describes how the state attempted to undermine her status as a mother by denying her access to her son as he lay dying in the street. She laments, "They took Mike Mike's body away and didn't even allow me to give him a proper goodbye. Maybe I wouldn't have wanted to see him like he was, but I'm his mama. That should have been my choice" (McSpadden 2016, 181). The state assumed control over Michael Brown's body, thereby denying McSpadden her authority as his mother.

In addition to the disregard of Michael Brown's familial relations, the state also advanced a demeaning caricature of Brown perpetuated by the Ferguson Police Department and the news media. The testimony of Officer Darren Wilson, Michael Brown's killer, revealed an intense hostility toward black men and an implicit bias that shaped his view of Michael Brown as an inhuman monster. In his testimony to the grand jury in the case of the *State of Missouri v. Darren Wilson*, Wilson describes Michael Brown in animalistic terms: referring to him with pronouns like *it*, Wilson expresses that Brown looked like a demon to him, and that attempting to physically engage him was like a "five-year-old holding onto Hulk Hogan" (*State of Missouri v. Wilson* 2014, 225). Most devastatingly, Wilson describes Brown as "almost bulking up to run through the shots, like it was making him mad that I'm shooting him" (2014, 228). Here, the testimony reveals that Wilson simultaneously saw Michael Brown as subhuman and superhuman. And because it is constituted in the official documents of Wilson's grand jury testimony, this depiction becomes the authoritative narrative on who Michael Brown was and how he met his end.

In her autobiography, McSpadden offers a picture of Brown that stands in sharp contrast to Wilson's description. To McSpadden, her son Michael is "Mike Mike," her firstborn child, beloved by his family and friends. In the narrative, she describes him as a child struggling with neighborhood bullies, being a typical young boy, and going on family fishing trips. McSpadden begins worrying about his education as Michael grows older; he has struggles in school, is diagnosed with ADHD, and eventually his high school graduation is in jeopardy (McSpadden 2016, 157). So, McSpadden places him in a program through the Positive Alternative to Learning Center (PAL). After much hard work and collective effort, he graduates high school. This fills McSpadden with tremendous pride, especially in light of the fact that she had to end her own schooling after giving birth to him. Through him, her dreams become realized in a sense.

I want to linger here on a scene from McSpadden's book that describes a family gathering that took place just before her son was killed. The memory reveals a great deal about Michael and the beloved community surrounding him. On a particularly nice summer day just after Michael turns eighteen, the family takes a trip to Spanish Lake, Missouri, where they listen to music, eat sandwiches, and go fishing. When it is time to leave, the family begins packing; however, Michael notes that he hasn't yet caught a fish and will not leave until he has. The family, although tired after approximately five hours at the lake, agrees to wait for Michael to catch one. McSpadden cheers him on and he finally catches a fish, which he holds up in the air with great pride (McSpadden 2016, 168–69). In this single vignette, we gain insight into Michael Brown's character that no police report can ever capture: here, McSpadden presents a determined young man who, after graduating from high school in spite of various odds, is unwilling to walk away from his goal. Notably, this picture contains his mother cheering him on, celebrating his accomplishment as his family bears witness. This is not the Michael Brown of Darren Wilson's testimony or the Ferguson police reports. Through her words, McSpadden is able to reframe his image and her own, reminding the reader of their humanity and value.

"The Single Mother and the Great White Whale"

Danielle Allen's *Cuz* charts a similarly tragic trajectory that leads to the death of her cousin Michael. Allen draws upon her unique standpoint as a Harvard political scientist and classicist to give insight into the social forces that determined her cousin's outcome. As mentioned earlier, even as Allen is the primary narrator, a significant portion of the work reads almost as a conarration with Allen's aunt Karen, whose experience is centered in the text. Allen recounts Karen's difficult circumstances (her battles with economic and domestic instability, violence, and addiction) that inform the precarity Michael A. and his siblings experience. Allen also highlights Karen's attempts to claim her maternal authority. Together, they produce a narrative that contextualizes Michael A.'s life, and not simply his death.

Danielle Allen describes Karen's efforts to help her children, even as social forces usurped her authority as mother, gradually moving Michael into the hands of the state. Like McSpadden, Karen experienced a number of physically and mentally abusive relationships that shaped her and her children's lives. She moved from place to place in search of an elusive stability. The interpersonal violence she endured was largely at the hands of her black male partners; Karen was routinely subjected to abusive relationships, her first significant one being with a man named Paul in Florida, who beat her so badly that she once arrived to work with an unrecognizably bruised face (Allen 2017, 154). She later married and moved to Mississippi with a man named Henry, where she constantly experienced physical violence. Other male figures threatened her daughter Rosalyn with rape while they lived there as well. Henry became so violent that Karen fled with her children to Georgia where they waited before making a move to California (Allen 2017, 184–85). From there, they underwent a series of moves to escape the onslaught of gangs and drugs bearing down on their communities. Allen recounts that "between the 1990 wedding [Karen and Henry's] and the summer of 1993, when Karen was finally resettled in Los Angeles with a measure of stability in a job that she would hold for more than a decade, Karen would go through four jobs and the kids through six mid-year school transitions" (2017, 186) During this time, Karen also had to contend with alcoholism and the effects of addiction on her family. The cumulative weight of these challenges proves to be devastating.

The domestic violence, addiction, and financial instability with which Karen had to contend functioned as compounding factors that contributed to Michael's move from adolescence to prison. Allen describes Karen as desperately trying to save her son from the "parastate" of gangs in Los Angeles. She writes,

> Karen and her brood came home to a war between two sovereigns: the parastate of a drug world increasingly linked to gangs on one side, and the California and federal governments on the other. When Michael stole that $10 in Georgia, and the judge dropped the charges, you might say Michael met the "forgiving world." When he shoplifted and stole the radio in Claremont in 1993, and didn't get any actual charges, you might again say that he met a "forgiving world." But by 1993, back in Los Angeles, Michael met a politically transformed world that was now unforgiving. (Allen 2017, 197)

The 1990s saw a rise in tough-on-crime policies that shifted the way the criminal justice system operated—a shift felt predominantly by black and brown residents of Los Angeles. Ironically, as Karen achieved a tenuous stability, Michael entered a heightened state of precarity. Karen's battle against the giants of the drug and gang world as well as the penal system was not enough to overcome the unforgiving world that ultimately punishes her fifteen-year old son as an adult. In Allen's description of this time—the advent of the war on drugs in LA—she reveals all the ways that Karen was powerless to help her son contend with these social forces. What Allen does not say—but what we can infer—is that Karen herself is victim of similar social forces that contribute to her own precarity as a black woman; therefore, it is unsurprising, even as it is tragic, that she is unable to facilitate better outcomes for her children. The compounding oppression with which Karen has to contend throws the afterlives of slavery into sharp relief (Hartman 2007). As Michelle Alexander explains, "More African American adults are under correctional control today—in prison or jail, on probation or parole—than were enslaved in 1850, a decade before the Civil War began" (2012, 180). This troubling statistic demonstrates the full circle of black captivity and its various iterations since slavery.

The ultimate effort to strip Karen of her maternal authority comes when Michael is finally sent to prison. Michael's arrest and trial for attempted carjacking came at a moment of cultural panic over crime in California: just ten days after Michael's attempted carjacking, Pete Wilson, governor of California, signed a bill that authorized the death penalty for people who committed murder during carjackings (Allen 2017, 75). When Karen handed over her son for trial to the state, she was surrendering custody of him for the last time. He would be sentenced to prison and not return home for another eleven years. Danielle Allen describes Karen as losing her ability to function—unable to have physical contact with her son during visiting hours, Karen would spend prolonged periods of time "lying on her daybed in the living room in a fetal position" (Allen 2017, 76). In losing her son to the penal system, she realized all the ways her authority as a mother had been taken from her. With Michael A.'s imprisonment, he became controlled by the carceral state, which hearkens back to the way slavery severed familial relations in the service of perpetuating itself as a system.

Throughout Michael's youth, Karen made a progressive effort to reclaim the authority refused to her by the state in an attempt to mother her child while he was imprisoned. At the age of seventeen, Michael was transferred to High Desert State Prison in Susanville, California (one of the most violent prisons in the system) making it nearly impossible for Karen to visit him (Allen 2017, 83). On a number of occasions, she petitioned to have Michael moved closer to home so that she could see him more frequently (2017, 83–84). Unfortunately, it was only when Michael died that Karen was able to have a true sense of authority over her child—now a man, dead at age twenty-nine. She elects to give him two funerals: one at the church where Michael was a parishioner, and another at Karen's preferred church, Bethlehem Temple. Here we see Karen making decisions on behalf of her son that she had long been denied. In her own way, she was offering a counternarrative to the state's, which even at his death depersonalized him—describing him as a "sleeping man" who was found dead in a car. No trace of Michael as a person comes through in the details of his death.

Cuz presents a deeper story to stand against the depersonalization of Michael at his death and arguably throughout his life in the California penal system. Throughout the book, pictures of Michael are shown, both in prison and posing with Allen at her wedding. Other artifacts such as his precise cursive handwriting, and letters and emails he wrote from prison, also fill the pages of the book. Allen attempts to capture that jurisgenerative black life that often gets lost amid the pervasive onslaught of black death. We can understand Allen's text through the rubrics of Christina Sharpe's *wake work*, a methodology that helps us to imagine new ways to live and survive in the wake of slavery. *Wake work* is a mode of "inhabiting and rupturing this episteme with our [black subjects'] known lived and un/imaginable lives" (Sharpe 2016, 17). Sharpe asks us to think through not only the slave system but modern modes of black captivity, including the prison system. It is against this backdrop that Danielle Allen aims to render Michael's life to her readers. She even devotes an entire chapter to his words: "Inferno, In Michael's Words." In it, Michael writes a compelling essay where he examines Dante's *Inferno* as a metaphor for his prison experience. Ironically, Michael is also a member of the prison unit's firefighting team, so even in the brief moments when he can escape the inferno of the prison, he spends that time beating back fires of another kind, ones for which he will receive little credit or pay for extinguishing.

Passing On a Different Story

In both texts, we see the effort to reframe narratives that attempt to obscure the humanity of Michael Brown and Michael A., two young black men caught up in systems of oppression that contribute to their untimely deaths. Correspondingly, both works reframe the narratives of their mothers, who also have been misrepresented or rendered absent-presences in the dominant narratives of their children's lives. In *Tell the Truth & Shame the Devil*, McSpadden works to offer a clearer picture of Michael Brown—one that is not framed by the state. She also offers new possible futures through her organization Rainbow Mothers,[6] a counseling and support program for mothers who have lost children to gun violence and other kinds of untimely deaths. Through this work, McSpadden provides space to mourn and affirm the value of black life while also creating important community that supplants the influence of the state and the violence visited upon these communities.

The same is true for Allen. She spends the last portion of *Cuz* affirming the countless efforts of her aunt Karen to fight against the social forces bearing down upon her and her children. At the end of the work, Allen names the problem (the parastate of gangs and mass incarceration), arguing that in naming it, we have the potential to "damage the generations to come less than we ourselves were damaged" (2017, 223). Alongside naming the problem of gang violence and the carceral system, she is also disrupting narratives perpetuated about black motherhood that denigrate mothers like her aunt Karen who, even amid her own precarity, fought to protect and defend her children.

Moreover, Danielle Allen places another story within our minds—a story she desires we hold and pass on. In a brief chapter called "My Heart's Locket," Allen writes:

> In my heart's locket, five gangly brown-skinned kids, cousins, will be forever at play in a pair of crepe myrtle trees bathed in a beneficent June sunshine. I loved to climb the trees as much as Michael. An arm here, a leg there, juts out from the trees' floral sundress, a delicate skein of pink and purple blooms. When we found unbloomed buds on the dichondra lawn, we would gently press at their nub until the skin slit and a fragile, crinkled blossom emerged whole. Meanwhile, inside the house, through the living room picture window, the adults, beloved, are forever passing their time in glancing distracted talk. (2017, 214)

This image of black affective life—of play, of innocence, of family, of love, of the mundane—stands in distinction to the tragedy that envelops their lives. Allen gives us this closing image along with the other to imagine another possible world—one where she and her cousins play forever in the trees while mothers like her aunt Karen simply pass the time rather than perpetually fight against the perverse narrative inheritances that structure and limit their lives.

Stacie Selmon McCormick is an assistant professor of English at Texas Christian University and the author of *Staging Black Fugitivity*. Her research focuses on twentieth- and twenty-first-century black literature, and its representations of gender, sexuality, visuality, and slavery's afterlives. She can be reached at s.mccormick@tcu.edu.

Notes

1. In recent years, there has been a rise in narratives produced by mothers who have lost children to state-sanctioned violence. One notable example is Sybrina Fulton and Tracy Martin's *Rest in Power: The Enduring Life of Trayvon Martin*, released in 2017. Due to the scope of this article, I examine McSpadden's and Allen's works for how they inform issues of unwelcome narrative inheritances; however, there are many possibilities for future scholarship that explores this growing body of work.

2. Although it does not diminish their authority in any way, it is important to note that both women's written accounts were made possible with the help of interlocutors (with LeFlore, an accomplished novelist, who coauthored *Tell the Truth & Shame the Devil*; and Allen, a Harvard professor, who conarrated *Cuz*). This fact highlights the ways both women inherit perverse narratives of black motherhood that place them outside of spaces which would allow them to be sole authors of their narratives.

3. Danielle Morgan argues that out of the Moynihan Report come other myths of Black maternal absenteeism and inherent alienation because black women were frequently out of their homes due to work (2018, 859).

4. We have even seen this emerge more recently in cultural discourse. For example, hip hop star Jay-Z recently spoke on a panel regarding police violence and mass incarceration, and made the claim that children in households led by single mothers contribute to the tensions between police and black children, because those children have an "adverse feeling toward authority" that causes them to tell police "fuck you" and ultimately results in the loss of lives (Shropshire 2019). In attempting to rationalize senseless police violence, Jay-Z lays the burden for problems such as police violence at the feet of black single mothers, which only furthers the notion that black single mothers cause harm to society.

5. See also Joanne Braxton's (1989) *Black Women Writing Autobiography: A Tradition within a Tradition* and Crystal Lynn Webster's (2017) "In Pursuit of Autonomous Womanhood: Nineteenth-Century Black Motherhood in the

U.S. North" for analyses of how black women have used life-writing to assert their legitimacy as mothers.

6. To learn more about McSpadden's organization, please visit their website (see Michael O.D. Brown We Love Our Sons & Daughters Foundation, n.d).

Works Cited

Alexander, Michelle. 2012. *The New Jim Crow: Mass Incarceration in the Age of Colorblindness*. Revised Edition. New York: The New Press.

Allen, Danielle. 2017. *Cuz: The Life and Times of Michael A*. New York: Liveright Publishing Corporation.

Ards, Angela A. 2016. *Words of Witness: Black Women's Autobiography in the Post-Brown Era*. Madison: University of Wisconsin Press.

Bailey, Lucy E. 2018. "Feminist 'Narrative Inheritances:' Revisiting, Pondering, Stretching a Concept." *Vitae Scholasticae* 35, no. 2: 93–113.

Braxton, Joanne M. 1989. *Black Women Writing Autobiography: A Tradition within a Tradition*. Philadelphia: Temple University Press.

Collins, Patricia Hill. 2000. *Black Feminist Thought: Knowledge, Consciousness, and the Politics of Empowerment*. New York: Routledge.

Freeman, Andrea. 2018. "Unmothering Black Women: Formula Feeding as an Incident of Slavery." *Hastings Law Journal* 69, no. 6: 1545–606.

Harney, Stefano, and Fred Moten. 2015. "Michael Brown." *boundary 2* 42, no. 2: 81–87.

Hartman, Saidiya. 2007. *Lose Your Mother: A Journey Along the Atlantic Slave Route*. New York: Farrar, Straus and Giroux.

McSpadden, Lezley, with Lyah Beth LeFlore. 2016. *Tell the Truth & Shame the Devil: The Life, Legacy, and Love of My Son Michael Brown*. New York: Reagan Arts.

The Michael O.D. Brown We Love Our Sons & Daughters Foundation. n.d. Accessed August 16, 2019. http://michaelodbrown.org/.

Morgan, Danielle Fuentes. 2018. "Visible Black Motherhood Is a Revolution." *Biography* 41, no. 4: 856–75.

Morrison, Toni. 1988. *Beloved*. New York: Plume.

Nadasen, Premilla. 2007. "From Widow to 'Welfare Queen': Welfare and the Politics of Race." *Black Women, Gender & Families* 1, no. 2: 52–77.

Raengo, Alessandra. 2017. "*Dreams are colder than Death* and the Gathering of Black Sociality." *Black Camera* 8, no. 2: 120–40.

Roberts, Dorothy E. 1993. "Racism and Patriarchy in the Meaning of Motherhood." *Faculty Scholarship*. Paper 595. https://scholarship.law.upenn.edu/faculty_scholarship/595/.

Sharpe, Christina. 2016. *In the Wake: On Blackness and Being*. Durham, NC: Duke University Press.

Shropshire, Terry. 2019. "Jay-Z Blasted for Seemingly Blaming Single-Parent Families for Police Brutality." *Rolling Stone*, September 3, 2019. https://rollingout.com/2019/09/03/jay-z-blasted-for-seemingly-blaming-single-parent-families-for-police-brutality/.

Spillers, Hortense J. 2003. "Mama's Baby Papa's Maybe: An American Grammar Book." In *Black, White, and in Color: Essays on American Literature and Culture*. Chicago: University of Chicago Press. 203–29.

State of Missouri v. Darren Wilson. 2014. Transcript retrieved from Documentcloud.org. Accessed August 10, 2016. https://www.documentcloud.org/documents/1370494-grand-jury-volume-5.html.

Webster, Crystal Lynn. 2017. "In Pursuit of Autonomous Womanhood: Nineteenth-Century Black Motherhood in the U.S. North." *Slavery and Abolition*. 38, no. 2: 425–44.

Queer Dis/inheritance and Refugee Futures

Ly Thuy Nguyen

Abstract: This essay investigates inheritance through queer reclamations of refugee lineage. I trace how queer dis/inheritance—as survival tactic, feminist epistemology, and aesthetic articulation—can make space for refugee futures. Looking at how Vietnamese American queer/artists navigate inherited traumas while fighting for belonging against xenophobia and racism, I forward queer dis/inheritance as a critical framework of refugee worldmaking beyond projects of recovery and recuperation. I read the refusal to make refugee experiences into something knowable, to preserve the silence and protect the unknown, and to rethink linear history into a sensory lineage, as manifestations of queer dis/inheritance. **Keywords:** Vietnamese LGBTQ; critical refugee studies; queer theory; refugee futures; Vietnam War; inherited trauma

"I will not carry it on. This bloodline ends with me," said Chrysanthemum Tran to audiences at the Asian American Writers' Workshop 2016 art show "Queerness and Our Refugee Mothers," featuring trans-queer-nonbinary Vietnamese American artists. Tran was speaking on their decision to not have children. This seemingly private revelation is well-known for followers of Tran, who was the first transfeminine finalist at the Women of the World poetry slam in 2016, and who won the Rustbelt Regional poetry slam with the poem "On (Not) Forgiving My Mother." In front of strangers, Tran announces, time and again, their disinheritance from the blood family that could only love them "with a fist / and a tongue slicked with poison" (2016, 3).

Centering the "intersection of diaspora and dysphoria," Tran's work

WSQ: Women's Studies Quarterly 48: 1 & 2 (Spring/Summer 2020) © 2020 by Ly Thuy Nguyen.

explores trans-queerness and mental health in relation to their mother's PTSD, and the refugee baggage they refuse to carry on. Their chapbook, *A Lexicon*, marks the rupture of queerness within a refugee lineage caught in the shadow of displacement. Their poems testify to the horrors of living with the rampant manifestation of war memory "leak[ing] through every ceiling tile / crawling inside walls like careful mold" (Tran 2016, 3), and in a body that was too much for their own mother—a Vietnam War refugee with PTSD. *A Lexicon* is filled with visceral details of how the war burns through generations, piercing across space and time to explode at them: "Sometimes a gunfire fist / a broomstick against the back / a volatile mouth naming me // *Disappointment, Mistake*" (Tran 2016, 3). For this, Tran permanently left home for a chosen queer family.

I begin this article with Tran's private grief made public to examine how queerness literally and figuratively tends to refugee futures. Tran's personal life and work both demonstrate the complex iterations of war's impacts in people's intimate lives. Their poems are ridden with contradictions that challenge idealized notions of restorative healing, wherein the attempt to refuse abuse also requires them to embody all the trauma. "This is the shrapnel of abuse," Tran writes, "a hereditary powder keg—all of this belongs to me" (2016, 4). Their refusal to "carry on" marks all the ways in which their life begins outside of violence. And yet, in announcing their dis/inheritance, Tran embodies the war memory that needs to bear borne witness. Their refusal calls attention to the ways in which U.S. empire functions as the source of violence: "All the war / still insulating this country / this home / this body" (2016, 4). The Vietnam War, through "this body," transports ongoing violence across time-space that is waged against the poor, women, immigrants, refugees, people of color, and trans-queer people in the United States.

Tran's delineation of queer dis/inheritance—a simultaneous embodiment and refusal of the refugee baggage—provokes me to ask: How do the intersections between queerness and refugeehood complicate inheritance as a conceptual framework and a reality? How do we situate inheritance in the ongoing reality of transnational displacement and the marginalization of refugees and their lives afterward? Furthermore, what are the possibilities for refugee futures from the vantage point of radical queer politics? To answer these questions, I bring together queer theory and critical refugee studies to address the larger conceptual and ethical concerns about world-(re)making possibilities surrounding trauma and loss.

Queer Refusal and Refugee Lineage

In the last decade, queer theory has embraced the theoretical turn to refusal politics. From Lee Edelman's *No Future* to Jack Halberstam's *Queer Art of Failure*, scholars have enunciated the divestment from a heteronormative capitalist society, its meaning-making function that (en)genders linear history, and its exploitative nature (re)produced as social "progress." Edelman's concept of *reproductive futurism*—how heteroprocreation ensures a hegemonic future—contributes to a consensus that queer time breaks with linear futures reserved for the nuclear family. Halberstam uses (re)productive failure to theorize queer time as "anticapitalist logics of being and acting and knowing" (2011, 20–21). These seductive proposals, indeed, build upon a genealogy of radicalism that challenges *that which must be inherited* to reimagine life beyond bio-industrial-capital reproduction (Marx's base and superstructure). And yet, as Kara Keeling notes, this queer antifuturism as a "(non)politics only for those for whom the future is *given*" reveals a lack of commitment to the material world wherein corporeal markers of difference and fugitivity are literally matters of life and death (2009, 568).

Keeling's critique evokes black feminists' discussion on personhood, property, and inheritance as predicated upon white possessive individualism. Inheritance, the legality of passing down wealth, is enabled via the violent bioreproduction of race, gender, and sexuality. Hortense Spillers (1987) interrogates how white patriarchal lineage emerged via the destruction of black personhood and bloodlines, wherein enslaved women's offspring became properties of—even when fathered by—white masters. Whiteness and its inventions, Cheryl Harris (1991) notes, undergird property law and legitimizing structures of settler capitalism through the bereavement imposed upon Native and nonwhite people. Further, M. Jacqui Alexander notes that the consolidation of white heteronationalism also manifested in newer instances of anti-immigration following the histories of Native displacement and slavery. Particularly, the 1870 immigration restrictions targeted Asian women for their supposedly sexual immorality, deeming them dangerous for white men and unfit for marriage with their male counterparts who were needed for the economy (2005, 293). Together, these scholars point to the mutual co-constitution of inheritable wealth and gendered exclusion of citizenship through American legal system.

To be given a future, then, is to inherit white supremacy, hetero-

patriarchy, private property—violent structures that simultaneously disavow, disappear, and recuperate (racialized m)others. These structures
also limit how we can imagine the dispossessed's biopolitical survival:
How can one become an inheritor beyond the racial scripts of American
possessive individualism? This question troubles me as I think about the
relationship between queerness, war, displacement, and refugee lineage. If
to *radically, queerly "inherit" life* through queer refusal is to reject, negate,
and oppose all that has been claimed and named by the global structures
of command, what do we make of the many worlds supposedly ended,
whose inhabitants must go on, even when their legacy and memory are
of trauma and war debris? For those whose bodies have been touched by
war and colonial conquest, how do we treat their reproductive futurism as
both a politics of survival and a site fraught with biopolitical temptations?
For racialized refugees, "failure" is never symbolic: it means to die in war,
go missing in the refugee passage, or to succumb under racist violence
after resettlement. There will literally be *no future*. How does one "carry
on" such historical traumas, and still dream of radical queer politics that
divest from upholding hegemonic futures?

In both queer theory and critical refugee studies, trauma is recognized
as a productive site of knowledge. It is the question of what constitutes
trauma and how it is recognized that these fields diverge from one another. For example, while state-structured and war-related intergenerational trauma constitutes a large conversation within refugee studies, Ann
Cvetkovich argues that historical trauma such as the Vietnam War "*constructed* as a wound that must be healed in the name of unity" is "used to
reinforce nationalism," unproductive insofar as it cannot account for the
queer(ed) traumas that occur in locations that are "too local or specific to
represent the nation" (2003, 16; italics mine). For Cvetkovich, archiving
queer trauma in its noninstitutionalized forms helps to form a counter-
public that necessarily refuses "public articulations" and "quick fix solutions" of representative inclusion (2003, 16). The Vietnam War, in her
work, appears as a ghostly metaphor, a peripheral reference for what *not* to
talk about, an epistemological and ontological dissonance within her proposed project of privileging "unpredictable forms of politics" outside of
institutions (16).

In other words, this imagining of queer trauma does not hold space
for Vietnamese American queer people. What is lost when their trauma is
dissociated from national discourses of war, displacement, "refugee debt,"

and diasporic identity? Vietnamese American queer people's trauma exists in the nexus of rampant American orientalist trans/queerphobia as well as through their families' homeland/diasporic sexual and gender politics, and especially through their parents' postwar experiences and war memory. The intersectionality of racialized queerness, diaspora, and refugeehood is rather obvious, and yet proves to be challenging for public imagination and scholarship alike. As viral as Vietnam was in American consciousness during and directly following the war, Vietnamese people continue to be narrowly represented in many fields of studies.

This essay, thus, makes an intervention into queer theory and Vietnamese diaspora/critical refugee studies to grapple with the question of how to radically, queerly "inherit" a *difficult* life. This article reminds scholars of queer theory to take seriously the lives and creativity of displaced people, and urges critical refugee scholarship to rethink inherited trauma beyond naturalized designations of generational legacy. *Queer dis/inheritance* marks a critical shift in how we understand refugee lineage and the possibilities of remembering outside of heteronormative, possessive individualist formations of familial structure. Centering refugee maternal relationships, this article points out the paradox between inheritance and dispossession beyond masculinist discourses of gains and losses, forwarding an intricate understanding of queer(ing) legacy.

Engaging with the "refugee repertoire" of Vietnamese American refugees and descendants' artistic productions (Bui 2016), I highlight a critical queer refugee consciousness, which centers refugeehood as "an enduring creative force . . . connec[ting] past, present, and future forms of displacement" (V. Nguyen 2019). The forms I analyze—spoken word, interactive art, experimental film—are deliberately nontraditional, wherein audiences and spectators become witnesses, participants, and at times, subjects, implicated in the narratives' critique. These artworks graft together a refugee lineage revealed through feminine affect and senses, enabling the living connection with the past to be (re)imagined, performed, and transformed toward a queer notion of refugee futures. The first section looks at Trinh Mai's installation *That We Should Be Heirs* to contour what I consider "refugee's abject form" of dispossession and inheritance. The second section analyzes how the short experimental film *Nước (Water/Homeland)* by queer writer-director Quyên Nguyen-Le—starring a real-life refugee mother and her queer child—enacts a queer temporality for refugee lineage. Together, these works' refusals to make refugee experiences into something knowable—through preserving the silence and protecting the unknown, speculating history and merging past-present-future into a sensory lineage—demonstrates what I call a queer dis/inheritance framework.

That We Should Be Heirs: Abject Inheritance

The central piece of Trinh Mai's 2019 installation is entitled *That We Should Be Heirs*, sharing its name with the entire exhibition of seven mixed-media, interactive artworks. In a vast white space, egg-shaped holes are punched into the wall. Some contain tiny paper scrolls bound tightly with red strings, laid under heavy rocks, stuffed with cotton and other debris. Others are sewn shut with strings dipped in water from the Pacific Ocean. The scrolls are a mixture of family letters and letters contributed by volunteers and workshop participants, buried in pockets. Trinh Mai asks visitors of the installation to write down their fears and secrets for the vaults and to literally *feel* those that were sewn shut—"open wounds" with scars—in hopes that the skin-to-skin touch between human hands and the materials will create a visible chemical reaction that changes the piece, further and further altering it into afterlives.

This section examines Trinh Mai's art piece as a form of abject inheritance—an honoring of refugee silence that calls attention to the dispossession endured by Vietnam War refugees. I take up what Marianne Hirsch calls *postmemory*—trauma transmitted across generations—to think about how the generation *after* reckons with an inheritance so ethereal, affective, fractured, and deemed nonvaluable. While many scholars have engaged with the term, Bui (2018) highlights Hirsch's concern for "postmemory's performative regime," or the complicated desire of Vietnamese refugee descendants to make sense of their transferred damage via spectators' eyes to navigate cultural citizenship and belonging (Bui 2018, 113–15). Here, I argue that Trinh Mai's piece holds space for silence and secrets, reconfiguring the afterlife of war into a process of collaboration and transformation among both insiders and outsiders to the refugee experiences.

In one of the vaults was Trinh Mai's late grandmother's collection of letters to family left in Vietnam after the war. The letters were collected in the two decades following 1975, each filled with stories of hardship and sorrow that her grandmother wished to keep hidden. Even after her grandmother had passed away, the artist did not open the letters, regardless of how they "have all the answers"—to family secrets, to belonging, to displacement, to the thing descendants were protected from knowing by the older generation. In this way, the unknowability of refugee experiences that her grandmother wished for was a sustained silence, an abjection that Trinh Mai inherited. This silence marks the fraught space in between knowing and feeling, sensing and becoming, showing its full "capacity to index structures of power, violence, and identity" (Espiritu 2014, 140).

In other instances of trauma inflicted by state terror such as the Holocaust, the Middle Passage, Japanese internment camps, or the Vietnam War, silence has been theorized as a host of survival tactics, colored by the survivors' and their descendants' paradoxical fear between knowing and forgetting, retraumatizing and healing. Here, I read Trinh Mai's art of silence differently. In her artistic articulation, silence is not a haunted space: it speaks loudly in its form, with a shape, a face, and many memories—memories to be kept anonymous, inaudible, to honor a refugee woman's integrity. Her piece offers audiences nothing: not descriptive testimonies, sufferable imageries, nor tragic lessons. Her refusal to comply with the public hunger for marginalized people's trauma does not allow audiences to be spectator, to know, to gain insights from, or to appropriate her grandmother's secrets. She heeds Hirsch's questions of ethical memory: Can we "carry [refugees'] stories forward without appropriating them, without unduly calling attention to ourselves, and without, in turn, having our own stories displaced by them?" (2008, 104). She asks: Can we hold and acknowledge a silence in its shape, can we remember refugees without demanding their trauma to be split open, testified, exhibited, to be consumed in our search for a common sympathy?

This installation continues Trinh Mai's art practices that challenge the racialized/gendered depiction of war victims as consumable spectacles, seeking to address the "hidden, overt injuries . . . the joy and survival practices . . . in the domain of the everyday" (Espiritu and Duong 2018, 588). A praxis of feminist refugee epistemology, her art addresses the "intersection between private grief and public trauma" (2018, 588) through the incorporation of found objects and debris and letter writing as a medium. These materials center the quotidian life of refugees, instigating "the unspectacular(ized)" to reclaim privacy as "a gendered space expressive of . . . refugee-making practices" (590). Furthermore, by asking audiences to contribute letters and interact with the piece, Trinh Mai expands the scope of refugee memory to include our current devastating immigration crisis. As audiences are encouraged to situate their present with refugees' "past," the fault lines that divide historical periodization become unsettled. Trinh Mai's reconfiguration of temporality transforms refugee's private grief into a critical site to acknowledge war's ongoing impact, allowing audiences to emerge in a subjectless, experiential "mode of relationality" that Vinh Nguyen (2019) calls *refugeetude*, to grapple with how our interpersonal lives are also shaped by a global regime that sustains itself through the perpetual production and management of displaced peoples.

Mai's installation illuminates what I consider refugees' abject dispossession, an out-of-place and untimely condition of existence that was produced out of America's race wars at home and abroad. Historically, the loss of political endowments from nation-states, of spatial orientation through uncharted waters and landscapes, of social and cultural claims to personhood accumulatively define refugees as "figures of lack" (V. Nguyen 2019, 113). Within the colonial and imperial history of the United States in North America and in Asia-Pacific, "lacking" was a perpetual condition for many populations. Subjugated peoples, and in particular Vietnamese people, were always lacking—humanity, democracy, modernity, ability to self-govern—and thus in need of foreign interventionism. As refugees, they are considered "losses" to a global political economy burdened with counterbalancing the costs of rescue. The humanitarian regime also obliged asylum-seekers to plead their cases through traumatic testimonials and political narratives—discourses exacerbating American exceptionalism. To appear legible to nation-states and humanitarian courts, many refugees mobilize the pervasive discourse about them as inherently lacking, utterly damaged people.

For women, who acutely experience the burdens of war differently from masculine soldiers and political prisoners, abject dispossession erases the particularities (marriage status, class background, education, etc.) surrounding the course of their refugee identities. As loss is presumed to encapsulate the refugee condition, it takes on a masculine order, rendering gendered experiences of refugeehood as marginalized and exceptional to the universal trajectory. Enduring the multiple levels of gendered violence embedded in patriarchal structures of war, revolution, reeducation, surveillance, borders, camps, and asylum procedures, refugee women's experiences escape the regime of knowability and the legal framework. As such, the deeply feminine nature of abject dispossession relays in its impossibility to be defined, fixated, and named in terms of national and institutional forms of memory and inclusion.

For the dispossessed, recovery is almost impossible: refugeehood persists in other forms of institutionalized "lacking." Disposable jobs, racialized ghettos, and imposed criminalization are rampant realities for resettled refugees. Vinh Nguyen (2019) notes the impossibility of refugees' domestication, arguing that the racialized economic structures of the United States are incommensurable to refugee survival. The only available path for the dispossessed—becoming capitalist workers and (re)settlers—is meant to exhaust any possibilities of imagining a future beyond capitalism. The abject dispossession of refugees, then, becomes a part of how the racialized, gendered, displaced body is implicated into the making of American capital.

At one point in her talk, Trinh Mai shows a piece of cotton from the vault, which she handpicked in the field where her father-in-law worked for many years alongside Mexican farmworkers upon arriving in the United States. In his previous life, Mai's father was a high-ranked official in the South Vietnamese army, and was imprisoned in a reeducation camp before escaping as a land refugee. By the time he made it to the U.S., he no longer had things to pass on. He landed manual jobs just to provide for his family of five, who all lived together in an apartment with another family of six. The story Trinh Mai tells perhaps serves mostly as context, an ephemera shared only in the moment of its telling. And yet, it demonstrates the double-meaning of the installation: *that we should (have) be(en) heirs*. On the one hand, she renounces the rescue narrative that erases refugees' material losses, making visible the conditions in which refugeehood was made humanless, propertyless, and futureless. And yet, in refusing to succumb to the narrative of loss and recovery, *That We Should Be Heirs* produces new ways to express refugee experiences, conceiving a queer possibility of inheritance in the way communities come together to silently and privately honor refugee legacy.

Transitioning from Trinh Mai's queer form of remembering refugee dispossession enacted through war and displacement, I move on to a queer articulation of refugee inheritance as outside of the material/reproductive logic of patriarchal property. In the next section, I provide a close reading of *Nước (Water/Homeland)*, a short film by queer writer-director Quyên Nguyen-Le to work toward a concept of *queer refugee lineage* that delineates the interrupted futures of refugees and engenders a reconfiguration of queer time as both embodying and emptying-out warring past.

Queer Futures of Interrupted Past

Nguyen-Le's *Nước (Water/Homeland)* is a short film that explores the intersection of being queer and a refugee descendant. The film title draws on the poetic meaning of the word *nước* in Vietnamese, which means both *water* and *country/homeland*, a familiar rumination in Vietnamese art. The film ponders a question: "How do you talk about trauma when you don't even speak the same language anymore?" This feeling of quiet alienation haunts viewers throughout the film—from the first scene in a darkroom where a moment of playful flirtation between two queer teenagers and questions about the accepting refugee-mother quickly becomes a gut-wrenching reflection of war and intergenerational trauma. This surreal, experimental narrative fiction redeploys iconic Vietnam War photography—Nguyễn Văn Lém's execution, the "Napalm-girl" Phan Thị Kim Phúc, carnations-on-gun-barrels Flower Power, and pictures of the Vietnamese boat-people crisis—as a spatiotemporal wormhole through which the protagonist bears witness to their mother's refugee history. Evoking a historical reality that operates within the psyche and the affect, *Nước* presents a sort of magical realism that patches together multiple timelines, and traverses through various sites, spaces, and bodies to make a stream of consciousness seamlessly running through multiple iterations of history. Most strikingly, through the maternal body, Nguyen-Le presents a practice of history writing that renders temporality through the mother-refugee's reproductive force, reconstructing a queer refugee future beyond unbecoming.

In the first scene, viewers are introduced to the mother-refugee through an intimate interaction between two queer teenagers in a darkroom, where the protagonist's lover breaks the moment by making a joke about the mother "watching" them. The following question about who the mother is—beyond a gaze in a picture—prompts the genderqueer protagonist to confess that they did not know much about their mother's story. "This is my mom," the protagonist murmurs, as viewers encounter a close-up of the mother's face upside down, reflection from a foot spa basin that quickly dissipates when a customer puts her feet in. In this bit of memory-scape, Nguyen-Le walks viewers through a lifetime of heartbreaks, as the mother-refugee, with her back against us, lowers her head to tend to the customer's feet in her lap. The imagery is symbolically telling, beyond Vietnamese refugee women's common sociality in the nail industry—itself a marker of complex class/social status within Vietnamese refugee communities—to make us wonder *what came before*. If *this* is the world the protagonist's mother occupies now, *what world did the mother leave behind?* Laden with confusion and the "rememory" of historical events "floating around . . . out there" (Morrison 1998, 36) beyond the protagonist's control, viewers follow their mind, jumping from one realm to another, mixing between the anamnesis and the real. The film's surreal style feels like a paper boat floating on water, and yet sternly anchors at the heavy questions of unspoken loss.

Eventually, we are dropped back into the darkroom, where the protagonist's love interest breaks the stream of memory: "Dude, Vietnam was such mistake." The response comes from guilt and liberal goodwill, evoking a prominent sentiment that transforms how America remembers the war, from a "good war" to a grave mishandling of power. The protagonist immediately snaps: "Vietnam is a country, not a war . . . We weren't there . . . don't idealize the war." The lines directly quote award-winning Vietnamese American novelist lê thi diem thúy, encapsulating the feeling widely expressed among cultural producers, artists, and scholars, who protest the American public's memory of Vietnam as solely an American tragedy. Nguyen-Le shares the sentiment, but also seeks to express a particular feeling that goes beyond being ignored by a larger society. Particularly, Nguyen-Le highlights the limits of a U.S.-centric queer radical politics that fails to recognize the complexities of the Vietnam War beyond race and the left-right binary. The two characters' conversation is a response to the polemic erasure of Vietnamese subjectivities in the American public discourses about the war—competing hegemonies where on one spectrum, all Vietnamese people are grateful refugees rescued by U.S. superpower, and on the other, they are heroic revolutionaries who defeated U.S. imperialism. After fighting the Cold War in Asia, the United States' ideological struggle to create a cohesive narrative of its role as a global superpower was brought back home with the arrival of refugees after 1975. Disrupting the bipartisan politics of "liberalism" and "conservatism," some Democratic congressmen were against accepting refugees, while other Republican politicians fought to embrace them. This conflict made visible the limits of the nation-state, as Vietnamese refugees entered a process of contradictory racialization that simultaneously make them hypervisible as rescued subjects—evidently reaffirming the United States as a benevolent savior—and rendered them invisible within the panethnicity of "model minorities"—submissive, hardworking Asians striving to be a part of the laissez-faire market. Vietnamese refugees pose problems and solutions for the nation-state: their isolated, exceptionalized traumas can only be dealt with through collective efforts to make them disappear into the "melting pot" of America. Through the reconfiguration of Vietnamese refugees into "good" immigrants, America rises again as the epitome of liberal democracy.

Trapped in this double bind, many Vietnamese refugees became invested in correcting the discourses, especially those who routinely made the news with their "over-the-top" anti-communist and hypermilitaristic patriotic demonstration to maneuver their complicated status as political agents and grateful refugees. In her work, Mimi Thi Nguyen (2012) explores how Vietnamese women also participated in this manner: aligning with South Vietnamese soldiers, they performed the role of hyperpatriotic benefactors of freedom who appreciate and, in the case of "Napalm girl" Phan Thị Kim Phúc, forgive America. But the mother-refugee in Nước (Water/Homeland) shows a different image of refugee subjectivity that quietly pushes back on such a corrective approach. As she silently eats porridge in the kitchen with her child one rainy day, sharing with them a favorite childhood memory about her own mother, she says in Vietnamese: "When I was young, whenever I'm sick, your grandmother would make me porridge." The protagonist—as many diasporic children who understand colloquial language but unable to speak in mother tongue—responds in English, and asks if she "ever missed Vietnam." The mother's answer—"Of course, but if I had stayed, I never would have had you, like I do today"—is simple, matter-of-fact. It is through this answer that Nguyen-Le marks out a queer lineage of refugee women: the mother's recognition that this lifetime is only one of many possible paths, suspended or otherwise, allows a future to start with a displacement without forever being lost. Refugee future, as such, is not ensured through capitalist success story or an inherited bloodline, but rather by enacting a sensory connection patched with, for example, favorite memories of mother's special homemade food for rare occasions, passed down as an invitation to include her children's queerness. In the final scene, we reenter this conversation to witness Mother telling her queer child to "invite your friend next time I make porridge," a gesture that we can read as latent recognition and acceptance of a queer lineage.

Nguyen-Le once shared that this conversation in the film comes from the familiar way many (immigrant/refugee) descendants learned about their family history: never an "origin story" passed down in full speech. It was always those fleeting moments, in the middle of watching a film or eating a meal, a parent would absentmindedly share something about the past, a memory that descendants sometimes could not dwell on. Here, Nguyen-Le's articulation of a queer refugee lineage is haunting/haunted by the omnipresent questions of trauma. This scene at once showcases a common diasporic reality of lost language, and a poignant critique of representational politics, casting doubt on the effects of traumatic testimonies and visualization. It asks: What language does trauma speak? Similar to Trinh Mai's enunciated silence, Nguyen-Le divests from the desire to demonstrate the refugee mother's personal stories as the points of inquiry. The protagonist, unable to learn the secrets, looks for answers widely available in iconic war photos. Falling into a dreamscape of alternative pasts, they insert themself into each historical moment, occupying Vietnamese bodies at the scenes, embodying the different roles of a witness-turned-perpetrator-turned-victim.

The "exceptional confusion" of the Vietnam War that Marguerite Nguyen (2018) writes of—Vietnamese's dismembered bodies and its function to obscure violence—was visualized here: in a series of fast-paced transitional vignettes, the protagonist finds themself sucked into the photos hanging in the darkroom. The replication of the Flower Power photo turns live; our protagonist stands among protesters in the 1967 March to Pentagon protests, watching their lover enacting activist George Harris sticking carnations in police's gun barrels drawn at protesters. The gun shots—viewers see the protagonist as both the South Vietnamese general Nguyễn Ngọc Loan shooting and the Viet Cong prisoner Nguyễn Văn Lém being shot. The protagonist jumps to another realm and becomes photographer Nick Út as he captures the Pulitzer Prize–winning picture of the Napalm girl. Instead of reproducing the image of a child's bare, burned body, Nguyen-Le makes Nick Út the centered object from the girl's point of view. In this sequence, Nguyen-Le makes visible the multiple gazes imposed upon the image of a traumatized war victim: the photographer's definitive lens, viewers' perpetual gazes, and the defining power that these viewings hold in the course of history. As he shoots, viewers become the captured subject. We become aware of the interconnected relationship between being and viewing: we are those who "weren't there" but who "idealize the war"—look what we've done. Under our gaze, the protagonist suddenly becomes trapped in the womb, cannot speak, only feel.

In making the protagonist inhabit the various bodies in these iconic images, *Nước* effectively highlights the ways in which these historical documents serve as sites of subject formation. It reworks the still images from the U.S. archive into a living history to be occupied and emptied out, carving out a trajectory for the protagonist to see their lineage as culminating from history's moving parts. Against these unfamiliar pasts, the protagonist arrives at the mother's womb—the only certain point of origin. In the womb, the protagonist struggles to cut off the umbilical cord that simultaneously connects and constrains them into a genealogy fraught with gendered violence. In an extreme close-up of their face in horror, we see an obscured projection of the famous scene in *Full Metal Jacket*, depicting a Vietnamese sex worker soliciting work with American soldiers occupying Saigon: "Me so horny, me so horny, me love you long time." Another iconic image—the infamous and fictionalized Saigon prostitute, reincarnation of Miss Saigon and Madame Butterfly, which stands in for orientalist (hetero)sexual desire—is etched onto the skin of our protagonist, a future queer body. This is the final straw; the protagonist rips off the umbilical cord and falls back into darkness, away from the nail-salon mother's lingering, piercing, almost resentful gaze. We see their mother at the nail-salon scene again, this time turning around and looking straight at the protagonist—past them—to us, breaking the fourth wall. The silent subject becomes a seer: her unspeakablity, unrepresentablity (like Gayatri Spivak's musing of the subaltern who unsettles Western formula of subject formation) does not negate a consciousness; she watched us watching her all along.

This scene and what follows encapsulates queer dis/inheritance. On the one hand, the ripping of the umbilical cord speaks to the disidentification that refugee descendants sometimes feel—as Nguyen-Le once mentioned, "The regretful feeling of not wanting your history to be full of trauma, and wanting to be free, to be your own person" (pers. comm., 2018). In the other hand, the scene also centers refugee women's reproductive force and agency as determining factors of history-writing. It posits her decision to have children, not simply as following naturalized patriarchal order, but as an enactment of future-making after displacement. When the protagonist opens their eyes, they see their mother attentively cleaning them up with a towel while looking at them with kind eyes, slightly nodding. The two are on a lone boat; the vast landscape around them, a dry desert. And then it rains. Throughout the overlapping of imagined realities and unvocalized

Fig. 1. Screenshots from *Nước (Water/Homeland)*. Courtesy of Quyên Nguyen-Le.

understanding beyond language, neither utters a sound. The quiet image holds all the sound of unspeakable heartbreaks: the desert—its soil, a graveyard for all the boat people who did not make it to land. The "absence of water"—*mất nước*, in Vietnamese, means *nation lost*.

This scene best depicts the refugee inheritance of war trauma, displacement, and loss beyond words. But then it rains, bringing water/homeland back in a different form, as the mother and child look toward the sky with an ambiguous emotion toward an uncertain future. The rain acts as a transition between realms, leading viewers back to the last scene in the kitchen, where the mother tells her child that they can bring their girlfriend next time, signaling a queer reconfiguration of her refugee temporality. As the mother and child quietly take in the moment, we hear the sound of the rain gently pelting outside the window like a gentle whisper of hope.

Conclusion

In envisioning refugee futures through a queer refugee lineage, this article shows the various affective strategies of refugee descendants who differently navigate "the things *refugees* carry" with special commitment to feminized concerns about gender, sexuality, and affects—intricate matters likely to be overlooked and sometimes unnameable. Situating refugee sociality through maternal relationships and women's history, this article contributes to feminist discourses on inheritance and on the gendered legacy of the dispossessed—namely, refugee (women) and their lines of descendants. Their unknown histories, which refuse to be displaced by public consumption, informed how Chrysanthemum Tran, Trinh Mai, and Quyên Nguyen-Le navigate war traumas and transnational dispossession while tacitly challenging corrective representation. Analyzing their work, this essay proposes *queer dis/inheritance* as a critical framework to articulate their enactments of refugee future—tending to the hurt and the trauma, imagining a healing, all the while rejecting damaging traditions of homophobia, transphobia, sexism, nationalism.

Acknowledgments

I thank the artists for their raw creativity and illuminating engagements. I'm grateful for Keva X. Bui, Athia Choudhury, Quyên Nguyen-Le, May Xiong, and the *WSQ* reviewers and guest editors for their generous comments.

Ly Thuy Nguyen is currently a PhD Candidate in the Ethnic Studies Department at University of California, San Diego. She can be reached at t0nguyen@ucsd.edu.

Works Cited

Alexander, M. Jacqui. 2005. *Pedagogies of Crossing: Meditations on Feminism, Sexual Politics, Memory, and the Sacred*. Durham, NC: Duke University Press.

Bui, Long T. 2016. "The Refugee Repertoire: Performing and Staging the Postmemories of Violence," *MELUS: Multi-Ethnic Literatures of the U.S.* 41, no. 3: 112–32.

———. 2018. *Returns of War: South Vietnam and the Price of Refugee Memory*. New York: NYU Press.

Cvetkovich, Ann. 2003. *An Archive of Feelings: Trauma, Sexuality, and Lesbian Public Cultures*. Durham, NC: Duke University Press.

Edelman, Lee. 2004. *No Future: Queer Theory and the Death Drive*. Durham, NC: Duke University Press.

Espiritu, Yến L. 2014. *Body Counts: The Vietnam War and Militarized Refuge(es)*. Berkeley: University of California Press.

Espiritu, Yến L., and Lan Duong. 2018. "Feminist Refugee Epistemology: Reading Displacement in Vietnamese and Syrian Refugee Art." *Signs* 43, no. 3: 587–615.

Halberstam, J. Jack. 2011. *The Queer Art of Failure*. Durham, NC: Duke University Press.

Harris, Cheryl I. 1993. "Whiteness as Property." *Harvard Law Review* 106, no. 8: 1707–91.

Hirsch, Marianne. 2008. "The Generation of Postmemory." *Poetics Today* 29, no. 1: 103–28.

Keeling, Kara. 2009. "LOOKING FOR M: Queer Temporality, Black Political Possibility, and Poetry from the Future." *GLQ* 15, no. 4: 565–82.

Morrison, Toni. 1998. *Beloved*. New York: Plume Books.

Nguyen, Marguerite. 2018. *America's Vietnam: The Longue Durée of U.S. Literature and Empire*. Philadelphia: Temple University Press.

Nguyen, Mimi Thi. 2012. *The Gift of Freedom: War, Debt, and Other Refugee Passages*. Durham, NC: Duke University Press.

Nguyen, Vinh. 2019. "Refugeetude: When Does a Refugee Stop Being a Refugee." *Social Text* 37, no. 2: 109–31.

Nước (Water/Homeland). 2016. Directed by Quyên Nguyen-Le. Visual Communications.

Spillers, Hortense J. 1987. "Mama's Baby, Papa's Maybe: An American Grammar Book." *Diacritics* 17, no. 2: 64–81.

Spivak, Gayatri C. 1988. "Can the Subaltern Speak?" In *Marxism and the Interpretation of Culture*, edited by Cary Nelson, Lawrence Grossberg, and Paula Treichler, 271–313. Macmillan Education: Basingstoke.

Tran, Chrysanthemum. 2016. *A Lexicon.* Providence, RI: Self-published.

Trinh Mai. 2019a. "Call to Participants." Trinhmai.com (website). http://trinhmai.com/call-to-participants.

———. 2019b. *That We Should Be Heirs.* Mixed media installation. San Diego Art Institute.

The Politics of Disinheritance

Meghana Nayak

Abstract: Why do my students from non-Western backgrounds often reveal and critique their family members' misogyny? To answer, I theorize the *politics of disinheritance*, or the disavowing of one's family, as part of colonial structures of knowledge production that require "native informants" to offer up tales of family oppression, particularly of gender violence. Disinheritance ultimately strengthens "rescue narratives" that offer "Western freedom" to non-Western women. I then use the work of transnational feminist writers to offer ways to politically engage with and retell family stories so as to disrupt the politics of disinheritance and to cultivate transnational feminist praxis. **Keywords:** disinheritance; native informant; gender violence; rescue narratives; family violence

"I'm sorry I said you are not a feminist." So begins a poem, "A Letter to My Mother," composed in 2012 by Esperanza Sobrado-Torrico, a student taking my Transnational Feminist Theories course at the time. The first verse continues:

> I'm sorry I wrote it in a paper for a women's studies class,
> And I'm sorry the department published it on the internet.
> I'm sorry that you found it there.
> I'm sorry my definition of "feminist" so narrow
> never fit you.

I reread this poem every year to think through what I call the *politics of disinheritance.*

The politics of disinheritance is part of colonial structures of knowledge production that rely upon and require women from marginalized

WSQ: Women's Studies Quarterly 48: 1 & 2 (Spring/Summer 2020) © 2020 by Meghana Nayak.

communities to mark some kind of distinction between themselves and their families, communities, languages, and countries, to be legitimized as feminists in Western contexts. To disinherit entails disavowing or disowning family members due to their misogyny, revealing family secrets about abuse and oppression, or engaging in acts of estrangement, separation, or "escape" from families. I posit that disinheritance is not simply naming or calling out oppressive practices within families but the intentional disruption of the intergenerational transmission of patriarchal, *non-Western* cultural and religious practices.

For example, in the paper in which Esperanza wrote about her "unfeminist" mother, she frames her mother's actions as a product of internalized machismo and Latinx Catholicism. Then, in a later line in her poem, she explains that her disconnect from her mother is a result of cultural differences about women's rights: "I'm sorry this clash of ideals comes from the inevitable cultural and generational disjuncture." But Esperanza then shares that she ultimately discovers the power of generational *connection*, and the role of "la conciencia de la mestiza," a phrase Gloria E. Anzaldúa (1987) uses to indicate an awareness of what it means to have more than one identity while straddling borders. So, while she initially describes her mother as a product of cultural and religious patriarchy, by the end of the poem, she eventually, through engagement with Anzaldúa's work, steps into the complex, contradictory space of rethinking and claiming anew her feminist politics and relationship with her mother.

In this essay, I breathe new life into feminist discussions about "native informants" in order to identify how "insider subjects" rely upon (or are expected to rely upon) acts of family disinheritance—namely, relaying stories of family misogyny and patriarchy to produce "authentic" information about their cultural contexts. I examine how colonial structures of knowledge production, which historically rely upon and strengthen asymmetrical power relationships between colonial officials/imperial feminists and colonized native informants, increasingly and systematically incentivize insiders to disavow their families so as to strengthen "rescue narratives." Thus, acts of disinheritance ultimately legitimize Western interventions in, governance of, and "saving" of non-Western places and non-Western peoples within the West (such as migrants). I do not intend to reinscribe a reductive binary of Western versus non-Western, but I use this flawed terminology to point to the persistence of oppressive (neo)colonial relationships.

My contributions are twofold. First, I enrich the discussions of the role of native informants in knowledge production. These conversations explore whether colonized voices can be recognized and heard (Spivak 2005), how marginalized people enter academic spaces to serve as tokens (Razack 2001), and the payoff of acting as feminist orientalists in order to earn power in Western feminist circles (Hussein 2008), or for strategic gain, such as applying for political asylum (Nayak 2015). In addition, feminists' attempts to critique patriarchal practices within their communities reveal the difficulty of doing so without reinforcing colonial representations. For example,

> feminists from the Middle East, especially those who write in English or French, are inevitably caught between the sometimes incompatible projects of representing Middle East women as complex agents (that is, not as passive victims of Islamic or "traditional" culture), mostly to the West, and advocating their rights at home, which usually involves a critique of local patriarchal structures. The problem with the latter is that it can easily be appropriated as native confirmation of already negative and simplistic images. (Abu-Lughod 2001, 107)

Through the lens of the politics of disinheritance, I challenge transnational feminist studies to more explicitly examine how native informing requires personal stories of oppression by family/kin. It is these stories that strengthen rescue narratives, or the idea that Western intervention, through neoliberalism, militarization, evangelicism, and other systems, is necessary to save women from their savage cultures. After all, if they are describing their own oppression at the hands of people who are supposed to love them, they are clearly seeking an escape from a bad country/culture to a good, enlightened country/culture.

My second contribution is to offer ideas for interventions into how we connect family oppression with feminist journeys. The same students who find Chandra Mohanty's "Under Western Eyes" (1984) or Lila Abu-Lughod's (2014) *Do Muslim Women Need Saving?* groundbreaking, mimic the representational practices they may critique otherwise. Typical comments include: "My mother isn't a feminist because she is a submissive Indian housewife; she had an arranged marriage"; "My father says horribly sexist things, but that's typical for Arab men." In other words, I want to demonstrate to my students that there are ways to retell family stories as political acts so that they do not feel like they have to choose between feminism and their families.

As an Indian American feminist located in the United States, I was inspired by Esperanza's turn to Anzaldúa to contend with her disinheritance. Western feminist contexts provide no space for me to think through my own flirtation with estrangement as a way to deal with my oppressive family experiences. So, I mined South Asian feminist work for stories of family violence in the authors' communities or homes; I searched for their achingly familiar struggles with feminism and family. I discovered four key writers who do not disinherit but rather politically engage with family violence and patriarchy so as to challenge colonial knowledge production.

Uma Narayan is an Indian-descendant philosophy professor at a U.S. university. She illustrates that non-Western feminist politics emerge *through*, not despite, engagement with family stories. Sara Ahmed is a Pakistan-descendant independent feminist scholar who rewrites acts of disinheritance as acts of feminist resistance and disobedience. Shahnaz Khan is a Pakistan-descendant professor of global studies and women's and gender studies at a Canadian university. She analyzes how state and global structures and processes, not simply *culture* or *religion*, make possible family violence. Shailja Patel is an Indian-descendant Kenyan poet/playwright who has lived in the United Kingdom and the United States; through her work, she explores family patriarchy and gendered expectations not in isolation but as responses to gendered and racialized oppression of colonialism and migration. As I note in the conclusions, it is not necessary to use one's cultural context to explore disinheritance, but doing so can make us more profoundly confront the damage of disinheritance.

Acts of Disinheritance

The middle of Esperanza's poem details her acts of separation:

> I'm sorry I only viewed feminism from a Western perspective.
> I'm sorry how that must've made you feel excluded
> and estranged
> from me.

> I'm sorry I critiqued you for staying with my father
> and I'm sorry I said I thought that made you oppressed.
> I'm sorry I always criticized you for trying to "assimilate" our family,

never considering how you looked to protect us.
I'm sorry I said I thought this made you brainwashed.

I'm sorry I never came out to you,
for fear of your religiosity.

I'm sorry I resented you for all those years
because I didn't feel I could ever tell you what really happened to me.
I'm sorry that I know the same thing happened to you.
And I'm sorry that I know the same thing probably happened to my
grandmother
and her grandmother.
I'm sorry that I know that the same thing probably happened
to every woman in our family.
And I'm sorry that is a dark and unspeakable part of our heritage.

I owe all my brazenness to you.
. . . I'm sorry, most of all, I never told them you taught me the meaning of
true power.

In this part of the poem, Esperanza invokes the Western context that alien-ates her from her mother; but, through the apologies, she starts to con-textualize her mother's actions and to acknowledge the intergenerational trauma that connects the women in her family. She attributes that violence to "heritage," a word ambiguous enough to mean "culture," patriarchal norms, or a cycle of violence specific to her family. But she also credits her mother for her feminist spirit. I contend that colonial knowledge produc-tion and the subsequent difficulty of narrating non-Western family stories in the context of Western feminist hegemony, *made possible* Esperanza's essay critiquing her mother, the act of "disinheritance" for which she apol-ogizes in her poem.

I do not have room here to survey the rich transnational feminist lit-erature on native informants, but an overview will suffice to explain what I mean by the colonial structures of knowledge production. Male colo-nial officials and imperial feminists retrieved, used, and distorted "insid-er" information from colonized men and women so as to designate the metropole and its civilizing mission as an indispensable force for good in savage and backward places (Grewal 1996). Gender and the family were principal sites for negotiating local and colonial power, as local patriar-chal actors attempted to exert their "expertise" about their cultures. For example, British colonialists obsessed with sati (widow self-immolation) in India confronted Hindu Brahmin upper-caste men, who offered their interpretations of scriptures in response; both groups excluded the perspectives of widows (Mani 1998). Colonized men may have asserted their insider knowledge in this case, but in other contexts, attempts at the rescue of colonized women served to emasculate and demoralize colonized men (Delphy 2015).

In addition, imperial feminists upheld the colonial project to show they shared a sense of "racial superiority" with colonial men and thus deserved equal rights. In European women's views, equal rights would truly illustrate the West was superior and civilized (Grewal 1996, 65–67). Towns (2010) argues that the legacy of European women's attempts at achieving equal political rights is the notion that the treatment of women is an indicator of how civilized a state is. I note elsewhere that stories about experiences with gender violence in particular continue to be useful in discursively generating hierarchies of "better" and "worse" states to be a woman (Nayak 2015).

Through new forms of replicating colonial structures of knowledge production, it is not only white men and white women but also nonwhite self-proclaimed feminists and women's rights activists, often located in the West, who engage in rescue narratives, whereby "'brown' wom[e]n [are saving other] 'brown women' from 'brown' men" (de Leeuw and van Wichelen 2005, 333). Because rescue narratives are institutionalized in governments, nongovernmental organizations and nonprofits, academia, and professionalized Western feminism (Bracke 2012), the colonial structure incentivizes insider subjects to provide the kind of information that will credential their inclusion in the West while reserving the right to critique, despite inaccuracies or lack of collaboration with those impacted by violence. The crucial move here is that the native informants are now proving their ability and right to speak on their own terms by narrating gory details about family gender violence as well as their "escape" from family misogyny.

Examples of these "new" native informants include Irshad Manji and Ayaan Hirsi Ali, as well as countless, lesser known others. Canada-based Irshad Manji is a queer woman of Indian descent born in Uganda. Postcolonial writers and Muslim reformists critiqued her 2003 book *The Trouble with Islam* for inaccuracies and inconsistencies, but she is increasingly receiving attention and legitimization from Western celebrities, media, and academia. As described in the book and multiple interviews, her feminist awakening is linked to a story of her father running after her with a knife when she was ten years old. Because they were refugees living in Canada, instead of in Idi Amin's Uganda from where they fled, Manji saw the possibility of freedom in a place with social services, police, and communities who "care" about this violence. But in an interview, she denies that her father's actions shaped her critique of Islam:

> There will always be people who assume that my trouble with Islam has to do with my childhood . . . Nothing could be further from the truth. People who say that give my experiences too much power. The fact that in the last 100 years more Muslims have been tortured and maimed in the name of Islam than by any other people—can that be laid at the feet of my childhood? (Bedell 2008)

Thus, while acknowledging that family violence is what made her appreciate her "rescue," she still posits a "universal" truth about Islam.

Or consider Ayaan Hirsi Ali, a Somali atheist, who writes and speaks frequently about Islam's oppression and was an elected Dutch political representative from 2003 to 2006. In her writing and interviews, Hirsi Ali details violence at her mother's hands, which she attributes to the unrelenting misogyny her mother faced. She also describes how her grandmother forced her to undergo genital cutting. She alleges she had to lie in the asylum claim when she fled from Kenya (where her family had settled) to the Netherlands in 1992 due to an impending arranged marriage because she feared that "family abuse" would not have been accepted as a credible reason for fleeing. Hirsi Ali asserts the necessity of escaping her family because she would, as noted in an interview (Hari 2007), "never let what happened to [her] mother happen to [her]." She was always open about fabricating her asylum claim, but after her election to parliament, a Dutch TV program investigated the falsehoods further, which eventually led to members of the government calling to remove her seat. Hirsi Ali left for the United States before the authorities removed her Dutch citizenship.

Crucially, both Manji and Hirsi Ali acknowledge that grants of asylum allowed them to live in countries with "freedom"; seeking asylum is a human right, but the act of granting asylum is increasingly intertwined with colonial rescue narratives. As I explain in my earlier work, due to transnational feminist activism, particularly based on stories of women's asylum claims being rejected when they were fleeing gender violence, family abuse is increasingly accepted by asylum-granting states as a form of persecution (Nayak 2015). Through my comprehensive analysis of "gender based" asylum cases in the United States, I discover that women who wish to claim gender persecution based upon domestic violence and female genital cutting are more likely to receive asylum if they present themselves as independent women fleeing violent *families*, and not just cultural/religious practices. As I note, "The family is seen as the key vehicle for reflecting and propagating 'cultural,' patriarchal expectations, roles, and relationships" (Nayak 2015, 73). The asylum seeker who convincingly expresses a desire to get away from family (whether partners, parents, or siblings) and represents her family as static and frozen in time, is desirable, particularly if she seeks to embrace the United States as a safe, enlightened place for women. Asylum seekers with more complex stories, or who do not wish to disavow their families, must still engage in acts of disinheritance in order to fit the frame Western immigration judges use to adjudicate asylum claims (Nayak 2015).

As insiders continue to tell family stories, purposely or reluctantly divorced from context or colonial legacies, they entrench colonial structures of knowledge production, which then delimit the kinds and forms of family stories that *can* be told. For example, if we examine the framing of "honor killings" in Western countries such as the United States and Canada, the state, media, and activists extract these acts of violence from the category of gender violence and frame them as exceptional, sensationalized forms of violence that signal the backwardness and danger of Islam/the Middle East/South Asia, particularly as brought *here* from *there* through migration (Abu-Lughod 2011; Olwan 2013; Jiwani 2015). People's own words about so-called honor crimes are ignored or distorted to support preconceived ideas about non-Western women's experiences with domestic violence, *over there*.

The more that native informants supply information about acts of disinheritance, the more entrenched colonial structures of knowledge production become. And so we must examine why feminist imperialism can be appealing for non-Western women who experience oppression at the hands of their relatives. Here I return to Ayaan Hirsi Ali, and share de Leeuw and van Wichelen's (2005) anecdote about a tense discussion between Hirsi Ali and Muslim women who were living in shelters for survivors of domestic violence. The women disagreed with Hirsi Ali's assessments and seemed to think that Hirsi Ali did not understand or hear them. One woman actually left the discussion. But Kiran Grewal (2012) argues that some Muslim women *do* seem to connect with Hirsi Ali. Grewal examines Ni Putes Ni Soumises (*Neither Whores nor Submissives*), a group in France created by Muslim immigrant women experiencing gender violence, poverty, and extremism. While Grewal critiques some of the group's premises as well as collusion with the French state, she notes that their affinity for Hirsi Ali is instructive. She comments that "it is th[e] combination of postcolonial feminism's need to embrace the emblematic figure of the 'Third World woman' and the reality of many non-western women's silencing that creates the conditions for a figure like Ayaan Hirsi Ali to gain such prominence" (2012, 588). In other words, Grewal claims that the desire to create space for women to tell their own stories, on their own terms, unadulterated and without Western intervention, has inadvertently and uncritically privileged insider voices. This puts us in the position of saying: We want to hear insider voices, but only if they say what we want them to say!

While one may grapple with or disagree with Grewal's assessment of postcolonial feminist interest in authentic non-Western voices, I highlight her point that insider voices are always made to speak for and represent all other insiders, regardless of intention. Instead, what people say about their experiences should be contextualized within an analysis of how individuals think about their privileges and oppression; how they negotiate colonial structures, particularly if they internalize them; if they feel pressured to choose between focusing on racial or gender oppression; and the "benefits" they may accrue from disinheritance, such as credibility within certain Western feminist sites, or career and publishing opportunities. Grewal thus introduces the concept of *postcolonial habitus,* of internalizing otherness such that one can overlook the contradictions and dangers in imperial feminism if that is perceived to be the only space to talk about sexism seriously (2012, 587).

Grewal notes that Hirsi Ali's "suffering is undeniable and her bitterness towards the traditional familial and cultural structures that she feels trapped her quite understandable" (2012, 572). Speaking about her family is not the problem; it is Hirsi Ali's conclusion that she had to disinherit her family, "Islam," and the entire Muslim world. The ultimate result is that Hirsi Ali and others who identify with her, are only understood through the lens of the violence that Westerners assume are non-Westerners' defining experience. Their identities are thus always already part of a colonial structure wherein they do not exist outside of their stories of violence and escape/rescue. Accordingly, the lesson to draw here is to examine one's "own" stories as partial, fragmented, intertwined with power structures, and somewhat unstable. Disinheritance will not grant greater ownership of one's story nor will it resolve the trauma, yet it can be appealing when it seems like there are no other alternatives. I turn next to other possibilities.

Interventions: Retelling Family Stories

I'm sorry I never told them how you called me your wild thing,
I'm sorry I never told them about the Spanish lullabies,
sung to stave away my greatest fears
I'm sorry I never told them how I was your cocita bonita
and how I still am.

I'm sorry I see us through the lens of consciousness doubled.
Where we represent two halves
two spirits
two localities
that can never be whole.

I am sorry our relationship can be reduced to this duality—
ever in search of reconciliation.

I'm not sorry that now I understand that our relationship
will always be in flux in this way;

Where you are the border
and I am the land

Or I am the land
and you are the border.

Constantly shifting
ever in motion
without respite.

Esperanza's poem ends with a mix of sorrow and hope. Since I started this essay with a brief contemplation about my students, I want to propose interventions to address their acts of disinheritance. While the following four writers are not the only South Asian feminist voices discussing family violence, I find that they offer distinct and clear lessons that speak directly to the *pressure* to disinherit.

First, Uma Narayan's (1997) *Dislocating Cultures* unpacks the concept of *death by culture*, or the narrative that women "elsewhere" die due to their "bad," murderous families and cultures. But Narayan's deft critique of this narrative is not the only reason to read this book. As I point out to my students, nestled in her introduction is a brief but crucial section:

> Telling the story of a person whose life is intertwined with one's own, in terms different from her own, is often a morally delicate project, requiring accommodation and tact and an ability to leave room for her account even as one claims room for one's own. Re-telling the story of a mother-culture in feminist terms . . . is a *political* enterprise. (Narayan 1997, 9)

Narayan points out that the process of connecting one's own experiences of family misogyny to others' similar experiences, is integral to "the history of women's movements" (1997, 11).

Narayan details how she confronts the politics of her family home, grappling with the contradictions of gender expectations, and of how her female relatives both endorse and resist misogyny. She notes that she was prompted to turn to Indian feminist work on gender violence not due to "westernization" or Western feminist influence but rather because Indian feminism helped her make sense of her mother's pain, of the "call to rebellion [rooted] in the mother-tongue" (Narayan 1997, 7). Thus, she notes that non-Western feminist critiques of their communities are very similar to the complex relationships between mothers and feminist daughters; in both cases, feminists navigate the mix of love, connection, fear, and anger felt toward their mother-cultures and mothers (10). Accordingly, Indian feminist responses to gender violence do exist, and "make sense" of family misogyny by formulating strategies and policies that will work best in the institutional, political, and legal contexts in India (95).

Narayan also contemplates the "political relationship" between Western and non-Western feminisms, drawing a parallel to the fraught encounters between hegemonic white feminism and women of color feminisms in the United States. She notes that the simplistic approach by hegemonic, Western feminisms toward "different" women precludes analysis of the rich diversity of perspectives held in various communities about patriarchy and prevents collaborative assessment of interlocking, border-crossing systems of oppression (1997, 152–53). She concludes that there is no need to disinherit or to distance oneself from one's community in one's feminist journey. Rather, we can ask why Western feminisms cannot hold the contradictory experience of claiming and critiquing family and community; we can explore how feminists who experience family violence can provide both solace and strategies in context-specific ways.

Second, and as part of the task of integrating family stories into feminist activism, we can rewrite acts of disinheritance as acts of feminist resistance and disobedience. Sara Ahmed notes that talking about her physically abusive father is "a feminist of color kind of complication" (2017, 72). However, as Ahmed writes, "We must tell these stories of violence because of how quickly that violence is concealed and reproduced. We must always tell them with care. . . . But it is risky: when they are taken out of hands, they can become another form of beating" (72). Ahmed links her father's verbal insults about her "will" with institutional structures (schools, moral standards, medical practices of "diagnosing" unhappy women, marriage, etc.) that seek to eliminate willfulness, which she defines as "not being willing to be owned" (74). Accordingly, she contextualizes her father's violence as part of larger oppressive systems of subordinating women, particularly women of color, whether through "enslavement . . . colonization . . . empire" (80), and connects how she yells back at her father's abuse to histories of feminist disobedience.

I will add here that Ahmed conceptualizes willfulness not as rebellious escape from a violent father; rather, it is a desire to protest violence in all forms and to be less willing to acquiesce to oppressive structures. And we are able to understand the importance of feminist activism *through* rather than *despite* her experiences with her father. This is not to valorize violence as the necessary sacrifice to become a feminist! Rather, it is to connect one's resistance to violence with multiple forms of feminist disobedience, a stance that seeks to dismantle rather than reinforce colonial structures of knowledge production.

Third, in order to study how family stories intersect with other stories about oppression, we should ask how state and global violence make possible family violence. Shahnaz Khan (2005; 2006) analyzes Pakistan's Zina Ordinance (enacted in 1979), which criminalizes illicit sex and allows family members to charge women with zina for adultery, prostitution, and being raped. Khan asks what makes family oppression possible, how and why the state is complicit with this violence, and how larger global processes shape this complicity. Khan traces how President General Zia-ul-Haq (1977–1988) saw the Zina Ordinance and Islamicization as answers to Pakistan's post-Partition problems, linking "the removal of impure and undesirable elements from society" to nation building (2005, 2019). Zia's crackdown on "impure" Pakistanis was bolstered by the financial and military assistance from the United States in the context of the Cold War.

In practice, there is a low conviction rate for women charged with zina—about 95 percent of women are acquitted (Khan 2006, 5)—but thousands of women who cannot afford lawyers are incarcerated until their trials. Women thus "suffer the effects of poverty, violence, and increased vulnerability to state and familial control over their sexuality" (Khan 2005, 2031–32). Khan argues that family patriarchy, even when blamed by women as the key culprit for their suffering, should be understood in the context of neocolonial militarization and neoliberalization of Pakistan, which increase poverty, illiteracy, and religious extremism, and thus enable and encourage the violation of women's rights (2005, 2032). Thus, we learn that family oppression does not operate apart from larger *political* processes, so even acts of disinheritance will fail to disrupt the political structures that enable and reward family oppression.

Fourth, we might retell family stories with an empathetic understanding of the pressures of oppressive systems. Shailja Patel's (2010) *Migritude* details her parents' experiences living in Kenya during Idi Amin's terrifying reign in Uganda, enduring a four-hour interrogation at a U.S. airport, and attempting to provide for their children despite their poverty. She reminds readers that migration, postcolonial conflicts, and class struggles comprise forms of gendered and racialized violence, and are worth discussing as part of one's feminist and family journeys. While she discusses sexism and expected gender roles within her family, she focuses her feminist rage on British soldiers' sexual assaults against Kenyans between 1965 and 2001.

Patel retells her family story by framing family patriarchy as a response to oppression. Using her mother's voice, she writes:

> I never wanted daughters. Women are never safe. My daughters make me so angry! They keep seeking out danger. After everything we've done for their security, they reject us. They choose the hardest, worst, most dangerous things. (Patel 2010, 23–24)

But Patel analyzes her mother's difficult words not simply as internalized misogyny but rather as fear of structural violence against women, and *particularly* during forced or unwanted migration. She notes that she accepts her mother's alleged desire for sons because "a mother's love in a time of danger can look and feel like rage, like rejection" (Patel 2010, 82). The reader may stop to consider that what feels like a family's rejection is what can prompt the politics of disinheritance, a reaction to the feeling of *being* disinherited or disavowed. I recall more of Esperanza's words:

> I'm sorry I resented your servitude to my brother and father
> I'm sorry I didn't tell you it just hurt to be treated differently.

So, with her recognition, Patel acknowledges how her mother both legitimizes and subverts gender norms. She further explains that she grew up thinking of the mangal sutra, a Hindu wedding necklace, as "a symbol of bondage" (2010, 92), but when her mother gave her one, she felt that her mother was validating her decision to not get married, to choose a path of her own. And yet, that path is intertwined with her mother's experiences and memories of colonialism, migration, and financial struggles.

Family patriarchy is dynamic, not static and timeless. Thus, I call for examining the interrelationship between the various sites of patriarchy, the family being just one of them. In so doing, family patriarchy, misogyny, and violence may be retold as part of feminist activism; as key to feminist disobedience; as indicators of how global power operates; and/or as flawed responses to oppression and discrimination.

Conclusion

At stake in addressing the politics of disinheritance is the potential of critical transnational feminist praxis, which Nagar and Swarr (2010) understand as creating space for collaborative self-reflexive dialogues, writing, and advocacy that challenge and remake *all* hierarchical relationships. If we are dedicated to challenging lopsided encounters and asymmetrical power relations, we should explore the fraught experience of naming misogyny and other types of oppression. Because acts of disinheritance play a role in colonial knowledge production, the way we tell our family stories can entrench or challenge hierarchies between Western and non-Western places.

I disrupted my own acts of disinheritance when I started to acknowledge how the effects of colonialism manifested as patriarchal oppression in my grandparents' generation and led to intergenerational abuse, colorism, and misogyny. And I concomitantly began to examine the feminist resistance of women and men in my family against these legacies. But I need to situate this retelling within transnational feminist praxis, which is and must be "inherently unstable" (Nagar and Swarr 2010, 9), always reassessing intersecting power structures.

So the first place to start is to imagine that retelling our family stories may disrupt disinheritance but might still reproduce violent power differences. For example, my family is Hindu Brahmin, so anything I say is through the lens of Hindu Brahminical casteist hegemony, which ignores the different and generally more equitable gender relationships in Dalit communities in India (Jeyaraj 2003, 69–70). Simply retelling my family story may confront the reductive Western/non-Western binary but may reinforce casteism for many Indian readers.

Second, we might ask whether we retell family stories primarily in Western academia, presses, and locations. Shahnaz Khan, whose work on zina I explored above, explains that as a Pakistan-born woman living in Canada and writing about Pakistan, she "extends the idea of the 'field' so that it includes not only the site *over there* where I search for answers to research questions but also includes a second site *over here* where my research will be read" (2005, 2022–23). Khan also remains committed to Pakistani feminist activism to support survivors of violence. I add a third site, *over there*, where the people researched *read* transnational feminist work. What if we retell our family stories *to our families*, whether they are "back home," or a migrant or minority in a Western or non-Western country? I know feminist researchers often maintain connections with those they interview, but I am curious about sharing the results of research and activism with loved ones. I read my research to my grandmother when she was alive. Our ensuing conversations challenged me to consider how to imagine our families and friends as part of our transnational feminist advocacy networks.

Third, we can examine whether the politics of disinheritance are limited to "our" communities. Esperanza's experience as a Latinx queer feminist negotiating her acts of disinheritance seems different from South Asian contexts, yet inspires me to theorize disinheritance. While we can look to writers within similar sociocultural contexts for tactics to disrupt disinheritance, we need to pay attention to the politics of disinheritance in multiple contexts, so that we can question whose disinheritance we rely upon to make claims about other places, and so that we can create anti-racist feminist spaces and coalitions to which people can turn.

Finally, as I contemplate the connection between disinheritance and transnational feminism, I end with the reminder that it is not just Esperanza's relationship with her mother that is "constantly shifting"; so, too, is her relationship with Western feminisms. The types of "work" we do *both* with our families and in our transnational feminist politics entail the decentering of Western knowledge claims and the transformation of interlocking oppressive structures, whether misogyny, racism, colonialism, neoliberalism, or others. I thus contend that a commitment to critical transnational feminist praxis requires an understanding of the politics of disinheritance.

Meghana Nayak is a Professor of Political Science and Chair of the Women's and Gender Studies Department at Pace University. Her work focuses on the politics of gender violence. She authored *Who Is Worthy of Protection? Gender-Based Asylum and U.S. Immigration Politics*. She can be reached at mnayak@pace.edu.

Works Cited

Abu-Lughod, Lila. 2001. "Orientalism and Middle East Feminist Studies." *Feminist Studies* 27, no. 1: 101–13.

———. 2011. "Seductions of the 'Honor Crime.'" *differences* 22, no. 1: 17–63.

———. 2014. *Do Muslim Women Need Saving?* Cambridge, MA: Harvard University Press.

Ahmed, Sara. 2017. *Living a Feminist Life*. Durham, NC: Duke University Press.

Anzaldúa, Gloria E. 1987. *Borderlands/La Frontera: The New Mestiza*. San Francisco: Aunt Lute Books.

Bedell, Geraldine. 2008. "'I Cringed When They Compared Me to Martin Luther.'" *The Guardian*, August 2, 2008. https://www.theguardian.com/books/2008/aug/03/women.

Bracke, Sarah. 2012. "From 'Saving Women' to 'Saving Gays': Rescue Narratives and Their Dis/continuities." *European Journal of Women's Studies* 19, no. 2: 237–52.

de Leeuw, Marc, and Sonja van Wichelen. 2005. "'Please, Go Wake Up!' Submission, Hirsi Ali, and the 'War on Terror' in the Netherlands." *Feminist Media Studies* 5, no. 3: 325–40.

Delphy, Christine. 2015. *Separate and Dominate: Feminism and Racism after the War on Terror*. Translated by David Broder. London: Verso Books.

Grewal, Inderpal. 1996. *Home and Harem: Nation, Gender, Empire, and the Cultures of Travel*. Durham, NC: Duke University Press.

Grewal, Kiran. 2012. "Reclaiming the Voice of the 'Third World Woman.'" *Interventions* 14, no. 4: 569–90.

Hari, Johann. 2007. "Ayaan Hirsi Ali: My Life under a Fatwa." *The Independent*, November 27, 2007. https://www.independent.co.uk/news/people/profiles/ayaan-hirsi-ali-my-life-under-a-fatwa-760666.html.

Hussein, Shakira. 2008. "Review Essay: 'Native Informants' and the Politics of Feminist Orientalism." *International Feminist Journal of Politics* 10, no. 4: 563–80.

Jeyaraj, Joseph. 2003. "Native Informants, Ethos, and Unsituated Rhetoric: Some Rhetorical Issues in Postcolonial Discourses." *Pretexts* 12, no. 1: 65–84.

Jiwani, Yasmin. 2015. "Violating In/Visibilities: Honor Killings and Interlocking Surveillance(s)." In *Feminist Surveillance Studies*, edited by Rachel E. Dubrofsky and Shoshana Amielle Magnet, 79–92. Durham, NC: Duke University Press.

Khan, Shahnaz. 2005. "Reconfiguring the Native Informant: Positionality in the Global Age." *Signs* 30, no. 4: 2017–35.

———. 2006. *Zina, Transnational Feminism, and the Moral Regulation of Pakistani Women*. Vancouver: University of British Columbia Press.

Mani, Lata. 1998. *Contentious Traditions: The Debate on Sati in Colonial India*. Berkeley, CA: University of California Press.

Manji, Irshad. 2003. *The Trouble with Islam Today: A Muslim's Call for Reform in her Faith*. New York: St. Martin's Press.

Mohanty, Chandra. 1984. "Under Western Eyes: Feminist Scholarship and Colonial Discourses." *boundary 2* 12, no. 3: 333–58.

Nagar, Richa, and Amanda Lock Swarr. 2010. "Introduction: Theorizing Transnational Feminist Praxis." In *Critical Transnational Feminist Praxis*, edited by Amanda Lock Swarr and Richa Nagar, 1–20. Albany, NY: SUNY Press.

Narayan, Uma. 1997. *Dislocating Cultures: Identities, Traditions, and Third World Feminism*. New York: Routledge.

Nayak, Meghana. 2015. *Who Is Worthy of Protection? Gender-Based Asylum and US Immigration Politics*. Oxford: Oxford University Press.

Olwan, Dana M. 2013. "Gendered Violence, Cultural Otherness, and Honour Crimes in Canadian National Logics." *Canadian Journal of Sociology* 38, no. 4: 533–55.

Patel, Shailja. 2010. *Migritude*. New York: Kaya Press.

Razack, Sherene. 2001. "Racialized Immigrant Women as Native Informants in the Academy." In *Seen But Not Heard: Aboriginal Women and Women of Color in the Academy*, edited by Rashmi Luther, Elizabeth Whitmore, and Bernice Moreau, 51–60. Ottawa: Canadian Research Institute for the Advancement of Women.

Sobrado-Torrico, Esperanza. 2012. "I'm Sorry I Said You Are Not a Feminist: A Letter to My Mother." Unpublished manuscript reproduced with permission of author, last modified January 15, 2019. Microsoft Word file.

Spivak, Gayatri Chakravorty. 2005. "Scattered Speculations on the Subaltern and the Popular." *Postcolonial Studies* 8, no. 4: 475–86.

Towns, Ann E. 2010. *Women and States: Norms and Hierarchies in International Society.* Cambridge: Cambridge University Press.

More Than and Not Quite: Exploring the Concept of the Human

Neda Atanasoski and Kalindi Vora's *Surrogate Humanity: Race, Robots, and the Politics of Technological Futures*, Durham, NC: Duke University Press, 2018
Megan H. Glick's *Infrahumanisms: Science, Culture, and the Making of Modern Non/Personhood*, Durham, NC: Duke University Press, 2018

Rebecah Pulsifer

For several decades, scholars in fields such as feminist science and technology studies, new materialism, and posthumanism have called into question several assumptions about the concept of *the human*. To what extent can humans be understood as rational and autonomous beings given the contingency of our understanding, and given that both interdependence and exploitation are integral to human experience and history? To what extent can humans be understood as bounded, agential subjects when our perceptions and reactions are shaped by ostensibly nonhuman forces, such as our microbiomes, our environments, and the objects with which we interact? How can we—and should we—disentangle the human from the conceptual divisions we have inherited, such as those between non-human animals, nature, and technology? And yet, if we do not distinguish the human from other conceptual categories, how do we name human responsibility in the Anthropocene?

To this rich area of inquiry, two new titles from Duke University Press add helpful terminology and provocative frameworks of analysis. In *Surrogate Humanity: Race, Robots, and the Politics of Technological Futures*, Neda Atanasoski and Kalindi Vora argue that contemporary discourse concerning technologies of automation and artificial intelligence (AI) draws from a key dynamic of liberalism: the surrogate relation between racialized others and subjects imagined to be paradoxically sovereign and vulnerable, self-determining and innocent of their actions' effects. *Technoliberalism*, the authors' term for our contemporary milieu, describes "the political alibi of present-day racial capitalism that posits humanity as an aspirational figuration in a relation to technological transformation, obscuring

WSQ: Women's Studies Quarterly 48: 1 & 2 (Spring/Summer 2020) © 2020 by Rebecah Pulsifer.

the uneven racial and gendered relations of labor, power, and social relations that underlie the contemporary conditions of capitalist production"
(4). Megan H. Glick's *Infrahumanisms: Science, Culture, and the Making of
Modern Non/Personhood* shows how beliefs about species categories, species relations, and species hierarchies form the ground from which ideas
about biological essentialism, humane behavior, and dehumanization
often grow. Glick argues that the *infrahuman*—that which is "'almost' or
'near' human"—is a malleable contrast category for "the management of
the human/nonhuman boundary" and, consequently, for "the justification of biological essentialism and the naturalization of social hierarchy"
(3, 10–11). Both books confirm that the human is a contingent concept: a
category whose definitions and meanings owe their inheritance to cultural
values regarding race, gender, nation, labor, and power. Moreover, both
books illustrate how efforts to distinguish the human and the nonhuman
often disguise or rationalize the positions of oppressed and exploited subjects whose humanity has rarely been recognized.

Surrogate Humanity presents six chapters that illustrate how contemporary "engineering imaginaries" often rely on all-too-familiar Enlightenment paradigms of invisible labor, "universal" rights available only to
some, and racialized hierarchies in which humanness is a quality to be
demonstrated or achieved (13). Drawing from Saidiya Hartman in their
theoretical framing, the authors argue that while we are often told that we
are in the midst of one or more technological revolutions, contemporary
technologies are the heirs of long-standing structures of liberal humanism
by reproducing the surrogate relation between slave and master, helpmeet
and complex subject. The authors also spotlight how contemporary discourses concerning automation, in particular, alternately promise liberation and threaten debasement while eliding the roles of racialized and
colonial subjects in producing the technologies and materials on which
automation relies.

Surrogate Humanity's first chapter focuses on the mid-twentieth century, tracing how robots held appeal under the ideologies of both liberalism for their promise of docile, deracinated workers. Chapters 2 and 3
show how contemporary labor arrangements such as the "sharing economy" and Amazon Mechanical Turk accelerate the inequalities of racial
capitalism while diminishing the material presence of workers. Chapter 4
clarifies one of the book's core arguments—that the concept of the human
relies on the surrogate relation—through a focus on "sociable emotional

robots" (25). Analyzing the functionalities of such robots in mirroring and displaying human emotions alongside Charles Darwin's assumptions about the emotional simplicity and exact correspondence of interiority and emotional display in nonwhite subjects, the authors observe that "humanity, as an essence, is always surrogate, not an essential quality of interiority" (131). In other words, the authors point out that in both liberal and technoliberal frameworks, humanity is never universal, but rather in need of constant verification. Chapters 5 and 6 focus on discourses concerning automation in contemporary warfare, discussing the paradoxes of "unmanned" drones that in fact act in response to human decisions and the anxieties around "killer robots," which they argue validate killings by humans as justified and ethical.

The book closes with a tantalizing yet all-too-brief exploration of AI-enhanced sex dolls as an instantiation of the surrogate relation. The authors argue that such sex dolls are designed to not only simulate humanness, but also to simulate consent, recapitulating the liberal formation of "a desiring subject that knows its own freedom only through the complete domination of the object of its pleasure, even when, and perhaps especially when, that body can simulate pleasure or reciprocity" (194). The authors' truncated analysis and intriguing claim that "there need not be such a thing as a feminist intelligence"—where intelligence is "one of the pillars of conscious autonomy, and as such can only be proven by self-possession" (196)—may be of particular interest to readers of *WSQ*, though the authors leave unexplored how liberal understandings of intelligence have changed and, perhaps, narrowed in a technoliberal age.

Whereas *Surrogate Humanity* focuses on the increasingly porous boundary between human and machine, *Infrahumanisms* takes up the historical instability of speciation to explore how the concept of the human is worked out in relation to other forms of life. The book is organized into three chronological sections: Bioexpansionism (1900s–1930s), Extraterrestriality (1940s–1970s), and Interiority (1980s–2010s). The first section focuses on the heritage of contemporary ideas about the concept of the human through the lens of the child and the primate, two subjects that appeared to bear liminal relation to humanness in the early twentieth century. Glick shows that while children were taken to be wild and animalistic, chimpanzees—though not gorillas, their darker-skinned, and consequently racialized, brethren—were presented as humanlike. The second section contains an intriguing exploration of the rich connections between extraterrestrial sightings and World War II photography. Glick argues that the "new visual reality" of Holocaust and atomic photography—like the proliferating accounts of gaunt, gray, humanoid aliens after WWII—were both "concerned about the boundaries of human embodiment, and both question the futurity of humanity" (87). The other chapter in this section explores how nascent posthuman discourse took hold in debates around fetuses and space travel. The third section contains chapters that argue discourse concerning HIV/AIDS emerged from the desire to mark and segregate racialized bodies and that connect porcine metaphors in discourse on obesity to anxieties about the decline of the white body. The book's epilogue walks through some observations about the microbiome that will be familiar to readers already acquainted with the work of Myra J. Hird and Elizabeth Grosz. In each strand of the book's argument, the presence of infrahuman bodies both clarifies and obfuscates the human subject.

Glick's methods and style in *Infrahumanisms* are bold and refreshing. The chapters unfold associatively, and the media through which Glick validates arguments are often unexpected yet convincing. The author does not shy away from speculation as a mode of argument, such as when she wonders in relation to HIV/AIDS, "Perhaps the ultimate form of dehumanization is complete silence, or the failure to recognize neither the human, nor the dehumanized self" (158). For these reasons, as well as the robust framework Glick builds for the term *infrahumanisms*, readers will find this book to be generous, opening up lines of inquiry that may be taken up elsewhere. The rubric that Glick lays out will be particularly generative for considerations of the monstrous and the disabled body as sites of infrahumanisms—instantiations that Glick mentions but does not explore in detail.

Surrogate Humanity and *Infrahumanisms* confirm that we have inherited a concept of the human that is both provisional and political: definitions of the human are often internally incoherent, and the implications of these definitions are powerful for subjects perceived to be on the borders of humanness. Together, these books suggest that historical assessments of the construction of the human through the exclusion of its perceived opposites can tell us much about the shifting ground upon which the concept of the human rests in our contemporary age.

Rebecah Pulsifer is a field services coordinator with the Ohio Federation of Teachers, and can be reached at rebecah.pulsifer@gmail.com.

PART VI. **STORIES OF INHERITANCE**

Knock

Kathryn Kulpa

Knock

I think of him in black and white. In a postwar world still clearing away its rubble, not quite ready to step into glorious Technicolor. I think of him knockingly, if knockingly is the word I want. If it's a word at all. He is the one who knocks. There's a black leather briefcase in the back seat of his car. There's a white possum foot hanging from the rearview mirror. For luck? It wasn't lucky for that possum. His sharp, questing chin. His foot in your door. All he needs is a moment of your time. All he needs is a chance.

Jerk

Here's one thing I know: when you were sixteen, you worked at a drugstore soda fountain. Back when drugstores had soda fountains. Pop Tate. And Archie, Betty, and Veronica sipping ice cream sodas through candy-striped paper straws. You were a soda jerk. Isn't that what they called them then? Was there a female version? A jerkette?

Chocolate, vanilla, strawberry. You learned to read the flavors in customers' eyes, knew which antsy, love-starved teenagers would choose chocolate, which resigned, tired-eyed mothers would settle for vanilla, which cheek-pinching old men would ask for strawberry, extra syrup, *Make it sweet like you!*

And then he threw you by asking for pistachio. There wasn't even a syrup for it, but you made it for him just the same, watched the chartreuse ice cream curling up against the frosty metal scoop.

I once had shoes that color, you said.

I have—right this very now—a car that color, he said.

WSQ: Women's Studies Quarterly 48: 1 & 2 (Spring/Summer 2020) © 2020 by Kathryn Kulpa. All rights reserved.

You imagined that car, parked outside, startling the sensible black Fords and tan Studebakers of Tiogue Avenue with its pale-green glamour, like a visiting luna moth. But he didn't offer, yet, to take you for a ride. He knew the power of the pause.

Hat Trick

It was a time when men wore hats. He wore one too. Pick the hat out of a hat. Stetson, homburg, panama, porkpie. A sharp hat for a sharp dresser. A flat sateen ribbon around the brim; a small, bent feather. On the inside of the sweat-stained lining, a two-inch business card tucked into a slit. LIKE HELL IT'S YOURS! PUT IT BACK! THIS HAT BELONGS TO _____.

He'd never filled it in. Not a man who feared hat thieves. Or maybe he'd stolen it himself, from some other man feckless enough to leave his hat unlabeled.

Maybe he'd stolen more than a hat. But you wouldn't have known that then.

Buckle

At the wedding you didn't wear white because it was a second wedding— not yours, but his. At the county courthouse in Laconia, New Hampshire. You wore a chartreuse shantung suit and shoes dyed to match, silk char-treuse shoes with patent leather buckles. You would have forgiven him a lot when he bought you those shoes. They were going places, those shoes. They were the kind of shoes that could only walk in one direction, up.

One, two, buckle my shoe. You used to jump rope to that rhyme. Not so long before. *Age of bride: seventeen.*

His shoes didn't have buckles, but his belt did. The belt was snakeskin leather and the buckle solid brass, rounded just enough that when it left a mark on your skin it looked almost like a smile.

Manicure

You didn't ask about the sales trips to Canada or the business calls made out of a series of phone booths or the identical black briefcases stacked in the linen closet. Those weren't things you needed to know about. He bought you a white fox fur. He bought you a dishwasher. No dishpan hands for my girl, he said. He enclosed your hands in his, planted a kiss on your pretty palm. In later years your hands would be sharp and knobby, every bone its own defined ridge, but at this point they were still soft as a child's hands. Your lifeline—long, curving almost into the wrist. Your knuckles, dimpled. Your nails always done, macaron shades, rosé and peony and coraline. You'd never even know those bones were there, beneath that smooth skin. He never hurt you anywhere that showed.

Gingko

You lived in a house with three stone steps up to the front door, always swept clean, and outside your bedroom window a gingko tree with fan-shaped leaves you loved, leaves like the print on your favorite dress, even though he said those trees made a mess of the lawn when they dropped their acrid fruit.

The fruit smelled like sick. You smelled it every morning, drifting in through the windowpanes, flooding your mouth with saliva. You'd pray it wouldn't happen again, not this morning, and then you'd run to the bathroom. Afterward you'd gargle, splash cool water on your cheeks. A touch of lipstick. Dab and blot. Check the mirror. Check the toilet. White porcelain and pink tile. Leave no trace. Everything was perfect.

Nothing stays perfect forever.

Sucker Punch

On party nights, you kept the chips and dip coming, freshened drinks, set down new ones, always with a new cocktail napkin underneath so the playing cards wouldn't pick up moisture. When the poker games were going, the men paid you no more mind than a waitress refilling their coffee cups, but they were always polite as they left: Sweet kid! You got yourself a peach there, Charlie.

That night you were cleaning up when the punch came without warning. You braced yourself against the table, retching, and he didn't stop. Something about bending over when you set the drinks down. Something about a neckline so low you were practically flashing nipple. You remembered almost nothing of what he said. Your mind was deep inside, past layers of skin and fat and muscle, curling into a caterpillar ball to protect what was inside. The one thing he gave you that you still wanted to keep.

Briefcase

Maybe he paused to rest his knuckles. Maybe he stopped to take a drink. You made it to the bathroom, locked the door. You heard him pounding with his fists, then something broader, heavier. A shoulder? Was this a neighborhood where neighbors call the police to report a disturbance, or the kind where they turn the TV up a notch louder, tell themselves nothing bad could happen amid these green lawns? Tell themselves: It's a private matter. A man's home is his castle. He might be Bluebeard, but no one's riding to your rescue.

You opened the linen closet, tried to fold yourself inside. At last you found out what was inside those briefcases. It was almost too heavy for you to lift with your shaking hands, but you did. You let your hands show you the things they learned without you knowing. When the door splintered, you had the hammer cocked. When the door slammed open, you had him dead in your sights.

I asked you once why you had no pictures of my grandfather. Why I'd only ever seen that one wedding picture, why it was at my aunt's house and not yours.

I'm the only grandparent you have, you told me. I'm all you get. I'm enough.

Kathryn Kulpa is a graduate of Mills College, Brown University, and the University of Rhode Island. She was a visiting writer at Wheaton College, taught at the Stonecoast Writers' Conference and Writefest at Rice University in Houston, Texas, and leads writing workshops in Rhode Island and Massachusetts. She is the author of the flash fiction chapbook *Girls on Film* and the short story collection *Pleasant Drugs*. Her work can be found in *Evansville Review*, *Smokelong Quarterly*, and *Superstition Review*. She can be reached at katekulpa@gmail.com.

Things

brenda Lin

My mother talks to me in fruits and vegetables.

On Tuesdays, the first day of the week traditional wet markets are open in Taiwan, red-and-white striped plastic bags will appear in my house, couriered across town by my mother's faithful driver/gofer/handyman. The bags will be filled with all of my children's favorite foods.

Because my husband is from San Diego, and because he is not Taiwanese, it constantly surprises and delights my mother when my children like foods that are very Taiwanese. The foods that she sends over include passion fruits with deep-hued purple skin, sent with handwritten notes reminding me to wait until the skin is puckered before consuming; small, soft guavas with an aroma so sweet and powerful, they perfume the entire house. Once, my mother observed the children clamoring for calamari rings at a family dinner, and ever since, if she finds freshly caught squid at the market, a bag of three or four will also appear, slick and glistening. If you hit it just so, the layer just underneath the translucent skin explodes into what looks like a million tiny stars. That's how you know the squid is still alive. Cucumbers are a staple, as are sweet potatoes and whatever leafy-green vegetables are in season—there is one called "*A* vegetable" in Taiwanese, which the children find hilarious, and will always ask instead for "*B* vegetable."

On the days she doesn't go to the market, boxes of fancy-grade fruit will arrive—giant green grapes the size of plums shipped from Japan or a species of wax apples dubbed "Black King Kong," because its skin is a deep red, richer and darker than the rosy skin of its more plebeian cousins. If not boxes of fruit or intricately packaged Taiwanese tea or nougats or the latest

WSQ: Women's Studies Quarterly **48: 1 & 2 (Spring/Summer 2020)** © 2020 by brenda Lin. All rights reserved.

award-winning pineapple or moon cakes, there will be takeout containers of various sizes and half-drunk bottles of wine. Judging by the contents of those boxes, or the name of the hotel restaurant printed on the paper bags in which they were carried, I can often guess which friends my parents dined with the previous evening.

When I first started living on my own in New York City after college, I loved having an almost-empty refrigerator, stocked with only the essentials I needed for the next few days. A visiting friend once opened up my cupboards one after another and grimaced: "You have no snacks!" I like having just what I need. This was before I knew about Marie Kondo or minimalism; for me, it just felt natural and made sense.

I have never liked complication or too much hassle. In fact, when too many things start piling up, my insides start squeezing tight and I feel a physical constriction. In Chinese, *hassle* is *ma fan*—a combination of the characters for numbness and irritation. That encapsulates how I physically feel when there are too many things around me. I've never named this feeling as anxiety, but I do think it's a form of it.

Lately, the things arriving daily at my house have become much more than just fruits and vegetables.

My mother has been retired for twenty years now. The first several years of her retirement, she traveled to remote parts of China and Southeast Asia to add to her collection of children's textiles made by indigenous tribes. She published books on her collection, organized by category—a book on children's hats, a book on baby carriers, a book on purses, another book on baby bibs and collars. She learned about the process of cultivating cotton plants and silk from silkworms, studied the ways dyes were extracted from plants and flowers, observed the different embroidery techniques used in different tribes, translated their signs and symbols into stories. She gathered her collection and organized exhibitions with local museums in Taiwan. She did what I imagine I would do in retirement—all the things she always wanted to do but which the daily minutiae in the life of a working mother prevented. After the books and exhibitions, she wanted to go on a monthslong homestay program in rural Japan to study the language, but in the end, she said my father wouldn't "let" her go. Maybe that's not entirely fair—she did admit to me that she didn't feel comfortable leaving my father, who has diabetes and a heart condition, for such a long stretch of time. So instead, she has been devoting her time to organizing her things, of which there are plenty.

Along with the bags of food that appear at my house now, there are also paintings and lithographs she has procured over the years of travel she'd had to do for work. There are also ceramics from Hong Kong and southwestern China, lacquerware from Japan to hold candies and nuts over the Lunar New Year holidays, multiple tea sets in blue and white, or dipped in cool celadon glaze. There is a box of twelve stone figurines of the Chinese zodiac, a replica of something from one of the dynasties. By other standards, these could be construed as tchotchkes. But my mother has impeccable taste.

I feel guilty when I complain to my husband that all of these things showing up at our house make my insides gnash together into a knot. So many more of our peers with aging parents have the opposite and unenviable burden of sifting through their parents' things for them. In the end, these are all just things, aren't they?

When the terracotta soldiers were discovered—an army of eight thousand life-size clay soldiers buried with Emperor Qin Shi Huang to protect him in the afterlife—it made me so sad. To think of all the work that went into creating each and every one of these figures, each one with a different face, different armor and accessories to denote rank. There are even chariots and horse cavalries. An entire village created with the sole purpose of being buried alongside the emperor so that he could be protected in the afterlife. Or is it so he wouldn't be lonesome? In my eyes, the foolishness and largeness of this gesture only magnify this sense of loneliness.

I take after my father in my dislike for buying things, and I remember growing up, hearing his annoyance over all the space my mother needed for all of her dong xi. *Things* in Chinese is *dong xi*—which translates literally to *east west*, hinting at the undiscerning vastness of a collection, everything under the sun. I think I was less privy to the amount and frequency that my mother bought than my father was. Plus, she was very good at organizing and putting all of these things away—I never felt there was visual clutter in our apartment and I would never describe my mother as a hoarder. We lived in an apartment building; there was a basement I never visited, and that's where she must have stored all of her larger acquisitions.

There were three special drawers that I remember in her room: one was filled with gifts—boxes of perfumes and soaps and trinkets she could wrap at any moment to bring as a hostess gift; another one was hidden under the trick bottom of another drawer that, when lifted, revealed all of her jewelry; the last drawer—my favorite—was filled with the artwork and poems I produced.

I enjoyed sifting through this last drawer, admiring my own work. One day, I came to my mother's room to do just that and was shocked to find that the drawer had been emptied. She didn't give me a clear explanation for where my things had gone, and I accepted that she had thrown them all away, begrudging her this act of cruelty for years to come. I dug in, and indulged myself in feeling hurt, thinking about the way she collected so many things—other people's things—with such passion and scope. The way she spoke about the intricacies of design in the textiles she collected literally brought tears to her eyes. I was moved, too, by the text in these textiles, the way in which language and stories were recorded and written in thread. I understood why she considered these exalted works of art, women's work that she saw for its elevated value and place in cultural history. But I yearned for a connection to this larger web of meaning; I wanted her to show me how I could also relate and belong to this same world that her collection described. And yet, when I showed her my work, she was tight-lipped with judgment. Once, I did a pencil drawing of a tree, which I found rather realistic and soulful with the gauzelike texture of the shaded areas. I laid it in front of her as she talked on the phone with a friend. Later, I was horrified when I saw she had fixed my drawing with a ballpoint pen, cross-hatching one side of the tree trunk to make the shadow more pronounced. I was in elementary school, when I just needed my work to exist on its own, as a testament to the innocence of childhood, before I was afraid to be creative, before I began to judge myself.

Does becoming a parent make you a hypocrite? Because here I am, thirty years later, judging my own children's writing and artwork, keeping only the ones I deem worthy of filing away, of taking up precious storage space in our house, and surreptitiously throwing away the bulk of the rest when no one is looking.

How does one begin the work of categorizing what stays and what goes?

My mother often sends things to the office of the family business my parents began in 1971 and have since retired from, and which my older brother and I have now taken over. On my office desk one day, I find a laminated piece of paper. It is a poem written in Chinese, with big, boxy characters—confident in its strokes, the plastic lamination protecting the softness of the pencil marks from smudging. The poem is titled "I often wonder," and ruminates on what clouds taste like, how it might feel like to scream into the ocean and have the crashing waves answer back, and whether heaven is a quiet place. It was written in 1986, when I was ten. I had been wrong about my mother. Being a parent to children who are ages *I* remember being often gives me the nagging sensation of my mother's vindication.

After my poem, the things arriving at my house begin to take on a different shade. My mother had salvaged a jade bracelet that had broken when my grandmother on my father's side was wearing it. Taiwanese people believe that if a jade bracelet breaks, it is because it was saving your life. So my mother mended the bracelet, screwing in some pieces of silver where the hard rock had split and placing the bracelet into a simple frame.

Everything my mother sends to my house comes with a note attached, usually on scrap pieces of paper she's come upon from around her apartment, the same apartment I grew up in, in downtown Taipei. Her handwriting used to be measured, the pen making featherlight contact with the paper. Now her script is loose and harried.

One day, a shopping bag arrives filled with different colored silk scarves. They are carefully folded and rolled into infinite folds of pinks, blues, and greens, like the velvet inner petals of peonies. *Most of these are from the sixties, worn by both amas. If you don't want them, you can return them to me.* My mother always gives me the opportunity to reject what she gives me. So I say yes.

Like any family before the digital age, ours has amassed a sizable collection of photographs over the years. There is one week when little gift bags show up at my house with Ziplocs filled with photos from the seventies, eighties, and nineties, all of them featuring me somewhere on the spectrum of cute, awkward, or cringingly bad. At the same time, my older brother is also receiving the same collated bags of photos, but with him as the focus. After the photos, I receive a small, flat cardboard box, this time without any note attached. Inside is a silver bracelet, so small it looks like an accessory for a doll. The chain is connected to a flat pendant with my name engraved on it. It isn't expensive—maybe something custom-made at the local mall in San Francisco, where I was born—but it had been kept immaculately, the silver still shiny and untarnished. I begin to feel like I am receiving my life in a backward reel.

So it is only appropriate that next, I receive an invitation to my parents' wedding. The envelope is cream-colored, as is the invitation within. The stationery has a feathery, unfinished edge. The writing is unadorned, simply announcing that Christi will be married to Eric at four o'clock in the afternoon at the Water Tree Inn in Fresno, California. The year on the invitation is 1970. And yet, because there isn't a single blemish of mold on the paper (the invitation comes to me wrapped in a small plastic bag), I would have believed it if someone told me it had been printed today, almost fifty years later.

My six-year-old daughter asked me recently what I would take with me if our house caught fire. I used to consider the same question—it's a good, if morbid, exercise to do to help whittle things down to the essentials.

"I would take xiao bei bei," she offered first. Her little blanket with the satin trim that my mother-in-law had given to her when she was born. When she was still a baby, she would suck on a mouthful of the satin edge in order to fall asleep. Now, she no longer uses her blanket as a pacifier, but she will rub the slippery satin material between her thumb and forefinger until she falls asleep. There are many places where the fibers have loosened into mere threads. Her blanket is the first thing she packs when we go away on trips. Really, it's less about the blanket than it is about the comfort it provides. I know if we forget to pack it one day, she'll eventually learn to sleep without it.

When I used to ask myself what I would bring, the answer was always my journals. Of course, now that I've been writing consistently for over thirty years and I have a trunk filled with leather-bound notebooks, it would be incredibly impractical to lug this trunk while a roaring fire chased after me. But hypothetical fire notwithstanding, what *is* my plan for these journals?

My mother wants to burn hers. She tells me this over lunch. I ask if I can read them before she destroys them. She doesn't hesitate before saying no. Would I allow anyone to read mine? This reminds me of the baby carriers in my mother's collection and how in some tribes, the mothers will burn the baby carriers in elaborate rituals as a way to protect the grown child's spirit. So this burning doesn't need to be seen as a severing or destruction of history, but rather, an embalming, a passing on. The recordings that my mother is specifically talking about getting rid of chronicle the times when she was resentful and confused and angry. She was uncomfortable rereading them, having them exist. If she could cremate those words, they would effervesce, change form, but they would not cease to exist.

I will change my answer to the fire question. All those words in my journals, the handwriting evolving over time, the letters tumbling over one another, falling down, floating up with heat. The physics of them don't matter. I have eaten them all.

In the book my mother wrote on her collection of centuries-old Chinese purses, I discover a paragraph describing a purse popular in the southern and northern dynasties (AD 220–589) called cheng lu nang. At the time, it was common practice to gather morning dew from the leaves of cypress trees, collecting the dew drops into these purses and using the liquid to sharpen one's eyesight. There was also a purse used to collect the purest air from high mountains and deep forests to present to the court. I wish there were a purse that could collect my daughter's breath in my ear when she pulls me down to tell me a secret.

I think about my grandmother's broken jade bracelet and how my mother put it back together again. If you could capture the moment when a life is saved, distill it into a piece of art, wouldn't you?

I still feel that numbness and irritation when things arrive at my house, but I've stopped resisting. I file and put them away. I devote drawers and corners of the house—places my children, even my husband, don't know exist, don't know to look—to these things. One day, I will pass them on.

Or set them ablaze.

brenda Lin's first book, *Wealth Ribbon: Taiwan Bound, America Bound*, is a collection of interconnected personal essays on family and cultural identity. Lately, she has been writing about the intersection between text and textile. She lives in Taipei and is the head of corporate social responsibility at les enphants Co. Ltd. She also teaches a creative writing workshop at Taipei American School. She can be reached at brenda.lin@enphants.com.

I, Who Set Out to Curse You

Mary Lane Potter

The love of the body of man or woman balks account, the body itself balks account,
That of the male is perfect, and that of the female is perfect.
                    —Walt Whitman, "I Sing the Body Electric"

Shall I, with the poet, sing the body electric, charged with the soul? Shall I, who have maligned you so long—this *woman's* body, *my* woman-body, my fraught inheritance—now gather up your treasures, your beauty in a song of praise, cataloging your wonders? Shall I, like that lackey prophet-for-hire Balaam, intent on cursing you, find my journey halted by a talking ass, my way barred by a flinty angel? Stymied and stuck unless I throw off the king's command to curse you and promise to bless you? Abundantly, and for all the world to hear?

For I have faithfully obeyed the king's command to dishonor and destroy you, that I might gain his favor and profit from his rewards.

When I was a girl, I raged against you, girl-body that demanded dresses, pinks and pastels, ribbons and ruffles, a quieted voice, a stilled body, softened footsteps, hands folding diapers, tending babies, pouring tea, leashing my powers, hiding my light. You were the prison house of my soul, from which I worked daily to escape—climbing trees, hunting wild grapes, following boys to wherever adventure awaited, running free until I was lost. But I could never escape you, and I cursed you, my jailer.

In the intellectual flowering of my youth, you were the millstone around my neck, dragging me down to drown in the deadening gaze of men,

WSQ: Women's Studies Quarterly 48: 1 & 2 (Spring/Summer 2020) © 2020 by Mary Lane Potter.

continually erasing me with the compliance and fears of women. How I hated you, beautiful as I knew you were, for blinding others to me, to my mind. You lay in wait for me at every turn. You were Satan itself, the Hinderer, and I cursed you, my enemy.

In the middle of my journey, you became my vehicle, the horse my ego could ride, the sturdy, wind-filled ship that carried me across the seas of the temporal realm to the shore of my true home, mind. You were my slave, chained to my will, whipped to do my bidding. I cared nothing for you. I despised you. I cursed you in my heart and with my lips.

And now, here I am, no longer young—and no longer foolish, I believed. Yet here you are, my beast of burden, my very own ass, refusing to carry me any farther on this path, speaking to me in the voice of a poet, asking, *Have you seen . . . the fool who corrupted her own live body?* Here you are, my sweet, stubborn angel, blocking my path until I answer the poet's question: *Have you ever loved the body of a woman?* and your own: *Have you ever loved your woman-body?* Here you are, my woman-body, the one who never abandoned me, a presence so constant you lived with me unseen until this moment you face me on the path. Here you stand, refusing to let me go on until I see you, in all your splendor, until I promise to leave off cursing you, until I praise you as my faithful friend and true companion, until I declare *the woman's body is sacred.*

What shall I sing then? Shall I sing with poets of your glories that can be seen and smelled and touched? Breasts, hips, embracing flesh, warming skin, lips, blood, bleeding, your openings and closings, your birthings and dyings, your irrepressible strength, your world-creating, world-shattering voice? Your glories abound, and I bless you.

Shall I sing with scientists of your glories unseen? The soul born of the body? Without you there is no beauty. Without you, no images, no memory. Without you, no desire, no emotion, no feeling. Without you, no thought, no communication, no meaning. Without you, no justice. No mercy. No compassion. No love. No joy. Without you, death. You are my life, and I bless you.

Shall I sing the body whole? The body giving, the body humble, the body disappearing, the body that brings us alive and keeps us alive and enables us to be this very moment, the body of a woman, the body sacred? I am yours, as you are mine, and I bless you.

Just in time have you stopped me on my path. Just in time have I come to recognize you. Just in time have I turned from cursing to blessing you. For one day you will cease and this tongue will be silenced forever. Until then, I sing of you, my woman-body.

Mary Lane Potter is the author of the novel *A Woman of Salt*, and books and essays on feminism, liberation theologies, and spirituality. All her work—from academic studies to fiction to creative nonfiction—explores the body-mind-spirit tangle, especially as it relates to gender and sexuality. She can be reached at potter.lane.m@gmail.com.

The Proper Name

Valerie Rohy

The first question was ordinary. When I was a kid in Southern California in the 1970s, I asked my mother why I was named Valerie. My mother said that before I was born, there was a senator who had twin daughters, one of whom was named Valerie. One night one of the sisters was killed by a stranger in their house. When my mother read about the incident in the newspaper, she thought, *What a pretty name.*

I asked which of the twins was named Valerie. My mother said she couldn't remember. Though I'd later doubt that response, by then I didn't trust my memory either; it didn't seem possible that I recalled such a thing accurately. So I returned to the story in my forties in a state of uncertainty. I searched the internet using the words I remembered—*senator, twins, murder, Valerie*—and was astonished to find that everything my mother had told me was true. But because I was a little girl when my mother told the story, I had assumed that the twins were little girls. In reality, they were twenty-one, and the murdered daughter was Valerie Percy.

Valerie Percy was the daughter of a Chicago businessman, Charles Percy, who was not yet a senator, but running for national office, which he later won. After her graduation from Cornell in June 1966, Valerie returned home to the wealthy enclave of Kenilworth, Illinois, to help with her father's campaign. On the morning of September 18, someone entered the house and killed her in her bedroom. The family, including her identical twin sister, Sharon, was asleep in the house, unaware.

In September 1966 my mother was twenty-four years old; she would have read coverage of the Percy case in the *Ithaca Journal* and the *Cornell Daily Sun*, which covered the crime extensively due to Valerie Percy's Cornell connection. My mother had earned both her BA and MBA at Cornell;

WSQ: Women's Studies Quarterly 48: 1 & 2 (Spring/Summer 2020) © 2020 by Valerie Rohy. All rights reserved.

my father was finishing his PhD in physics. They'd been married for a little over two years. She was a first-generation college student from a large family that had moved around the Connecticut River valley when she was a child; he was the son of a California pharmacist. My mother must have read the Percy articles in the apartment she and my father shared in an old farmhouse on Ellis Hollow Road in Ithaca.

The Percy story ran daily for almost a week in the *Ithaca Journal*, alongside updates from Viet Nam and the NASA space program, as well as ads for Bass Weejuns, Salem menthols, hi-fi stereophonic sound, DuPont Dacron blazers, Ayn Rand books. The newspaper described Valerie Percy in diminutive terms: she was one of her father's "comely blonde twin daughters"; she was "gracious"; she "always wanted to do the right thing." On the other hand, one of her former professors said she was "exciting and stimulating to know." On the front page of the *Cornell Daily Sun* on September 19, 1966, she appears in a studio portrait, dark-eyed, demurely dressed, smiling slightly. She doesn't meet the camera's gaze—nor does she in the more candid, badly reproduced photograph in the same day's *Ithaca Journal*. The articles included graphic details: the *Ithaca Journal* said that Mrs. Percy had been "awakened by a moan." She found Valerie "dying of a crushed skull and more than a dozen stab wounds," and ran to activate the burglar alarm. By the time a doctor from the neighborhood arrived, it was too late.

Writing this feels like a cruel repetition, but it's what my mother must have read.

An investigation began immediately and soon involved the FBI. The *Ithaca Journal* offered updates on the Percy case well into 1967, revealing potential clues. Valerie's mother had caught a glimpse of the assailant, a white man, before he fled. There was no attempt at robbery. Police found bare footprints leading to a beach on Lake Michigan; a wet woolen glove; a green station wagon; a hole in the glass of a French door. Other items appeared later: a fourteen-inch bayonet found in the lake, a bloody handprint, a lone moccasin. Early news articles noted that the Percys' dog, a Labrador retriever, did not bark and speculated that the assailant must have been someone the family knew. As in the Sherlock Holmes story about "the curious incident of the dog in the night-time," silence has substance and absence has meaning. But despite these clues and the intense investigation, the case was never solved.

My research was not exactly gratifying; indeed, it raised further questions. What kind of mother names her daughter after a murder victim she doesn't even know? What kind of mother then *tells* her daughter about this gruesome naming? And having done all that, why did my mother lie about not knowing which daughter was named Valerie? It's possible that she really didn't recall which one was Valerie when I asked. But she knew when she named me. Of course it was the unlucky twin. I was the unlucky twin.

Hearing this story as a child hadn't frightened me, but as an adult, I felt there was something indecent about picking a name from the police blotter. Both the naming and the telling seemed to show a lack of empathy, a want of concern—in advance or afterward—for another person's distress, both mine and Valerie Percy's. While I was not particularly invested in social proprieties, I was pretty sure people didn't *do* this—neither the naming nor the telling.

People didn't, but my mother did. She had been the oldest of five children and had taken on both responsibility for the younger children and the impossible task of keeping peace between her warring parents. Her toughness must have come early. She was determined that our family not repeat her own upbringing, and, in fact, our house was quiet. My parents never raised their voices to each other. My brothers and I were safe; we got help with our homework. But there was always a detachment, an opacity, between my mother and me. As a child, I hid my little sorrows. As a teenager, I hated who I was supposed to be. Whoever Valerie was, she wasn't me. Did I remember that she belonged to a world where girls got killed in their beds? I only knew that Valerie was "pretty," well-mannered, and feminine, and I was not.

Still, after my research, I had to acknowledge that Valerie Percy, a person who died before I was born, was a part of me. Names matter. Jacques Lacan argues that each of us is "the slave of language," specifically the language "in which his place is already inscribed at birth, if only by virtue of his proper name." Before we enter the world, we are put in our places by our names, and with names come stories. I have carried this story with me, first as mythology, then as history, for over forty years. As long as I thought it was apocryphal or untraceable, a figment of my childish imagination, it could be cordoned off. Somehow knowing it was true seemed to give it, retroactively, a formative power.

I grew up with another story that belongs with Valerie Percy. In December 1962, when my mother was an undergraduate at Cornell, she was walking across a snowy quad when someone stabbed her in the back, knocking her down and then running away. The assailant turned out to be the troubled teenage son of a professor, who had attacked another female student a few weeks earlier. The *Cornell Daily News* reported the incident when it resumed publication after winter break. Under the headline "Ithaca Over Vacation" we read that on December 19, 1962,

> a 14-year-old boy was reported by police to have admitted stabbing a 20-year-old University coed in the back on Wait Ave. shortly after 5:30 p.m. the day before. The youth also confessed to the dusk assault of another University coed in front of Risley Hall Dec. 1.

The other woman had apparently been unharmed, but my mother, the article continued, "received a three-quarter inch deep wound inflicted by a paring knife. Her screams brought a sorority sister to her aid."

My mother told this story several times when I was a kid; she didn't seem upset by it. She had not been badly injured, and in her account, there was even an upside: after the incident, my father started walking her home from the library at night, so they got acquainted and eventually began dating. The crime became a catalyst. My mother was twenty, my father twenty-two. They were engaged by the time they visited his family in Santa Barbara a year later, Christmas 1963, and they got married the following June, right after my mother graduated.

So by chance I came into being, as my particular parents' child and as the person of my proper name, between two acts of violence against women. Though the first incident, involving my mother, was a small premonition of the other, and the second, the murder of Valerie Percy, a horrifying escalation, they are mirror images. In fact, they are a hall of mirrors. The elements double and redouble: two attacks, two female victims, two male assailants, twin sisters and sorority sisters, two Valeries. My mother and the other Cornell woman who was accosted by the professor's son are like the Percy sisters: lucky and unlucky. The elements begin to form patterns.

Virginia Woolf describes how moments of "shock" are "followed by the desire to explain"; each moment, she goes on, "is or will become a revelation of some order; it is a token of some real thing beyond appearances." For many of us, the response to shock is that desire to explain, to look for meaning in patterns, but we never know the precise contours of "the real thing." My effort to make sense of these stories leads from the speculative to the coincidental. Valerie Percy and my mother were both sorority members at Cornell at the same time; they surely crossed paths somewhere on campus at some point. Uncanny, too, is that I was conceived on almost precisely the day Valerie Percy died; my birthday, in June 1967, was forty weeks later. This can't possibly have any meaning.

I seize on patterns to fend off chance, because so much about these stories seems arbitrary. Why was Valerie the unlucky twin, and not her sister—or another family member? The *Ithaca Journal* reported that "the intruder crept up a staircase. At the top landing were three doors. He chose Valerie's—whether accidentally or by design is not known." The difference between accident and design can be elusive. Why was it my mother and not another young woman walking across the quad? Without the motives of the assailants, we can't answer these questions. In the Percy case, there is nowhere to start. We don't know whether the killer knew anyone in the family. In my mother's case, the teenager's identity has been lost. The newspaper didn't identify him; my mother only recalled that his father was a math professor. In any case, the teenager didn't know her; he seems to have chosen her at random. Everything that resists pattern, suspending cause and effect, makes both assaults seem like ghastly accidents.

At the same time, they aren't accidents at all. Violence against women is systemic, part of a clear pattern. That pattern doesn't mean it stops being uniquely traumatic for victims and their families. But we can't say the crimes are arbitrary. There is a much longer story. Violence is something our culture repeatedly does to women—*does*, by accepting it as normal. Inaction and inadequacy are not passive, but active. Yet the attacks on my mother and Valerie Percy were aberrant in one way: most violence against women is committed by men they know, not by strangers. While we attend to the horror of "random" attacks, we may turn away from crimes born of intimacy and known intent. In that sense, my mother's story and Valerie Percy's are at once typical and unusual—not unusual in the crimes, merely in the identity of the perpetrators. That said, systemic violence doesn't mean equally distributed violence. It makes the death of Valerie Percy no less appalling to acknowledge the other women whose murders never get in the newspapers.

As it happened, Chicago's CBS-affiliated television station cancelled what would have been the first TV showing of Alfred Hitchcock's 1960 film *Psycho*, scheduled for September 23, 1966, due to Valerie Percy's murder. The film, in which the fate of Marion Crane is sealed by a simple mistake—she takes the wrong road—eventually premiered in June 1967, on a New York City station. In the process, the famous shower scene was reportedly reedited, reducing it from twelve stabs to three in deference to viewers' sensibilities. But the story remained the same: a woman, Marion Crane, is killed after her random meeting with a sick individual, a "psycho," the prototype of the brutal intruder and the professor's son. Of course, *Psycho* is also a film about how a dead person can determine the fate of the living, about the persistence of the past, a perverse amplification of the parental influence that shapes all of us.

The hall of mirrors is larger than I thought. I am caught in the web of human relationships circulating through these stories, women obscurely sharing each other's trauma. The Greek word *trauma* means *wound*, although trauma is now understood as largely mental, not physical. Cathy Caruth notes that trauma can have a traveling quality—the wounded party may or may not be the traumatized party, and the voice of trauma, the cry of the witness, might originate in either place. Caruth says that "one's own trauma is tied up with the trauma of another," leading to strange encounters, other people's voices. The greatest trauma, I know, belongs to the Percy family. My mother intruded on it in naming me, and I intrude in writing about her. But our stories connect us.

Did the story of Valerie Percy's death awaken the forgotten trauma of my mother's own assault? Whose trauma are we talking about? How many people are part of it? It can't be pinned down. It's like the way people feel compelled to tell their tragedies to their friends, who tell *their* friends, in widening circles, like ripples from a pebble thrown into a pond, to ever more distant people, until finally its energy has been dissipated: it reaches someone who doesn't need to pass it on. That's a pattern, too, and I'm in it.

I get stuck on one line of the 1962 news article: "Her screams brought a sorority sister to her aid." (This is my mother's good fortune. If Valerie Percy had time to scream, she might have survived.) In a way, my mother's scream seems more terrible than her injury. A scream is inarticulate, inhuman; it's Marion Crane's scream in *Psycho*. I have never heard my mother scream; it seems impossible. Yet, as in Elizabeth Bishop's story "In the Village," the scream can't be taken back. In Bishop's story, a young girl recalls a scream that, we learn, is her mother's: "A scream, an echo of a scream, hangs over that Nova Scotian village. No one hears it; it hangs there forever." Because her mother is suffering a series of mental break-downs, the child feels that her scream never goes away; it always threatens to recur. My mother's scream is suspended in time by opposite forces: she is by no means mad, or even excitable. That's the mystery. I can't connect the coed's scream in the *Cornell Daily News* to the absolute determination of a woman who, in her seventies, stood between her house and a California wildfire with a garden hose, as the neighbors' house burned and its propane tank exploded.

And I can't understand the scream because my mother retells the story impassively, just as she told the story of my name. The only emotion she ever attaches to the incident is annoyance. Instead of seeking damages for the injury, my grandmother wrote to the assailant's father, the professor, asking to be reimbursed for the cost of the clothing that was ruined in the attack. He sent the money, but none of it ever reached my mother, only an enduring grievance. Maybe that's why she kept the coat she was wearing when she was stabbed. When I brought up the story some time ago, she said, "It's right here," and produced from the hall closet a black raincoat with a small cut in the back.

Even if you're the kind of person who keeps everything forever, wouldn't you want to get rid of such a grim reminder? And if you really needed your raincoat, wouldn't you at least mend the hole? My mother is an accomplished seamstress who made most of her high school wardrobe herself to keep pace with wealthier classmates, yet she never mended this coat. I have pictures of her wearing it during her engagement visit to my father's family the following December. Here she is, making an imperious gesture at a small dog, posing on a blue sofa with Dad's mother and grand-mother, sitting on his lap under some fiercely awful modern lamps. All in the black coat with the hole. Her attitude is consistent—why would she feel a sympathetic shudder about Valerie Percy's murder if her own assault didn't haunt her? Maybe to her it wasn't a grim reminder; maybe it didn't mean anything.

But the black raincoat means something to me. If my mother's scream, as reported in the newspaper, seems excessive, the unmended hole in the raincoat, conversely, holds the place of something missing. The wound is long healed, but something else has remained undone, something I've in-herited. The hole is an opening to another time, to the unknown, to unan-swered questions. It's the fact of a dog not barking, the unsolved murder of Valerie Percy, the oblique angle of her gaze.

Valerie Rohy is professor of English at the University of Vermont and author of *Impossible Women: Lesbian Figures and American Literature*; *Anachronism and Its Others: Sexuality, Race, Temporality*; *Lost Causes: Narrative, Etiology, and Queer Theory*; and *Chances Are: Contingency, Queer Theory and American Literature*. She can be reached at valerie.rohy@uvm.edu.

PART VII. **POETICS OF INHERITANCE**

Shared Scars

Abby Manzella

I share a scar with my father and brother.
Our abdomens marked as kin.
My father's a slicing long and wide,
a question how life was resewn.
My brother's, he says, "like bullet wounds,"
and mine just dots, bleached-out stains.

The genetic, the hereditary,
the failures of the body
passed from one to the next,
aim indiscriminate and true.
Fathers to sons, not the only path.
An inheritance evading primogeniture.
The gall of the vitriol,
a pain like fireworks of stone.
But there's progression in the science,
diminished harm with knowledge.

I learned from them,
but the doctors said they learned mnemonically.
Four *F*s they said:
female, family, forty, and fat.
No insult intended to the woman before them,
who defied the categories wielded,
except their definitions of family.

I do not know what my father (or his grandfather) felt.
I do not know when he grasped the source.
I did not yet exist.
For my brother, it took weeks,
but he, I saw,

WSQ: Women's Studies Quarterly 48: 1 & 2 (Spring/Summer 2020) © 2020 by Abby Manzella. All rights reserved.

not quite adult,
slapping the steering wheel
to cut the ache,
extracting himself from his car
with hand to roof rack,
the wracking hurt so great,
the displacement insufficient.
Still I cooled his head and called for help.
The organ must go
to deplete yellow from skin,
to drain the pain from his eyes.

We can survive with much less.

When my turn came,
I knew the smack of the heel
against my bathroom floor to quell the agony.
I knew.
My mirrored eyes were my brother's.
I thanked him for this knowledge,
if not all my ancestors for the pain.
Still my scar and quick solution
came through their suffering.
Their detriment, my benefit.

This is family.

Abby Manzella has taught and written on contemporary American literature and film, particularly as they relate to issues of race and gender, at the University of Missouri, Yeshiva University, Centre College, Tufts University, and the University of Virginia. She has been published in *Feminist Studies*, *Frontiers*, *Women's Review of Books*, *Ms.*, *BUST*, and *Literary Hub*. Her book, *Migrating Fictions: Gender, Race, and Citizenship in U.S. Internal Migrations*, was named a Choice Reviews Outstanding Academic Title. She can be reached at abbymanzella@hotmail.com.

Mitochondrial Eve 11.20

Bettina Judd

Somewhere buried in the dirt,
is a common woman, a common
mother, with a common pelvis
commonly made degenerate
her common bones fossilized,
we hope, that we may exhume,
examine our commonality
and go unquestioning how
common it is for a woman
like her to be uncovered
carried to a museum
and presented for her
peculiar.

WSQ: Women's Studies Quarterly 48: 1 & 2 (Spring/Summer 2020) © 2020 by Bettina Judd. All rights reserved.

Laura: Mitochondrial Eve

Bettina Judd

According to science, grandmothers
hold the promise of two generations:
her own child and the eggs of
her not yet grandchildren.
Which means that in the late month
of 1951, and the earliest months of 1952,
you held my mother, who held me,
if not as an idea then, as a fact

It wouldn't be the first time, mother of
mothers, you held a thought before flesh could
form it alive. You, poet laureate of my heart,
gave me words before I knew sound

Every dream for us carefully winked,
charted, and documented in notebooks,
on the backs of envelopes, a graduation,
a new job, the first of yet another generation

Every celebration, a newly minted song,
every equation of our needs penciled and
solved. Every terror pressed out by the
hallowed bend in your knees

What sliver of paper would
hold our day of ghostly hearts?
Which one of us will wave goodbye from our
earth porch as you sail away from us?

We hold to each other feeling for
our flesh inheritance, our spirit

WSQ: Women's Studies Quarterly 48: 1 & 2 (Spring/Summer 2020) © 2020 by Bettina Judd. All rights reserved.

heirlooms, and come up wanting
more than the you in ourselves

According to science, grandmothers
carry the promise of two generations
holding and then, carefully, and firstly
breathing, pushing, letting go

Bettina Judd is currently assistant professor in the Department of Gender, Women & Sexuality Studies at the University of Washington. Her poems and essays have appeared in *Torch*, *The Offing*, *Meridians: feminism, race, transnationalism*, and other journals and anthologies. Her collection of poems, *Patient.*, tackles the history of medical experimentation on and display of Black women, and won Black Lawrence Press's Hudson Book Prize in 2013. She can be reached at inquire@bettinajudd.com.

Endless Relations

Susan Facknitz

Borderline freak-show ugly,
their faces claim me
from pages of a battered album
my father handed me
claiming not to know
who they were.
His mother's people,
the dark Dutch of the upstate,
they dress like china dolls
and waistcoated men
in borrowed clothes
from the photographer's studio,
whose embossed name is splashed
across their nameless bodies.
In New Paltz or Saugerties,
their coarse faces rise above Victorian frills,
hover over tender lace.
Blunt hands grip canes and walking sticks,
pigskin gloves and Spanish fans.
On facing pages beautiful children
swing in fairyland settings,
blond and fine: preludes or postscripts?
It isn't clear whether theirs
is a parable of the promised land
read backward
or the immigrants' curse
that warps them into the pages
that come later in the valleys of New York.

WSQ: Women's Studies Quarterly 48: 1 & 2 (Spring/Summer 2020) © 2020 by Susan Facknitz.

Susan Facknitz has published in *Southword*, *Room*, *Poetry East*, and *New Orleans Review*. She leads creative writing workshops at a community college and in a homeless shelter after teaching for thirty-three years at James Madison University. She can be reached at facknisx@jmu.edu.

Reclaiming Perspective

Lauren Camp

Confession: the week after you saw him, he walked
through the city's headlights
in a suit. A stranger

returned him through pinpricks of sunrise. And again.
And again—with calls each time
to report his aimless shadow.

He could end anywhere and it's that absolute
that scared me. You want to believe I'm shame-
sewn, faulty. You want to know

why he's in there? Do you think I don't see
the other residents nod off or pace out
broken thoughts? I'm grateful now

the doors fight back. He must not amble to the pitch
of a whim. Oh he's durable, my father,
but each day he wakes with a little less

truth. Or truth that won't help him.
His window looks to a lodged plum tree.
He no longer repeats

his regrets. His small room
is grand enough to put his name on the wall
six times. He has enough space

in his day and mind for unpredictable syllables
and stock prices that roll and saddle
his screen. They gleam, painless.

Misnomers and "accidents" no longer
torment him. True, he has bones
for concrete. Sometimes his old city creeps over his face.

I can't break him of that. I had to decide
how far to unravel. For months, he piled unopened mail
on his bed, size-sorted. All September he gorged

on weeping. I wanted to wake knowing
that the dark hadn't held him
at knifepoint. Believe me—his life is a lot

to absorb. I still expect him to remember to sleep
and kiss and mete or shutter the sun
when it chunks through his windows. Let soon

not come yet to his doorway. In phone calls, he pulls out
any name that sounds about right. We laugh
at his small creases, and the losses

don't scare me like they did. Maybe I'm paying
for him to be outlined in the blousy sun
and to cup casual melodies each night.

Nothing is insignificant, but I know the room
holds all of his history. There's no doubt he's dipping below
membranes. I gather his failure

at the corners of my mouth
to use on relatives who intercede: *He's softening
to broad, precious pauses. He's safe*, I'll tell them.

Take the week he started wearing his socks
eight days in endless conservation, his toes grown
with fungus. Take the days he spoke

the immediate future as an ancient alphabet.
A time will come. His brain is dismantling,

but he isn't waiting. His identity is not where he left it.

I never want him to know
he's been wrong. He breathes through his teeth,
then takes them out. There's always crud

on the underside, and I'm so tired
and unprepared for this. How many rules and lessons
make a whole life? He can't say, but of course I know.

"U.S. Tariff & Import of Japanese Velveteen"

Lauren Camp

Throughout his apartment, each fist
of paper, his desk surrendered
to unbidden cyphers and diagonal lines.

In closets, mini motel soaps and sloping shoe trees
in a combustion of naphthalene. Moths fold
dead and thin in the bathtub. A sign

on the faucet, "pull up—
with love," which is cheerful until I recall
the architecture of his once concentrated

anger. In the bathroom, a pair
of stretched briefs hangs in stout crests.
And everywhere ample paper napkins

folded to each narrow inch
and nested in cracks and slips
of his dresser. In hollows, small trinkets, keys,

broken things without motion. A tin can
of okra. Outside the window, more than half the city
scrawls, and after that, the bridge.

But I am pulled to a complete periphery
and entire duration: names
written in steady order, intricately wrapped

in rotting rubber bands. Pulses
and swells of Arabic cursive, his ancient report cards
and reddish cylinders of nickels. I see

what others rarely locate: the marrow
of my father. And blue
umbrellas, his partial dentures in pink resin, each

with more teeth than the last. Every murmur of clutter
is answer. Of course I'll keep the thesis,
his translucent words held to surface. This is the consolation

of not being on the flat side
of his death yet. I finger the firm hand
of his signature, spilled large and dark below the title.

Resilience

Lauren Camp

There are thirty-one words in the Pledge of Allegiance,
which I started reciting in first grade with the beauteous
Miss Steinberg, whose long hair I drew on all
my construction paper. I drew her in pink dresses that went
to her toes. Last week, I learned the first twenty-four
United States presidents by teaching my seven-year-old nephew,
who recited their surnames in order while swinging a plastic
baseball bat in his kitchen. His grandmother says he'll remember
his whole life, his mind holding the rhythms, but won't he
think of Taylor Swift and her smile, not of Zachary Taylor?
And will he know Fillmore as Millard? And Buchanan
(number fifteen), whose name he said was *Im-possible*,
until I said to think of the compulsive destiny of a cannon
and, boom, he suddenly knew it (but not the leader's meager
accomplishments). Not to change the subject, but all our memories
are doomed. My father's words are already vacant. Every day
more disappear, and the bell of the phone can seem irrational
in his pocket, though he answers and simultaneously paces,
hoisting one word to his ear at a time. When he thinks
to say something, he offers his name, which swings up to me
whole, but gentle, uncertain. Exhumed from the past.

Lauren Camp is the author of five books of poems, most recently *Took House*. Her poems have appeared in the *Los Angeles Review*, *Pleiades*, *Poet Lore*, *Slice*, and other journals. Winner of the Dorset Prize, she has also received fellowships from Black Earth Institute and the Taft-Nicholson Center, and finalist citations for the Arab American Book Award, the Housatonic Book Award, and the New Mexico–Arizona Book Award. She can be reached at lauren@laurencamp.com.

WSQ: Women's Studies Quarterly **48**: 1 & 2 (Spring/Summer 2020) © 2020 by Lauren Camp. All rights reserved.

Confabulation Shovel

Regina Marie

After Rumi's "I am so small"

The third time she fisted my chest I
saw stars, reeled slightly, didn't fall. Am
I a punching bag hanging from my vows? If so,
I was shaped for this. "There is nothing small
about my forgiveness," I repeat out loud. "I
am softened by your suffering, I can
hear your history in each smack—barely
bruises." Because I'd practiced, I let her blows be,
but the *thud, thud* made me stutter. I'd seen
this before—my shame-coated tongue. How
I cradle her knuckles, how she spits. Can
I hold myself aside, separate myself from this
latest rendition of as a girl she'd endured great
secrets? She'd slammed her mouth shut for love.
Her spit spelled *heal me*. Would her stiff lips be
made supple if I tenderly took the blame? Inside
me, all her unbending nest. Cottoned me,
confused as clouds, whisked by her fists. Look
at my leather, pocked by her punches. At
what point would I break open? *It's your*
fault I hide. You're the reason I lie! she cried. My eyes
pooled, and what glimmered there—how they
filled her hands with diet pills and cock. Who were
those parents who whispered *never tell*, forced her small
mouth to swallow words and worse, even now. But
who am I, swinging in the shadow of the life they
gave her—my heart synced to her jabs. See
me spill out. My surrender an enormous
stain on the floor. See me cleave to married things.

WSQ: Women's Studies Quarterly 48: 1 & 2 (Spring/Summer 2020) © 2020 by Regina Marie. All rights reserved.

Regina Marie started writing with great urgency after a long career designing software. Her poem "Fall" was published as a finalist in the Frontier Poetry Open. Her work has also appeared in *Poet Lore*, *CALYX*, the *Briar Cliff Review*, *Permafrost*, *Puerto del Sol*, and *Crosswinds*. She received her MFA from Sarah Lawrence College, and works with Citizens Climate Lobby in Salt Lake City, Utah. She can be reached at reginamariepoet@gmail.com.

Portrait of Her Father as Meteor

Pam Crow

sometimes he is the smallest of his kind, a speck of dust

sometimes a rough stone effigy she walks around to reach the stereo

he tamps down tobacco with a small silver tool

threads a wooly caterpillar through his pipe

it emerges smeared with black tar

the night sky is polluted with light

smells of smoke and cherries

at night, a body of matter

a matter of body   a broken-

off particle

sometimes he is heading straight toward her

she is the crater he leaves behind

Pam Crow lives in Portland, Oregon, where she works as a clinical social worker. She won the Astraea Emerging Lesbian Poets prize in 1998, and published her first book of poems, *Inside This House*, in 2007. Her poems have appeared in *Southern Poetry Review*, *CALYX*, *Seattle Review*, *Ploughshares*, and others. Last year she won the Neil Shepard Prize in Poetry from *Green Mountains Review*. She can be reached at pamcrowlcsw@gmail.com.

WSQ: Women's Studies Quarterly 48: 1 & 2 (Spring/Summer 2020)

Inventory

Ann Cefola

And now, before six, the sun hitting Her things, crowding my room inside
these pink walls, stoic brass lamps with cream pleated shades, colonial
chandelier on its side, rusted flour sifter, glass baking trays, five—from
lasagna to brownies; blue bucket of household cleaners, red aerosols, and
white spray cans; kitchen stool facing down, maroon photo albums with
their black felt pages' and white-penciled inscriptions; iron next to paper
cups, spatula, and slated spoon; a Lord & Taylor's box labeled *mementos*,
stack of medical files over five years; ice bucket, wine glasses cleaned and
stacked in a brown paper bag, red sleigh of artificial holly and pine, empty
file cabinet, glass plates and matching bowls, nesting French soufflé dishes;
Her Lenox, Golden Wreath, discontinued 1980, layered and lopsided in
Her monogramed blue towels in several open baskets, as if for a picnic;
box of lightbulbs and yellow sprinkler with last name printed in magic
marker; paintings by mother-in-law, watercolors of Vermont, against a
wall; black-green marble patterned tray tables; Shakespeare's works in six
volumes atop a backgammon box, Teddy Bear with blue ribbon, and the
small sculpture, jade green, nude carrying water bowl in crook of her neck,
without identity, her one purpose in life, to hold that bowl, to be admired,
to find a place on the shelf; but she has put the bowl down now, wiped her
brow, and returns to find it empty, no reflection, no water, no arms, and
I cannot find her either in this ether, among remnants of the kingdom,
sun sparking the gold chandelier, light green through an old sailor's jug on
the wall, how life gets dismantled, and we, once children, anthropologists,
fingering recipe cards like hieroglyphics, breathing into the quiet, the
extraordinary quiet, after a reign, after it is done, court dismissed, castle
breached, handmaiden without hands.

WSQ: Women's Studies Quarterly 48: 1 & 2 (Spring/Summer 2020) © 2020 by Ann Cefola. All rights reserved.

Inheritance

Ann Cefola

Because they left the body behind, because they lived in the damp rain
of their gray-pink brain, labyrinth without exit, because they drank
what they called *nightcap, chaser, hot toddy, brew,*
ate linguini and clam sauce, tapped into ice cream late at night,
took red pills prescribed by doctors who knew it was hard to quit,
because their exercise was to walk to the station or car, lay in bed, faces
    flickering blue,
often said they were happiest asleep, groaning in dreams,
because one turned orange and died at sixty-nine,
because the other gulped fear and popped worry until no one could stand
    her,
because they left the body behind, I

pull myself like a shipwreck survivor onto the moist shore, imprint its sand,
because they left the body behind, I am the flag waving on the pole set in
    this new land,
sun rising from the sea and reddening at night, I am breath and air and
    electric blue
twilight, I am one billion pores like stars, salt and water and circuitry,
I am praise.

Ann Cefola is the author of *Free Ferry* and *Face Painting in the Dark*; and the translator of *The Hero* and *Hence this cradle*. She can be reached at annogram@aol.com.

WSQ: *Women's Studies Quarterly* 48: 1 & 2 (Spring/Summer 2020) © 2020 by Ann Cefola. All rights reserved.

The Politics of Love & Other Invisible Structures

Sheree La Puma

To a ghost that never dies.

I had my first drink at fifteen, the same year my grandmother took her last, washing down two bottles of codeine with gin. I watched them wheel her out of her apartment on a gurney, zipped up tight. My soul died there. Some talk of funerals. She read the obituary every morning with her coffee. Her death came fast and silent like a traitor. I wept until earth became clay, and clay became chalk, then I erased her memory.

Forty years later, our bodies like urns, cupping our animal hearts. Mom buries her hope inside an old sycamore. I tear at the roots with my hands. Tired of the fury, that loud, ugly, spit-in-your-face anger. The fuck you kind of rage women aren't allowed to show. I want to make my darkness visible, so I sell plasma on the corner for $60 a pop.

Sheree La Puma is an award-winning writer whose personal essays, fiction, and poetry have appeared in or are forthcoming in *JuxtaProse*, *River Heron Review*, the *Rumpus*, *Plainsongs*, the *Main Street Rag*, and *I-70 Review*, among others. She received an MFA in writing from California Institute of the Arts and taught poetry to former gang members. She can be reached at sheree@shereewrites.com.

***WSQ: Women's Studies Quarterly* 48: 1 & 2 (Spring/Summer 2020)** © 2020 by Sheree La Puma.
All rights reserved.

PART VIII. ALERTS AND PROVOCATIONS

A Love Note to Our Literary Ancestors: Then and Now

Jamia Wilson

On a crisp November evening, encircled by a lively cadre of writers, agents, publishers, editors, and philanthropists, I stood in a brightly lit mahogany- and rosewood-adorned architectural studio overlooking Madison Avenue. As I waited at the bar for a tumbler of pinot noir, I watched the guests catch up over drinks and dart over to newly acclaimed writers to congratulate them on their recent publications while reaching for the hors d'oeuvres being passed around.

The pleasant din quieted suddenly when the warm yet stately New Orleanian memoirist and soon-to-be National Book Award–winner Sarah Broom began speaking. Broom reflected on how being awarded the 2016 Creative Nonfiction Grant from the Whiting Foundation had impacted her life and work. She tied her writing process to stories about her family's home, history, and resilience in a complex and oft mythologized city. As *The Yellow House* author named the 2019 Whiting Award winners amid enthusiastic applause, I looked at the bookshelves lining the walls and then at the hopeful faces of this year's victors, including Channing Gerard Joseph, author of *House of Swann: Where Slaves Became Queens.*

In celebrating these writers, I thought about Broom's and Joseph's relationship to other authors from underrepresented communities who have received this award, including Feminist Press author Brontez Purnell. Contemplating the lineage of those who paved the way for rooms like this to showcase and support intersectional literature, diverse insurgent voices, and LGBTQ authors of color, I wondered what our literary ancestors would think about this moment.

As I connected with an author whose debut book with the Feminist

WSQ: Women's Studies Quarterly 48: 1 & 2 (Spring/Summer 2020) © 2020 by Jamia Wilson. All rights reserved.

Press springboarded them into a publishing juggernaut, I remembered an anonymous voice mail I received during my first week at the helm of the Feminist Press in July 2017: "Our ancestors planted seeds and you are the flowering of their dreams." I'd jotted the message down on a fuchsia Post-it and had tucked it away in my wallet for safekeeping.

This anonymous message helped support my entry into an industry that is notoriously homogenous and systemically less accessible for communities of color; it is this type of intergenerational support, too, that Layla Saad describes in her book *Me and White Supremacy* (2020) as being a "good ancestor" in the present. As I surveyed the room, I saw editors, writers, and others who had been touched by the transformative magic that brought me to the Feminist Press as a reader when my mother first handed me a copy of the foundational Black feminist text *But Some of Us Are Brave*. It was then that I thought about how that inaugural voice mail shaped my intentions and goals for my service as the youngest and first woman of color executive director and publisher of FP. At a time when Pew Research studies show that the person most likely to read a book in any form today is a college-educated Black woman (Bump 2014), it feels fitting that this granddaughter of sharecroppers—whose Carolinian ancestors fought for the right to read and preserve their language and stories—is midwifing books that document our past and carry on our lineage of imagining a more powerful, complicated, innovative, and inclusive feminist future.

As I walked home later that night, I unraveled the Post-it note that the memory of that auspicious voice mail inspired. "Be a good ancestor because your ancestors dreamed you and this moment into existence. What will be your imprint? (Pun intended!)" In the spirit of the women and allies who banded together, shared their resources, and offered their time to create a space for marginalized voices to amplify our voices, unearth "lost" narratives, and speak truth to power, I reflect on this idea as a guidepost every day. How are the books we're publishing speaking to the next generation? Who is missing from our list and from the room? What are our books, programs, and leadership structure saying about who we are, and about how we have or have not evolved to the people who will read our texts fifty years from now, and beyond?

Through that voice mail, I realized that the lineage built by our Feminist Press founder, Florence Howe (who celebrated her ninetieth birthday in 2019), and our other foreparents, created a world where having access to the Feminist Press was my birthright. Every day, I marvel at the fact that I was born into a world where the Feminist Press has always existed. The culture we live in is better for it.

My own parents taught me early on about the importance of reading as a means of education and consciousness-raising, as well as a tool for resistance. From them, I learned that literature is transformative—it holds the power to change minds and hearts, build community, and inspire action. As a lifelong activist, I have been sustained by the books inhabiting my shelves. Since childhood, I have drawn courage and insight from Feminist Press titles such as *But Some of Us Are Brave*, *Still Alive*, and *I Love Myself When I Am Laughing*. These books gave me hope and stirred me to fight for gender, racial, and economic justice—and more.

In 1970 the Feminist Press was born to fill this need, and to foster an inclusive, intersectional feminist community for all people who are underserved by mainstream literary culture. In 1972 the *Women's Studies Newsletter*—which, in 1981, became *Women's Studies Quarterly* (WSQ), as we know it now—made history as an interdisciplinary peer-reviewed academic journal. This is just one of the many examples of literary and scholarly endeavors that FP has championed since its inception. Indeed, from the Feminist Press, I've learned how to midwife stories that fuel movements and keep feminist authors' ideas alive and immortalized through generations. We operate on the principle that both feminism and literary culture should reflect the vast complexity and diversity of humankind, and should be accessible to an unbounded audience. Countering the traditional gatekeeping practices of the publishing industry, we invest in emerging authors and thinkers with bold new voices, creating space for ideas deemed too risky, radical, or controversial by larger publishers. I'm grateful for Florence's insistent follow-through on the urgent need to provide people of all ages, races, and genders, and from all sectors of society, with books that will help them expand their possibilities as artists, thinkers, and human beings. Minds and hearts have been moved as a result of FP's thoughtful and complex publishing, and discourses have shifted from classrooms to *Saturday Night Live*.

In a climate where many of our sibling feminist publications are shuttering due to the harrowing political economy of media both on- and offline, inheriting this chapter in the Feminist Press's story imbues me and our team with energy and inspiration to ensure that our books also provide a road map for the next generation of advocates working to advance gender justice. Our community has kept us alive for fifty years because of our mission to create a more just world where everyone recognizes themselves in a book. Now, as *WSQ* moves on to a new home, we look forward to sharing the fruits of our inheritance with new communities unknown. Although the future is uncertain, we know we'll keep building and creating with good ancestors, courageous resisters, informed educators, and compassionate creators in our hearts, minds, and words. Like blood memory, it's in our DNA.

Jamia Wilson is the executive director and publisher of the Feminist Press. She is the author of *Young, Gifted and Black*, *Step Into Your Power*, and *Big Ideas for Young Thinkers*, coauthor of *Road Map for Revolutionaries*, and wrote the introduction and oral history to *Together We Rise: Behind the Scenes at the Protest Heard Around the World*. She is the recipient of the 2018 NYU Graduate School of Arts and Sciences Distinguished Alumnae Award, the Planned Parenthood Southeast "Legend in the Making" award, and her work has appeared in numerous publications, including the *New York Times*, *Essence*, Rookie, Refinery29, CNN, the *Washington Post*, *Elle*, and more. She can be reached at jamia@jamiawilson.org.

Works Cited

Bump, Philip. 2014. "The Most Likely Person to Read a Book? A College-Educated Black Woman." *The Atlantic*, January 16, 2014. https://www.theatlantic.com/culture/archive/2014/01/most-likely-person-read-book-college-educated-black-woman/357091/.

Saad, Layla F. 2020. *Me and White Supremacy: Combat Racism, Change the World, and Become a Good Ancestor*. Naperville, IL: Sourcebooks.